The Single European Currency in National Perspective

A Community in Crisis?

Edited by

Bernard H. Moss
Associate
Institute of European Studies
London

and

Jonathan Michie
Professor of Management
Birkbeck College
University of London

First published in Great Britain 1998 by
MACMILLAN PRESS LTD
Houndmills, Basingstoke, Hampshire RG21 6XS and London
Companies and representatives throughout the world

A catalogue record for this book is available from the British Library.

ISBN 0–333–72548–4

First published in the United States of America 1998 by
ST. MARTIN'S PRESS, INC.,
Scholarly and Reference Division,
175 Fifth Avenue, New York, N.Y. 10010

ISBN 0–312–21531–2

Library of Congress Cataloging-in-Publication Data
The single European currency in national perspective : a community in
crisis? / edited by Bernard H. Moss and Jonathan Michie.
    p.   cm.
Includes bibliographical references and index.
ISBN 0–312–21531–2 (cloth)
    1. Monetary unions.   2. Monetary unions—European Union countries.
3. Monetary policy—European Union countries.   4. Monetary policy-
-European Union countries.   5. Money—European Union countries.
6. European Union countries—Economic policy.   7. Europe—Economic
integration.   I. Moss, Bernard H.   II. Michie, Jonathan.
HG3894.S57   1998
332.4'94—dc21   98–13924
                                                             CIP

Selection and editorial matter © Bernard H. Moss and Jonathan Michie 1998
Chapters 1, 3, 7 © Bernard H. Moss 1998
Chapter 2 © Jonathan Michie 1998
Chapters 4–6, 8–10 © Macmillan Press Ltd 1998

This book is printed on paper suitable for recycling and made from fully managed and
sustained forest sources.

10   9   8   7   6   5   4   3   2   1
07   06   05   04   03   02   01   00   99   98

Printed and bound in Great Britain by
Antony Rowe Ltd, Chippenham, Wiltshire

THE SINGLE EUROPEAN CURRENCY
IN NATIONAL PERSPECTIVE

Also by Bernard H. Moss

THE ORIGINS OF THE FRENCH LABOR MOVEMENT

Also by Jonathan Michie

CONTRACTS, COOPERATION AND COMPETITION: Studies in Economics, Management and Law (*edited with Simon Deakin*)

FIRMS, ORGANIZATIONS AND CONTRACTS: A Reader in Industrial Organization (*edited with Peter Buckley*)

THE ECONOMICS OF RESTRUCTURING AND INTERVENTION

THE POLITICAL ECONOMY OF SOUTH AFRICA'S TRANSITION (*edited with Vishnu Padayachee*)

Contents

v

List of Tables

Preface and Acknowledgements

All the material collected together in this book was commissioned and written specifically for publication here. We are therefore grateful to the authors for having undertaken this work and for having responded quickly yet fully to all editorial suggestions. Early drafts of some of the papers were presented and discussed at a conference on 'The Single Currency in National Perspective' held in London in October 1996. We are grateful to UACES for having hosted that event. Of course, responsibility for the views expressed in the following chapters is solely that of the respective authors. We are also grateful to Linda Auld and Sunder Katmala of Macmillan for the speedy and efficient production of the book.

Bernard Moss would like to add his acknowledgements to Professors Francis Snyder and Alan Milward of the European University Institute in Florence for introducing him to the subject, to Drs Steven Jeffreys, Valerio Lintner, and Amy Verdun for reading portions of the manuscript, to the anonymous reader for *Contemporary European History* for comments on an article drawn from material in this book, and to René Mouriaux of CEVIPOF for his insights and friendship over the years.

Jonathan Michie would like to add his thanks to, first, his colleague and co-author Michael Kitson of St Catharine's College, Cambridge, for joint work on these and other topics. Chapter 2 draws on some of that work. Secondly, to John Corcoran for having commissioned a guest lecture on the topic at the University of Sunderland Business School, the text of which became the first draft for Chapter 2. Thirdly, to Bernie Moss for having suggested this book in the first place and subsequently driving the project through to completion. And fourthly, to Robyn May for assistance in editing the manuscript.

Finally, this book would not have been possible without the love and support of our families and we would therefore like to add a special thanks to them; from Bernard Moss to his wife Neysa and son David, and from Jonathan Michie to his wife Carolyn and sons Alex and Duncan.

Bernard H. Moss
Jonathan Michie
October 1997

List of Contributors

John Corcoran is Senior Lecturer in Economics, Economics Division, Sunderland Business School, University of Sunderland.

Jörg Huffschmid is Professor for Political Economy and Economic Policy at the University of Bremen. His specialisms are in European integration, economic concentration, the European arms industry and, recently, financial markets.

Miguel Martinez Lucio is a Lecturer at the University of Leeds.

Jonathan Michie is Professor of Management, Birkbeck College, University of London. He was previously at the Judge Institute of Management Studies, University of Cambridge, and before that worked in Brussels as an Expert to the European Commission.

Bill Morris is General Secretary of the Transport and General Workers' Union (TGWU).

Bernard H. Moss is a professor of history, associated with the Institute of European Studies in London, who has written widely on modern and contemporary France. With an LL.M. from the London School of Economics, he has expanded his interests to the European Union.

Andy Robinson is *Business Week*'s correspondent in Madrid and an economic journalist on Spain's financial daily, *Cinco Dias*.

Annamaria Simonazzi teaches economics at the University of Rome – 'La Sapienza'. She has written extensively on monetary policy and unemployment, competitive deflations and the European Monetary Union.

Fernando Vianello teaches economics at the University of Rome – 'La Sapienza'. Among his publications are the entry on the Labour Theory of Value in the *New Palgrave Dictionary*, and a number of essays on growth and income distribution, the investment function, the Italian economy and the 1992 EMS crisis.

Introduction

Most books about Europe take the European Community (EC) or Union (EU)[1] as the point of reference for an association that is composed of nation states. The literature, which is vast, tends to be descriptive, seldom interpretive or critical. Most Europeans view the EU through the lens of national culture and politics, but the national perspective is largely absent from the literature. The prevailing narrative is that of the weakening of the nation state and the growth of the EC towards ever closer union. The single currency and Economic and Monetary Union (EMU) are often viewed as the last great step toward a supranational government, the culmination of a process of trade integration begun in 1957.

This book offers a different perspective. It is concerned with the interaction between the EU and EMU and national politics and economies. It highlights in particular the negative effects that the policies of monetary union introduced in the 1980s have had on jobs, social welfare and growth in Europe. It describes the cumulative process by which the EC and member states achieved the liberalization of markets, the effects of which on wages and employment have caused disaffection and protest in member states and a change of government pledged to reflation and job creation in 1997 in France.

The contributors to this book include political economists, a historian and lawyer, an economic journalist and the General Secretary of the Transport and General Workers Union (TGWU). The book is explicitly interdisciplinary in approach. It aims to be of use and interest to both academic and general audiences.

The book is critical of the current approach towards European integration. First, as we have noted, the literature is heavily weighted in the other direction and a systematic critique of both the EU and EMU is sorely needed. Whereas the Brussels perspective has no end of articulate defenders, criticism of the EU tends to be partial, fragmented and partitioned, hidden away in national debates. Europe has become an article of faith in many countries and among many academic specialists. It has not always been easy to find specialists willing to question the faith. Yet, by all reckoning the EC has not fulfilled the hopes of its founders and advocates, either as a supranational state or as a promoter of economic growth and social justice.

In Britain, where this book originates, almost all the criticism of the EU in recent years has come from the Conservative Right. Tory Eurosceptics object to the extension of EU power on both nationalist and market grounds because it threatens national sovereignty and because it is – albeit minimally – regulatory. Practically nothing critical about the EU has been heard from those concerned about labour and employment. If we, the editors, are Eurosceptics, it is not because we are nationalists but because we are sceptical about the market agenda currently controlling the EU.

Considerable attention is devoted to France, which has played both a pivotal and contrapuntal role in the EC. With strong Gaullist and Communist parties the French were sceptical of both its supranationalism and market orientation. Integration could only go so far as the reluctant and inflationary partner, France, wanted. The turnabout of François Mitterrand in 1982–83 from interventionism to monetarism provided the thrust for the completion of the single market and creation of the single currency. The future of the latter depends very much on the compatibility of French and German policies, which pull in opposite directions. The French are important not just for the pivotal role they played, but for the counter-point they offered in the form of proposals for planning and industrial and social policy as well as their current demand for an economic government for Europe to control EMU.

Some believe the dissatisfaction created by the single currency will induce demands for such a government, but further substantial transfers of sovereignty from members to the EU are unlikely. First, as we try to show, the EU does not possess constitutional and institutional foundations for government. Second, it lacks the democratic legitimacy to assume such a role. Third, increasing policy divergence among members, particularly France and Germany, due to disillusionment with monetarism, makes agreement on economic and monetary policy problematic. Dissatisfaction with the results of EMU is more likely to result in a reaction against federalism and a recentering of economic policy in the nation state.

It is commonplace to hear that globalization, particularly the internationalization of financial markets, has vitiated the effectiveness of national policy. Globalization has been encouraged by the adoption of neoliberal domestic policies and the abdication of national responsibility by politicians bowing to market pressures.

The EC, serving as an instrument for national deregulation and global free trade, has been an accelerator of globalization. Though the extent of globalization has been exaggerated, there is a long-term trend toward the internationalization of markets that makes purely national policy less effective. The EU can provide minimal levels of social protection and perhaps some degree of fiscal harmonization. International cooperation in areas like high technology is necessary, but the greatest achievements like Eureka and Airbus have often been achieved through inter-governmental arrangements rather than the EU.

The EU as presently constituted is not empowered to become an instrument for social and economic governance. For it to become more than a common market, which is probably all that the founding members bargained for, would require a refoundation. But any such deepening of the EU is made increasingly unlikely by the renationalization of economic policy in France and Germany and by the prospect of enlargement, as the minimalist treaty concluded in Amsterdam in June 1997 made clear. The nation state remains as the chief locus of loyalty, solidarity and regulation in Europe. To recognize this fact is not to promote an atavistic nationalism, but to identify the real levers of economic governance and social welfare in a market system that, left on its own, will produce only more unemployment, insecurity and inequality.

STRUCTURE OF THE BOOK

Following an introductory 'overview' chapter by Bernard Moss, which sets the current phase of European integration in its historical perspective, the book is divided in two Parts. As briefly outlined in the remainder of this introduction, Part 2 contains four thematic pieces, preceded in the first part of the book by chapters on each of the five major countries of the European Union – Britain, France, Germany, Italy and Spain. The first of these, on Britain, sets out the economic issues involved in a move to a single currency. The record of the Exchange Rate Mechanism is discussed, and the particular provisions of the Maastricht Treaty's blueprint for moving towards, and then administering, a single currency are critiqued. The implications of no longer recording balance of payments between member states is also discussed. The present proposals for a single currency are found quite badly wanting on a number of grounds. Firstly, the degree of economic, political and institutional integration between the member states falls far short of that required for successful monetary union. Secondly, the particular proposals reflect an economic, financial and political orthodoxy whose priority is the defense of existing relations of wealth and power in society rather than the pursuit of broader economic or social development. This orthodoxy and this policy approach are neither neutral nor new. They will provoke the same sort of economic and social problems that they have in the past, and will call for the same sort of political response to overcome these problems and reverse the approach.

Chapter 3 explores the relationship between the EMU, unemployment and the social divide in France. Until 1983 most governments had relied upon market intervention, easy money, devaluation and administered credit to sustain growth and maintain social peace. The divergence of French policy from German made European economic and monetary union impossible. In reversing course and adopting monetarist policies, Mitterrand laid the basis for the single market initiative and EMU but his sound money policy caused high unemployment and opened up the crisis of representation and confidence known as the social divide. The chapter examines the social divide as expressed in elections, particularly the 1992 referendum on Maastricht, and in the 1995 transport and public service strike. The divide led in June 1997 to the election of the red-rose-green government of Lionel Jospin, which was pledged to job creation and wage reflation, a program that was not compatible with the monetarist constraints of EMU.

The integration of Germany within a Western European framework has been one of the central pillars of successive German governments since the establishment of the Federal Republic. Unified Germany has continued to drive towards a widening and deepening of the European Community and was one of the prime movers at Maastricht. But Germany has found that the convergence criteria it so readily agreed to in 1991 have become far more difficult and controversial. The changing economic structure, economic strains and the effects of fierce global competition have resulted in only modest growth rates, increasing budget deficits and high unemployment rates. Chapter 4 examines the economic difficulties which have confronted Germany in the 1990s and the related shift in domestic political attitude to European integration.

Chapter 5 analyses the case of Italy. It argues, firstly, that there are fundamental political, social and economic reasons for the country to have had somewhat shaky public finances historically. But, secondly, the persistence of primary deficits in the 1980s was mainly the fault of a corrupt, irresponsible political class squandering public money, seeing in public expenditure a means of self-enrichment as well as the cement to reinforce their systems of patronage. However, ironically, this political class accepted with reckless nonchalance the Draconian conditions of the Maastricht treaty, as the deficit reached 10 per cent of GDP while the public debt soared past the 100 per cent mark. Amongst other things, this provided a justification for a severe downsizing of state-owned industry. And after forty years the so-called 'extraordinary intervention' in the south was brought to an end. A more constructive approach, it is argued, would have been to divert spending in the south from the system of personal subordination it had created to one favouring autonomy, initiative and industriousness. The EU initiative, not sufficiently resisted by the Italian government, went in exactly the opposite direction.

The impact of monetary integration in Spain is usually measured in terms of the extent of financial restrictions within the state and the general constraints imposed on welfare expenditure. Spain has had to reform economic and social intervention to meet the Maastricht criteria. This has been difficult due to the bureaucratic legacies and dysfunctional processes that were inherited from the dictatorship. Governments have tried to balance the economic imperatives for public expenditure control against social imperatives pushing for social welfare. Spain is still as far behind other member states in per capita income as ever. Monetarist policies have emerged at the expense of a proactive industrial policy, making Spain a consumer rather than producer of high technology. They have also led to deregulation in the labour market and an obsession with cutting labour costs. Chapter 6 argues that what appears to be happening is the fragmentation of state intervention in the social ambit, with an emphasis on cost rather than value-added strategies taking its toll in industrial development.

Part 2 opens with a chapter that asks whether the EC has been politically and economically neutral. It argues that the treaties, law and institutions of the Community have contained a free market bias that was exploited by neoliberal governments in the 1980s to create the single market and currency. The EC has been successful in accomplishing negative integration, the sweeping away of national impediments to free trade, but has failed in areas requiring constructive intervention – transport, commercial, industrial, regional, social and employment policy. The social deficit is linked to the democratic one, the absence of a legislative process that reflects popular needs and opinion, particularly that of labour. Hopes placed in an interventionist EU supra-state are ill-founded. The EU lacks the constitutional and institutional foundations for social and economic governance.

Chapter 8 then describes the background to the single currency proposals in the form of the 'single market' programme. It was as part of this movement that all member states were required to abolish their currency controls, and once this had been achieved, the Commission argued that it no longer made sense to have separate currencies, hence their proposals for a single currency. As Chapter 8 demonstrates, though, a single currency requires a degree of political unity and convergence of national economies that does not appear to have been attained in Europe. National markets, national business cycles, and national political economies appear to be still entrenched.

In Chapter 9, Bill Morris argues that although as late as 1996 it appeared to many – including him – that Europe was on course for the introduction of a single currency, proceeding on schedule and on a sound basis, events since then have forced a modification of this view. In particular, for far too long the whole question of a single currency for Europe was discussed without any reference to its likely impact on employment. The absence of this element from the debate is, Bill Morris argues, one of the reasons for the decline in popular support for the European Union and the rise of 'Euroscepticism' in one form or another across so much of the continent.

The concluding chapter looks at the latest attempts to force through the single currency, whether from Britain's 'new Labour' Government, or from the born-again deregulators who emerge in all manner of guises but whose central message remains drearily constant. The election in 1997 of a Labour Government in Britain and a Socialist one in France should have called a halt to the monetarist blueprint for Europe. And certainly the French Government appear committed to economic objectives other than price stability. But for such commitments to survive the post-single currency Stability Pact will require some fundamental changes. So far the implications of this have been swept under the European carpet. This has proved possible because of the widespread fatalism in face of what is seen as an inexorable process of European integration. But if the current proposals for a single currency are really forced through, it will then demand a political reaction. The two alternatives appear to be either a Eurokeynesian programme to overthrow the Pact, or else the wholesale rejection of EMU so that economic and industrial policies can once again be pursued by the individual member states.

Notes

1. The EU formed at Maastricht in 1992 still contains the EC, founded in 1957 by the Treaty of Rome, as one of its three pillars.

1 The Single European Currency in National Perspective: A Community in Crisis?

Bernard H. Moss

INTRODUCTION

The single currency scheduled for launch in 1999 was, in the minds of many, to be the culmination of a long process of European integration leading to the formation of a supranational state. Instead, the single currency arises in a period of doubt and uncertainty for the European Community (EC)[1] or Union (EU). The movement for monetary union begun under the Maastricht treaty of 1992 has paradoxically halted momentum for European unity. The European Commission under Jacques Santer has put a quietus on constructive forms of integration such as social and industrial policy. Public opinion, oblivious to the conferral of citizenship under Maastricht, has turned sceptical to the benefits of the EU, especially where Economic and Monetary Union (EMU) has, by artificially raising interest rates, increased unemployment.[2] By imposing a deflationary strait-jacket, EMU has stifled growth and employment and forced cuts in social expenditure, undermining the credibility of national governments and causing the worst crisis in Europe since the 1930s.

The intergovernmental conference at Amsterdam, revising Maastricht, produced minor adjustments that left open the tough decisions about institutional reform to accommodate enlargement for the future. Already slowed in its decision-making with 15 members, the EU risks being unable to take constructive action with enlargement, reinforcing its tendency to become merely a free trade area. The new British prime minister Tony Blair, expected to give a boost to social Europe, turned out in his enthusiasm for the 'flexible' labour market to be not so different from Mrs Thatcher. The adoption of a resolution on employment and growth, reflecting this enthusiasm,

8

did nothing to bridge the gap between the monetarist Germans and interventionist French, who are finding fewer interests in common than they have had since the war.[3] Attempts to formulate common foreign and defense policy founder as in Bosnia and Albania, and European security seems to hang more than ever on NATO and the American armed forces. Analysts are beginning to realize how much European unity depended upon the Cold War and memories of WW II that are now faded.

Most books about Europe take the EU as the point of reference for an association that is still composed of nation states. The institutions and decision-making of the EU are treated as flowers cut off from their roots, as *sui generis* phenomena unconnected to national politics and constitutions. Of literally thousands of books on the subject almost none offer a national perspective, one concerned with the impact of EU policies on member states and their reaction to them.[4] Yet, the majority of Europeans view the EU through the lens of national culture and politics. The EU has had a tremendous effect in eliminating barriers to free trade, but with a budget that is only 2 per cent of those of its members its constructive intervention or degree of positive integration has been insignificant.

The literature on the EU in Britain tends to be descriptive rather than interpretive or critical.[5] The main theoretical framework adopted in the US was that of neofunctionalism which, loyal to the spirit of Jean Monnet, founder of the European Coal and Steel Community (ECSC), was economistic and teleological, assuming the automatic translation of market links into political unity. The realist critique of this perspective has until recently been chiefly concerned with the high politics of diplomacy and little with the social bases of national politics.[6] The prevailing narrative is that of the weakening of the nation state and growth of the Community toward ever-closer union.[7] Because the EU shares some of the features of a nation state, a single internal market and a sovereign legal system, and has now embraced a single currency, many assume that it is on its way to replacing the nation state as a supranational government.

THEORIES AND HOPES OF FOUNDERS

This trajectory is consistent with the hopes and aspirations of the founders and theorizers of the EC, who believed that the customs union created by the treaty of Rome would lead inevitably through a process of spillover and linkage to economic, monetary and political union.[8] Most, after WW II, were impressed with the US experience of federalism and the grand market. Two kinds of logic, often confounded, operated. Monnet based his plans for integration on the involvement of domestic producer and interest groups in a transnational project and the spillover effects of integration from one economic sector to another while the EC of 1957 relied, to a much greater extent than the ECSC, on free market principles.

Realizing he could not challenge the power and legitimacy of the nation state directly, Monnet sought to circumvent and surround it by setting up in the High Authority an independent body of officials and experts that would enmesh ever-expanding networks of producer and interest groups in support of transnational policies.[9] National governments and democratic assemblies were to be kept at arms' length from this process. The history of customs unions like the Zollverein in nineteenth-century Germany had shown that wars and revolutions, not markets, made nations. But Monnet hoped that the accretion of small steps of economic solidarity would obviate the need for a big bang to create a European state. The hope was that the integration of coal and steel would create pressures for the integration of related sectors like energy and transport. The removal of protection from one sector did not produce economic pressures for the liberalization of others, but it might make the remaining barriers more visible and thus create political demands for further integration to remove disparities until the entire economy was involved.

While inheriting the institutions of the ECSC in modified form, the EC did not grow out of it but resulted from a great leap forward toward a new order based on free market principles. Gone was the interventionism of the ECSC, which had funds for industrial reconversion and retraining and emergency powers to fix prices and quotas. Negotiators for the Common Market had always insisted on the need for positive social and industrial intervention to correct the inequalities generated by the market.[10] Assistance for industrial reconversion and retraining was featured in the Spaak Report that set the groundwork for the Common Market. The French in particular insisted on the prior upward harmonization of social policy and wages, along with national planning targets, in an unabashedly socialist program.[11]

Yet, rather inexplicably they accepted a treaty that in the words of the former premier Pierre Mendès-France was 'based on the classical liberalism of the nineteenth century, which holds that competition pure and simple resolves all problems.'[12] Fear of economic and diplomatic isolation after the Suez crisis and Hungary forced the French to back down. In the turning point of the negotiations the French conceded to the Germans that social improvement would have to come primarily from the functioning of the market. The other partners rushed to conclude an essential trade agreement while the French iron was still hot. Few realized that they were acceding to a new liberal order in Europe.

The logic of competitive markets was incorporated in the new order. The treaty instituted a common market free from national regulations and distortions to competition on the model of an internal domestic market. It favoured economies with stable prices and exchange rates, which with the bias against devaluation pointed the way to fixed exchange rates, if not a single currency, and to a European government responsible for economic and monetary policy. The implicit ideal was a 'natural market' free of regulations and controls. For the abolition of tariffs to be effective, it would have to lead to the removal of all other forms of discrimination such as differential transport, tax and exchange rates. By blunting the instruments of national economic policy, such harmonization would lead to a federalist union. The first European Commission under Walter Hallstein shared this aspiration for a single currency and a federal executive responsible to a democratic European parliament.[13]

But the conception of the 'natural market' underlying the treaty was no less political and 'psychological' than Monnet's assumption of sectoral spillover, as Hallstein admitted.[14] The elimination of tariffs, which resulted in a 630 per cent increase in intra-EC trade in the first twelve years,[15] did not produce economic pressures for the fixing of exchange rates. The treaty did not actually mandate the abolition of exchange controls, which were only ended by the major states in the 1980s after they had decided on the liberalization of their own domestic markets. Financial dependency came from the deficit in energy and high technology with the US and Arab states. The internationalization of financial flows had more to do with the breakdown of Bretton Woods, the floating of exchange rates and the domestic neoliberal policies of the 1980s than with intra-EC trade.[16]

Trade interdependence as measured by the proportion of GDP going to EC exports grew from 6 per cent in 1958 to 13.3 per cent in 1992. It reduced the effectiveness of national economic policies,[17] but much more so in small trading nations like Belgium with an interdependency rate (intra-EC imports and exports as a percentage of GDP in 1992) of 82.5 per cent than in France with a rate of 21.8 per cent or Italy at 17 per cent.[18] Intra-EC trade in manufactured goods has stagnated since the mid-1980s and actually declined among founding members since 1973. Most of the growth in intra-EC trade moreover consisted of intra-industrial competition, especially that offering quality ranges, rather than sectoral specialization.[19] This means that it especially concerned luxury goods that enhanced the quality of upper middle-class life, like the German Mercedes that helped undermine the Mitterrand experiment for which there were perhaps less imperious national substitutes. Trade interdependency alone does not explain EMU.

Despite a certain logic the federalist project contained its contradictions and self-inhibitors. The EC was always a head without a body, relying on the nation state to make its final decisions, supply its revenue, defend its territory and administer and enforce its laws. Under the rule of unanimity it could only advance as fast as its slowest member. It sought a closer union among the European peoples, acknowledging there was no European people or demos to found a supranational state. It set up a complex and remote system of law-making, giving ultimate power to national governments and largely consultative powers to parliament, thus inhibiting the growth of European movements of opinion. It trusted in 'permissive consensus' from the public and discouraged the active involvement of citizens. Moreover, its design for a common market free from state regulations and distortions to competition, with its bias against social or industrial intervention, limited the potential for state construction.

The six nations which signed the treaty were not all persuaded of the desirability of a federal state. Their concerns were more immediate and trade-oriented. The US, with the Marshall Plan, had demonstrated the benefits of freer intra-European trade for national growth. The six represented natural contiguous trading partners with resurgent economies that after the war lacked means of payment.[20] The post-war economy revolved around Germany, which supplied not only machinery and capital goods to the other five, but which also offered an expanding market for semi-finished manufactures from its partners. France under its economic plan needed a system of protection from world prices for its agriculture and industry within the context of a larger market that would spur investment and innovation. The Benelux countries wanted to guarantee sales to Germany and France, and Italy the export of textiles and manpower and new found markets for white ware in Germany. For these governments the EC was essentially a mechanism for sustaining the high level of growth of the 1950s through intra-European trade.[21]

FRENCH RESISTANCE TO SINGLE CURRENCY

Progress toward union could only go so far as France, the reluctant partner, wanted. With strong Gaullist and Communist parties, the French were sceptical of both the supranationalism and economic liberalism of the treaty. Despite serious misgivings General de Gaulle, who took over in May 1958, accepted the obligations of the treaty as a means of disciplining and modernizing the French economy and securing German markets. The French viewed the Common Agricultural Policy (CAP), whereby farmers were guaranteed a high level of prices and protected from world competition, as compensation for freeing up industry. The policy was contrary to the competitive method indicated by the treaty but since all members practised some form of protection, a common approach was necessary. Still, it took marathon bargaining sessions and threats of walkout and exit and more than 12 years before the French obtained their CAP.

Faced with the federalist projects of the Commission, de Gaulle tried to offer an alternative vision of a political union in a confederation of states. The Fouchet Plan, presented in 1962, which would have subordinated the EC to an inter-governmental political union, was actually approved by all members except the Netherlands under British influence. This flirtation with Gaullism showed how superficial the adhesion to federalism in the EC was. When the Commission tried to link the completion of the customs union with an extension of its own and parliamentary power in 1965, de Gaulle conducted a six month boycott. The crisis of the 'empty chair' ended with the Luxembourg Compromise whereby France asserted the right of each member to veto legislation on all very important matters. In his cantankerous way de Gaulle expressed reservations that most states had about the extension of central power. The asserted veto power put an end to the Commission's activist projects, including that of a single currency.[22]

The Commission had been pressing for a common economic and monetary policy that was in the logic of the treaty. The treaty talked of the Community 'progressively approximating the economic policies of member-states' in article 2 and the Council of Ministers (council) coordinating economic and monetary policy in article 104. It viewed the exchange rate as a 'problem of common interest' and protected the victims of devaluation. In the 1962 opinion of the Monetary Committee the treaty pointed to a system of fixed exchange rates. In 1962 also Robert Marjolin, the only *dirigiste* on the Commission, proposed an action program for the convergence of national economic policy that included sectoral forecasts and indicative plans on the French model. The medium-term program, drafted by national representatives, recognized the need for regional and industrial policy and envisaged fixed exchange rates and a reserve currency by 1970. In 1966 the Commission proposed giving the power to decide the volume of national budgets to ECOFIN, the council of finance ministers. Nothing came of these projects. The Germans objected to planning while the new French finance minister Michel Debré in 1965 saw a single currency threatening the integrity of the state.[23]

New life was given to the project of a single currency by the plan put forward by the newly appointed Commissioner Raymond Barre, a liberal French economist, in 1969. Assuming that trade interdependence limited the autonomy of national economic policy, Barre called for prior consultation and monetary cooperation. The crisis of the Bretton Woods system with the collapse of the dollar gave urgency to monetary cooperation. The resignation of de Gaulle and election of the more pro-European president Georges Pompidou in April made the French government more receptive to the plan. The Werner Report proposed a ten-year plan to achieve a single currency with the formation of an independent central bank and a 'centre of decision for economic policy' responsible to the European parliament. The plan, which tempted the French, was vetoed in December 1970 by Pompidou, who argued that the nation state was the only organism capable of assuring social order and justice. Despite a new agreement about monetary union in 1971 the only immediate result of the Werner Report was the formation of the European 'snake' within the 'tunnel', which tried to maintain fixed margins of fluctuation among the currencies.[24]

There was, however, too much divergence between the strong D-Mark and Dutch guilder and other weaker currencies for the 'snake' to work; the inflationary French were forced to withdraw in 1974 and again in 1976. Underlying monetary divergence were profound differences in political economy, relating to the nature of the labour movement in each country. The French relied upon easy money to sustain growth and guarantee social peace. Deflation, they feared, would produce social division that would be exploited by the Communists. The government had conceded large real wage increases of 8 per cent in the strikes of May–June 1968. Faced with a volatile work force and the threat of a united Left, Gaullist governments continued to increase the money supply, promoting growth and higher real wages as the key to social peace even after the oil shock of 1974.

Led by the Bundesbank, German policy was deflationary. The Germans inherited a fear of inflation from the 1920s, but they also disposed of an independent bank dedicated to price stability and to trade unions which, unlike the French, were highly integrated through centralized bargaining and company co-determination into the profit-making system. The Germans met wage increases with tight money that induced recession, welcoming higher unemployment and unused factory capacity in their battle against inflation. This divergence between German and French political economies made monetary union impossible.

Under Barre, appointed prime minister by Valéry Giscard d'Estaing in 1976, the French began to approach the German model. Barre instituted wage guidelines, stabilized the budget, restricted the money supply and, following a victory over the Left in March 1978, began to remove price controls. Still hounded by the Left, however, he went only half way, doing nothing to reduce social transfers, especially unemployment insurance, or state aids to industry and allowing inflation to reach 13 per cent in 1980.

It was in the context of French liberalization that Roy Jenkins, new president of the Commission in 1977, proposed a European monetary system. The French liked the idea because they thought it would serve as an external discipline for internal austerity and create a haven of stability against the dollar. Helmut Schmidt, the German chancellor, wanted to stop the appreciation of the mark *vis-à-vis* the dollar and demonstrate German willingness to take responsibility for European cooperation. There was no talk of economic convergence as in 1969. With divergence indicators and credit facilities the Exchange Rate Mechanism (ERM) gave slightly more protection to currency margins than had the 'snake'. The Germans warned they would not prop up another currency if it threatened their price stability. Preference for responding to major imbalances was given to realignments, which would be subject to mutual consent. Under ERM the EC Monetary Committee became responsible for the collective management of state finances in a crisis, a system tested under François Mitterrand.

POLITICAL ECONOMY: TURNABOUT OF MITTERRAND

Monetary union required the breaking of the strength of the Communists in France because it was the fear of a social explosion led by them that prevented governments from adopting tight money policies. Mitterrand became the instrument of liberalization and monetary union by outmanoeuvreing the Communists, first adopting then vitiating their program. He was elected president in 1981 on a platform that included the nationalization of major industrial firms and banks, an increase in wages and social benefits and the reconquest of the domestic market through a large – eventually 240 per cent – increase of state aids to industry. Mitterrand, however, showed signs of hesitation and improvisation; his policies lacked the coherence that a large initial devaluation and industrial plan combined with perhaps temporary measures of protection might have afforded.

Mitterrand maintained growth and employment during a cyclical down-turn, despite escalating American interest rates, at the cost of falling reserves and a rising trade and growing inflation deficit with Germany. Deciding against a large devaluation at the outset, he resorted to three smaller devaluations involving collective management, largely German, of the French economy, which reversed his expansionary thrust. The turning point came in Spring 1982 when, after consulting the Germans and the Commission, he proposed a wage and price freeze to accompany devaluation. The freeze brought about a loss of real wages and a deindexing of wages from prices, a historic reversal in distributive policy which henceforth would favour profits. When the franc again came under pressure in 1985 Pierre Bérégovoy, finance minister, raised interest rates, inaugurating the policy of the *franc fort* that tied the franc to the D-mark.

Most commentators conclude from the reversal that the outcome was dictated by international market forces and that there was no alternative.[25] These forces had been strengthened in the 1970s by the internationalization of short-term financial flows caused by the break-down of Bretton Woods. But an economic alternative to austerity may have been possible. Like de Gaulle in 1958 Mitterrand might have solved the trade problem by a large devaluation or float, preferably at the outset, accompanied by measures of trade protection, state aid to industry, lower interest rates and wage controls.

What Mitterrand lacked was a political majority for the alternative. Only 39 per cent of the public wanted a radicalization of policy. Divided and demoralized, the Communist-led unions were unable to resist the plant closures and job losses dictated by the adoption of sound money. Mitterrand had come to power by breaking the electoral force and prestige of the Communists, who were made vulnerable by the loss of industrial jobs, and by incorporating social liberals like Jacques Delors and Michel Rocard into his coalition. The constraints of the ERM and financial markets operated politically through the Europeanists in Mitterrand's government who opposed departure from the ERM. The neoliberal turnabout of 1983 was inscribed in the nature of Mitterrand's electoral victory of 1981.

MITTERRAND AND DELORS: SINGLE MARKET

This reversal made possible new initiatives on Europe that led to the single currency. Europe provided a new goal and moral justification for the domestic policy reversal. Mitterrand's conversion to monetarism levelled differences between him and the British and Germans. In shuttle diplomacy he discovered a common denominator in the desire to complete the internal market in goods, services and capital with the elimination of non-tariff barriers. The internal market was inscribed in the treaty, but progress in the harmonization of national rules and standards was blocked by the requirement of unanimity. The Single European Act (SEA) provided for the harmonization of regulations by qualified majority. In the absence of harmonization the principle of mutual recognition, whereby each state accepted the equivalence of standards of every other member, applied. This meant that the lowest level of regulation, that which imposed the least cost, would probably prevail.

The appointment of Delors to head the Commission gave renewed impetus to the campaign to complete the single market by

1992. Delors was not a social democrat but a social Christian, who had come up through Catholic unionism. As a social Catholic he valued the market in so far as it preserved individual autonomy and responsibility and produced the wealth without which there was no social progress. There was no progress without a competitive market, but the market required social consensus.[26] With his belief in the Church doctrine of subsidiarity, he preferred voluntary cooperation and dialogue among the social partners to state intervention, and qualitative issues like working time and conditions to wage ones, which were to his mind materialistic and conflictual. Delors however was more concerned with achieving consensus than real reform, which was undercut in any event by his commitment to competitive markets.

Delors obtained labour support for the single market and currency by promising to develop a social dimension to the EC. The results were disappointing. The SEA contained provisions for health and safety legislation by qualified majority voting and for a social dialogue between unions and management leading to agreements on a European level. Since UNICE, the powerful employers' confederation, was opposed in principle to European-wide regulation, the dialogue was only a simulacrum of bargaining. In 1988 Delors proposed a social charter, a statement of fundamental employment rights, but as it emerged from negotiations it contained no legal force. Britain, which refused to sign, vetoed measures of implementation. The social protocol attached to the Maastricht treaty, designed to circumvent the British veto, was also restrictive in scope and minimalist in approach. The only major legislation passed under it was a subsidiarist version of works councils legislation that had been in the pipeline since the 1970s.

A major justification for the SEA was the need to overcome the growing European technological deficit with the US and Japan. A title of the treaty was introduced to strengthen the scientific and technical base of European industry by encouraging research and development in firms, research centres and universities. This provision ran up against the reluctance of states to transfer resources. Only 4 billion ecu were spent for the framework program and Eureka, an inter-governmental program of assistance for technological research, as against 67 billion spent for industry by members in 1990. Restricted to pre-competitive projects, the policy was vitiated by the bias toward deregulation, a tough mergers policy and control on public purchasing.[27] The treaty of Maastricht gave the Commission the power to enhance the competitiveness of EC industry by assisting firms and fostering cooperation among them. But this provision, which clashed with the requirement of fair competition, was stymied by the unanimity rule and the turn against interventionism. Dominated by the Germans, council repeatedly denied money for minimalist versions of Delors' public works proposal for trans-European energy and transport networks.

The principles, institutions and practices of the EC militate against constructive intervention in areas of social and industrial policy. The emphasis of the original treaty was on negative integration, the elimination of state barriers to competition, tariffs, quantitative restrictions, state aids and monopolies.[28] Much of the negative integration written into the treaty was either directly applicable in law, when clear and precise, or self-executory by the Commission. Positive integration, establishing new institutions where allowed by the treaties, usually required unanimity in council. Under the treaty interventionist policies could not be allowed to discriminate against firms or distort competition, which they almost inherently do. Business lobbyists in any event could usually find a country in council to block them. Seriously redistributive measures would require democratic pressure and legitimation, which is missing in the European parliament. The legal and institutional legacy of the EC virtually precludes the development of an interventionist European state.[29]

1988: FROM SINGLE MARKET TO SINGLE CURRENCY

The move to monetary union under Maastricht was a by-product of the single market initiative. France had asked for monetary union in the SEA, but Germany had insisted on the prior need to end exchange controls. In 1988 Mitterrand agreed to the ending of exchange controls by 1990 in return for a promise of fiscal harmonization that was not kept. All major states had renounced the use of monetary policy to regulate employment and growth. The combination of fixed exchange rates under ERM and the free movement of capital in the single market made national monetary policy untenable.[30]

In the context of the EC this combination implied a single currency controlled by an independent central bank committed to price stability – that at least was the conclusion of the Delors Committee, consisting of central bank governors, who fixed the stages for monetary union. The Delors Report saw the need for the coordination of national economic and central bank monetary policy and the strict control of national budgetary deficits. Governments were to refrain from intervention with subsidies and in the wage and price formation process. The burden of adjustment for differences in competitiveness would fall on wages and labour, which would have to respect the limits of productivity growth.[31]

There was practically no debate or discussion of EMU, not even among experts.[32] The Emerson committee of economists who justified the choice for the Commission had links with the employers' union.[33] Employers hoped that the single currency would end exchange-rate risk and save on transaction costs, which amount to only one quarter of one per cent of GDP. Their underlying aim was, through the deflationary pressures generated by EMU, to depress wages and social costs.[34] The Emerson committee rejected older economic theory that recognized the value of devaluation as a spur to investment and the existence of a trade-off between inflation and employment. Unlike the report on the single market and the Delors Report, this one denied that the single currency would aggravate regional problems, requiring government intervention. Like the Delors Report, it expected labour to absorb shocks of competitive adjustment. As product markets became more competitive national unions would lose the power to impose higher wage levels, which would then be set in local factor markets.[35]

In his rush to European unity after the reunification of Germany in 1990, Mitterrand abandoned proposals to flank the bank with an economic government responsible for fiscal and budgetary policy. The treaty consecrated the German vision of an independent bank insulated from domestic political influences in order to maintain price stability. So independent is the European Central Bank (ECB) that officials are forbidden from trying to influence it and its statutes can only be changed by international treaty. Council is authorized to set internal parities and external rates for the euro – there is even some dispute about this – but it must act without prejudice to price stability and in accordance with competitive principles. Despite the creation of an inner euro council at French behest the independence of the ECB remains untouched.[36] The fate of the European economy has been entrusted to an unaccountable board of central bankers, who lack legitimacy.

SINGLE CURRENCY: NATIONAL DIVERGENCE AND CONFLICT

The basic disagreement on monetary policy between France and Germany, the leading partners, widened after the victory of the French Left in the elections of May 1997. France wanted a weak euro, Germany a strong one; France inclusive membership, Germany an exclusive one, France ministerial control of the Bank, the Germans complete independence; France a socially responsible Europe, Germany a liberal one. To assure price stability the German government, backed by the Bundesbank, popular opinion and the Constitutional Court, insisted on strict application of the convergence criteria that limit budgetary deficits to 3 per cent and public debt to 60 per cent of GDP. The inflationary history and high indebtedness of Italy disqualified it in German eyes despite strenuous efforts to lower the budget deficit. Spain and Portugal might qualify but Greece had no chance at all. In view of the risks involved Sweden decided against joining the first wave, as did the British government for essentially electoral reasons. Both countries condition membership upon approval by referendum, which would be hard to obtain. However liberally applied the Maastricht criteria will create a two-speed Europe.

The deflationary model on which EMU is based is drawn from German experience. Germany was able to enjoy a long period of non-inflationary growth in post-war Europe because it possessed technological superiority based largely on its system of technical training, a cheap abundant labour supply drawing upon reserves from the east and south, and a trading network supplying capital goods, representing 80 per cent of its exports, for European industry. Because of its high level of productivity and monopoly position – the low price elasticity of demand for its goods – German industry did not suffer from its deflationary domestic policies and the rising external value of the D-Mark. German export-led prosperity depended on the deficit financing and devaluation in France and Italy that Germany condemned.[37] Ironically, Germany is imposing these same policies on Europe at a time when they no longer work for a Germany threatened with unemployment and underconsumption by the spread of technology to Eastern Europe and other low-wage economies.

The same model may not work for countries such as France,[38] Italy and Spain, which at least in the past have depended upon devaluations, fiscal stimulus and some inflation for growth. Inflationary growth in France and Italy favoured wages and employment at the expense of interest rates and profit; by reducing real interest rates this inflation assisted growth. The goal of price stability is particularly damaging to the southern countries where sectoral disparities in productivity growth give rise to differential price increases and a structural inflation. Deflation might not be so harmful for these countries if there were mechanisms for adjustment through labour mobility and fiscal redistribution such as exist in the US. While fiscal redistribution is able to compensate for 40 per cent of economic loss in the US, it only returns 1 per cent of such losses in Europe. Low labour mobility in Europe makes fiscal redistribution that much more important. Yet, even national fiscal policy is severely constrained by the convergence criteria of Maastricht.

In a report to the Commission in 1987 experts signalled the danger of the single market creating regional imbalance, helping the technologically advanced core regions but causing a spiral of decline and ruin in the periphery. It was to avoid this imbalance that Delors doubled the structural funds for backward and declining regions in 1988 and that the treaty of Maastricht created a new cohesion fund for the four poorest countries. The fact remains that money appropriated for social cohesion is a pittance, a mere one quarter of one per cent of EC GDP in 1991. The Delors II budget plan in 1992 aimed to increase the Community budget by 31.4 per cent and structural spending from 28 per cent to 31.4 per cent of the budget by 1997. Mildly redistributive, Delors' budget was opposed by the wealthier members.[39] An unpublished study of the Directorate of Social Affairs in 1993 showed that the combination of minimal fiscal flows with wage and price inertia would condemn less competitive regions under the single currency to low growth and substantially higher unemployment.[40] Yet, in 1993 the Commission concluded that governments could handle the shocks and that EU action beyond a slight increase of the budget to 2 per cent of EU GDP was not necessary.[41]

The Emerson group admitted there was little connection between low inflation and growth. Econometric studies show that devaluations may still be effective in stimulating growth in medium-sized countries like France. The countries which left the narrow bands of the ERM in 1992 – Britain, Spain, Italy, Denmark – benefited greatly from devaluation.[42] It was because Italy and France were growing with the help of rising prices and devaluations in the past that they were able to import German goods and guarantee German prosperity. European economic history has always been marked by periods of rising and falling prices just as by those of expansion and recession. Moreover, the trade cycles of member states are not synchronic; they move at varying rhythms and in different directions, requiring different monetary policies. Their divergence has increased since the 1980s.[43] This is particularly true of the British economy, which is currently running closer to the American than to the continental. The assumption underlying EMU of continual growth based on stable prices and balanced budgets everywhere is a myth.

This deflationary model may not survive member states protesting, under popular pressure, its rigid strictures fettering national growth. EMU contains the seeds for endless disputes, blockages, compromises and package deals involving non-monetary matters. Rather than provide a new elan for Europe, EMU is likely to compound the existing policy paralysis in the EU. Frustrated in their attempts to alter ECB policy in conformity with national requirements, members may finally consider exit as they did from the Latin Monetary Union last century. EMU could also be subject to continual challenge in the court by individuals who contest the interpretation of the treaty. The German Constitutional Court has held that strict compliance with the convergence criteria is a matter of fundamental constitutional importance for Germany; presumably it would not feel bound by any European act that violated the criteria.[44] A currency subject to so much dispute and uncertainty and bearing the indebtedness of states like Italy and Spain stood little chance of achieving stability and world class status if it survived at all; fall-out from a collapse of the euro could do immense damage to the EU.

LIMITS OF EUROPEAN GOVERNMENT AND SURVIVAL OF NATION STATE

With the single currency, the EU encroached upon national fiscal and budgetary policies without taking up responsibility for them. Under an 'asymmetrical' EMU[45] governments would be spread-eagled between monetary policy set by Frankfurt and social and economic policy decided within deficit limits at home. The treaty provides in article 103 for council to formulate broad guidelines for national economic policy but without an enforcement mechanism and without the coordination with the ECB that the Delors Report recommended. Under article 104c and the Stability Pact approved at Amsterdam, national economic policy is circumscribed by the convergence criteria. It must be subordinated to the ECB's pursuit of price stability.

At the core of EMU is the absence of European government. Further transfers of economic sovereignty to the EU, suggested as a response to the inequalities EMU will generate, are unlikely. First, as we show, the EU does not possess the constitutional and institutional foundations for economic government. Second, it lacks the democratic legitimacy and accountability before a European people or demos to assume such a role. Third, policy divergence among members, especially France and Germany, caused by disillusionment with monetarism, make agreement on macroeconomic policies extremely problematic. Finally, states may have reached the limit of their transfer of sovereignty without losing their coherence as constituting bodies for their society.

Forty years of integration have not produced a transfer of loyalties, expectations and political activity from the nation to the EU, not even among the farmers, the interest group that at least initially most benefited from it.[46] The federalist movement itself has probably never been weaker. The EU has not, as the German Constitutional Court noted in its Maastricht decision, created the sense of a European people or demos bound together by a common culture and destiny.[47] The common adherence to market values and rapid communications have not brought nations together. The historian might argue that despite all the cultural exchanges between France and Germany under their treaty there is less mutual knowledge and understanding today than there was on the eve of WW I. As in the 1960s their elites are probably more familiar with America than with each other.[48]

Most of the Europeans who identify with the EU see it as an aid to the nation state not its replacement. European identity comes second to the national one in all member states.[49] The EC disposed until recently of a fair-weather or 'permissive consensus.'[50] The EC was supported as long as it did not require obvious sacrifices and offered the prospect of expanding market opportunities and social mobility, especially to professionals and the upper middle class,[51] who also appreciated access to a broader range of quality consumer goods. The Europhilia of the 1980s coincided with the market enthusiasm generated by neoliberal governments. Can it survive a long period of stagnation and unemployment now associated with EU policies? Support for the EU has dropped dramatically with the onset of mass unemployment.[52]

The nation state has proven to be hardier and more resilient than federalists expected. It still commands the primary loyalty of its citizens, who look to it to provide basic physical and economic security. It is responsible for welfare and social security; its policies still set, within limits – partly self-imposed – the parameters of economic growth and wealth distribution; it still enjoys the monopoly of physical force and constitutional sovereignty, which give it the power in the final analysis, if the costs of membership become unbearable, to quit the EU.

Globalization, which can ruin firms, industries and regions, makes the nation state even more important as the main focus of regulation and the strongest bastion of solidarity. To say this is not to deny the pressure of market forces, but to recognize the power of national governments based on popular coalitions to channel and tame them. The state remains the most powerful institution to regulate markets, for purposes of employment, education, research, health, financial integrity, job training, labour relations, infrastructure, and justice. Even with globalization the nation state still has the capacity to secure markets and industry and attract long-term investment. It has no peer as a source of public power for economic governance.[53]

GLOBALIZATION AND EC

The actual extent of globalization relative to the past is highly exaggerated. The dependence on exports of European states – an average of 21.7 per cent of GDP in 1992 – is not much greater than it was in 1913; the rate of overseas direct investment is less, particularly with respect to the Third World. Financial flows were more global before 1914 than they are today. Globalization occurs in waves and drawbacks.[54] The commercial threat from low-wage countries such as China acquiring sophisticated technology is more a long-term than current problem. The present threat to national autonomy comes from multinational firms, which control sources of high technology, and from international flows of short-term speculative capital, which has limited effect on long-term investment. As for the multinationals, they are to a large extent national firms with international operations. They are nationally based and structured, as are their assets, shareholders, research, and management, and can be nationally regulated and controlled by governments with a desire to do so.[55]

In any event, liberalization in the EC was an ideological principle that preceded and encouraged economic globalization. The external commercial policy of the EC, which is about the most liberal in the world, did nothing to strengthen European industry. Contrary to free trade theory, protectionism has been effectively used – in nineteenth-century Europe and contemporary Japan and East Asia – to strengthen national firms for international competition.[56] In the EC the competitive internal market alone was to prepare enterprises for this competition. Under American pressure in a succession of GATT rounds, tariffs on manufactured goods were reduced to an average level of 6 per cent, half that of the US and a third that of Japan.[57] The EC came to depend much more on international trade than the US and Japan, with a share of imports of 24 per cent of GDP in 1991 compared to 7 per cent and 9 per cent respectively for those countries.

The EC failed to adopt an industrial and technological policy to reduce external dependence. The Commission rejected French proposals in 1966 to promote the formation of transnational firms. Council ignored proposals made in the 1960s by the Committee on Medium-Term Economic Policy for aid to industry and failed to take up recommendations of the 1970 Colonna Report for an industrial policy to encourage industrial cooperations and mergers. Instead of taking up new French proposals for a voluntarist and protectionist policy in 1983 the Commission approved the privatization program begun in Britain, which eliminated the motors of investment in Europe. With the neoliberal turn of the 1980s and loss of direction 'national champions' had to make their own arrangements – joint ventures and investment – with US multinationals, selling off national subsidiaries. Competition policy in the EU makes no allowance for efficiency or effective competitiveness. Competition criteria alone were used to stop the proposed takeover of the Canadian aircraft maker De Havilland by ATR, a French-Italian consortium.[58]

Globalization has been as much a political as an economic process. The formation and deepening of the EC, with the sweeping away of barriers, protection and regulations, were a regional instrument of this process. Globalization was a self-fulfilling prophecy, a cumulative international and domestic process. Leaders used the presumed ineffectiveness of national action in the face of globalization as an excuse for inaction, which only worsened dependency. They transferred more responsibility and sovereignty to the EC in order to tie their own hands – manifestly in the cases of France, Spain and Italy – which made them even more helpless before market forces.

EMU MONETARISM AND ITS DISCONTENTS

EMU incorporates the result of a sea-change in European thinking, the neoliberal revolution of 1980s which saw the defeat of radical alternatives in Britain and France, and the decline of organized labour.[59] The decline of labour was based on real structural changes, the loss of industrial jobs and expansion of the polymorphous service sector. These structural changes do not however mean an end to the labour movement. The blue-collar working class, while diminished, has not disappeared; among the employed it has become more highly skilled. Moreover, there are signs that it is being joined by ranks of white-collar employees sharing similar conditions and pay and more than ever vulnerable to the insecurity of the market place.[60] The strikes that have been conducted, particularly in France, against the cuts dictated by Maastricht and the victory of the Left there in the May 1997 elections, show signs of solidarity stretching far beyond blue-collar workers to public sector, white-collar and even managerial personnel. A basis exists in the expanded working or wage-earning class for a labour movement to challenge the deflationary strictures of Maastricht.

Governments have had to cut budgets, particularly main item social expenditures, and to depress economic activity in order to meet the Maastricht criteria. In France the policy of the *franc fort* associated with Maastricht stifled growth by at least 1 per cent a year, reduced industrial production by 5 per cent and raised unemployment from 9 to over 12 per cent from 1990.[61] The unemployment and sense of insecurity it generated produced strong opposition to Maastricht in the referendum of 1992 and provided broad support for the public sector strike of 1995. The election of May 1997, called by the president Jacques Chirac to legitimate further austerity measures needed to meet the criteria, resulted in their repudiation. But the new Socialist-Communist government of Lionel

Jospin, elected on a program of reflation and job creation, failed to alter the criteria and signed the Stability Pact at Amsterdam in June 1997.

Protest against the effects of Maastricht, fragmented and uncoordinated, had not yet taken an explicitly anti-European turn. Strikes broke out in Germany, Belgium, Italy, and Spain to protest austerity measures hitting the poor and wage-earners. Since 1991 public support for the EU in Spain and Portugal has plummeted, but this has not affected government determination to meet the criteria.[62] The Italian government, made up of former Communists, after making $60 billion in cuts, ran into resistance over plans to reduce pensions, but few in Italy were yet willing to challenge the European 'imperative'.

Faced with both the highest unemployment since the war and French demands for reflation, the German public, once staunchly Europeanist, turned largely against EMU. The government of Helmut Kohl, determined to meet the criteria, was blocked by the refusal of social welfare cuts by the Social Democrats, tax increases by the Liberals and creative accounting – the revaluing of gold reserves – by the Bundesbank. Without meeting the criteria Germany could lose its moral authority to dictate terms to others. The Bundesbank and Constitutional Court stood guard over the *dreikommanullprozent*, the three per cent deficit limit, which like the French soft euro, which was rejected, became an article of popular conviction and national faith. At the end of 1997 France and Germany, benefiting from a slight upturn in the economy in the third quarter, planned to approach the 3 per cent limit, but the world financial crisis spreading from Asia threatened to throw their projections into a cocked hat.

A single currency, Delors and Hans Tietmeyer of the Bundesbank agreed, required a certain degree of political unity, which was actually unattainable. A single currency that was not responsible to a single people and state would necessarily be either over-valued by an independent bank or under-valued by quarrelling nations. So, in the words of the British foreign secretary Robin Cook debate was polarized between 'a softer euro, which would not be workable and a harder euro, which would not be popular.'[63] EMU opened a dangerous gap between a political and economic elite determined to pursue the project and a growing number of people – at least 40 per cent – who were hostile to it.[64] In the long term, in a community of nation states the single currency was not sustainable.

Notes

1. The European Economic Community, established by the Treaty of Rome in 1957, continues under the Maastricht treaty of European Union.
2. Cameron, 1996, pp. 345–6, 356.
3. *Le Monde*, 22 May, 1997, p. 4. *International Herald Tribune*, 3 July 1997, p. 1.
4. Cf. the EC Membership Evaluated Series, for example Dreyfus *et al*, 1993, and the model of Moravcsik, 1993.
5. Cf. Holland, 1980.
6. Hoffmann, 1982, 1966.
7. Cf. Wallace, 1994, with Milward, 1992, p. 468.
8. Hallstein, 1962, 1972, and Haas, 1968.
9. Featherstone, 1994.
10. Milward, 1992, pp. 188–90.
11. Marjolin, 1986, pp. 286–8.
12. Cited in *ibid.*, p. 293.
13. Dyson, 1994, pp. 67–8. Hallstein, 1962, pp. 39–45 and 1972, pp. 24–9.
14. Hallstein, 1972, p. 29.
15. *Ibid.*, p. 87.
16. Cf. Hirst and Thompson, 1996, esp. p. 197.
17. Cooper, 1972.
18. Dyson, 1994, pp. 292–3.
19. Fontagné *et al*, 1997.
20. Milward, 1983.
21. Milward, 1992, ch. 4.
22. Newhouse, 1967. Neunreither, 1972.
23. Dyson, 1994, pp. 69–71. Marjolin, 1986, p. 347. Holland, 1980, pp. 34–7.
24. See Chapter 3 on France.
25. Cf. Rand Smith, 1995.
26. Ross, 1993, pp. 61, 72–3.
27. Sharp, 1993.
28. Cf. Pinder, 1979, with Tinbergen, 1965, pp. 77–9.
29. Cf. Streeck, 1996.
30. Dyson, 1994, pp. 154–8. Padoa-Schioppa, 1994, pp. 4–7.
31. Committee, 1989.
32. Verdun, 1996, p. 69.
33. Dyson, 1994, p. 250.
34. Verdun, 1996, pp. 75–80.
35. Emerson, *et al*, 1992, pp. 10, 13, 21–24, 27, 136–77.
36. *Le Monde*, 24 Apr. (p. 15), 18, 19 June, 1997. *Le Monde Economie*, 29 Apr. 1997, II.
37. Zinn, 1978.
38. Cotta, 1991.
39. Scott, 1993.
40. Dyson, 1994, p. 247.
41. European Commission, 1993, pp. 6–7. Verdun, 1996, p. 71.
42. Connolly, 1995.

43. HM Treasury, 1997, pp. 11–12.
44. Zuleeg, 1997.
45. Verdun, 1996 and 1997.
46. Cf. Haas, 1968, p. 6, with Averyt, 1977.
47. Minc, 1990, pp. 195–230. Weiler, 1995.
48. Lindberg and Scheingold, 1970, p. 265. *International Herald Tribune*, 3 July 1997, p. 1.
49. *The Guardian*, 11 June 1996.
50. Lindberg and Scheingold, 1970, pp. 176, 264–74.
51. Percheron, 1991, p. 393.
52. Cameron, 1996, pp. 345, 356.
53. Boyer, 1996. Epstein, 1996. Streeck, 1996. Hirst and Thompson, 1996. Cf. Strange, 1995, and Horsman and Marshall, 1995. Even the World Bank under Japanese influence recognized the economic role of the state in its 1997 development report.
54. Bairoch, 1996. Hirst and Thompson, 1996.
55. Wade, 1996, pp. 78–82. Porter, 1990, p. 19. Hirst and Thompson, 1996, ch. 4.
56. Bairoch, 1994. Jeanneney, 1978.
57. Hine, 1985, pp. 75–9. Prate, 1995, pp. 92–9.
58. Saint-Martin, 1996, p. 189. Monnier, 1996. Holland, 1980, pp. 26–75. Hallstein, 1972, pp. 194–5. Hayward, 1995, pp. 7–8.
59. Cf. Overbeek, ed., 1993. Jobert, ed., 1994.
60. Todd, 1995, pp. 102–3.
61. Interview with J.-P. Fitoussi, O.F.C.E., 2 Apr. 1997.
62. Cameron, 1996, p. 351, table 13.2.
63. *The Times*, 9 June 1997.
64. See poll conducted by the European Commission in *International Herald Tribune*, 28 November 1997.

References

Averyt, Jr., W. (1977) *Agropolitics in the European Community: Interest Groups and the Common Agricultural Policy*. New York: Praeger

Bairoch, P. (1996) 'Globalization Myths and Realities: One Century of External Trade and Foreign Investment', in Boyer, R. and Drache, D. (eds) *States against Markets: The Limits of Globalization*. London: Routledge

Bairoch, P. (1994) *Mythes et paradoxes de l'historie économique*. Paris: La Découverte

Boyer, R. (1996) 'State and Market: A New Engagement for the Twenty-First Century?' in Boyer, R. and Drache, D. (eds) *States against Markets: The Limits of Globalization*. London: Routledge

Cameron, D. (1996) 'National Interest, the Dilemmas of European Integration and Malaise', in Keeler, J. and Schain, M. (eds) *Chirac's Challenge: Liberalization, Europeanization and Malaise in France*. New York: St. Martin's Press

Committee for the Study of Economic and Monetary Union in Europe (1989) *Report on Economic and Monetary Union in the European Community*. Luxembourg: Office for Official Publications of the EC

Connolly, B. (1995) *The Rotten Heart of Europe: The Dirty War for Europe's Money*. London: Faber and Faber

Cooper, R. (1972) 'Economic Interdependence and Foreign Policy in the Seventies', *World Politics*, 24: 159–81

Cotta, A. (1991) *La France en panne*. Paris: Fayard

Dreyfus, F.G., Morizet J. and Peyrard, M. (eds) (1993) *France and EC Membership Evaluated*. London: Pinter

Dyson, K. (1994) *Elusive Union: The Process of Economic and Monetary Union in Europe*. London: Longman

Emerson, M., Gros, D., Italiener, A., Pisani-Ferry, H., Reichenbach, H. (1992) *One Market, One Money: An Evaluation of the Potential Benefits and Costs of Forming an Economic and Monetary Union*. Oxford: Oxford University Press

Epstein, G. (1996) 'International Capital Mobility and the Scope for National Economic Managements', in Boyer, R. and Drache, D. (eds) *States against Markets: The Limits of Globalization*. London: Routledge

European Commission (1993) 'Stable-Sound Finances: Community Public Finance in the Perspective of EMU', *European Economy*, no. 53

Featherstone, K. (1994) 'Jean Monnet and the Democratic Deficit in the European Union', *J. of Common Market Studies*, 32: 15–60

Fontagné, L., Freudenberg, M. and Péridy, N. (1997) 'Trade Patterns Inside the Single Market', *Document du travail*, no. 97–07. CEPII.

Haas, E. (1968) *The Uniting Europe*, 2nd ed. Stanford: Stanford U.P.

Hallstein, W. (1962) *United Europe: Challenge and Opportunity*. Cambridge, Mass.: Harvard U.P.

Hallstein, W. (1972) *Europe in the Making*. London: George Allen & Unwin

Hayward, J. (1995) 'Europe's Endangered Industrial Champions', in Hayward, J. (ed.) *Industrial Enterprise and European Integration: From National to International Champions*, Oxford: Oxford University Press

Hine, R.C. (1985) *The Political Economy of European Trade: An Introduction to the Trade Policies of the EEC*. London: Harvester

Hirst, P. and Thompson, G. (1996) *Globalization in Question: The International Economy and Possibilities of Governance*. Cambridge: Polity Press

HM Treasury (1997) *UK Membership of the Single Currency: An Assessment of the Five Economic Tests*. London

Hoffmann, S. (1966) 'Obstinate or Obsolete? The Fate of the Nation-State and the Case of Western Europe', *Daedalus*, 95: 862–916

Hoffmann, S. (1982) 'Reflections on the Nation-State in Western Europe Today', *J. of Common Market Studies*, 21: 21–37

Holland, S. (1980) *The Uncommon Market*. London: Macmillan

Horsman, M. and Marshall, A. (1995) *After the Nation State: Citizens, Tribalism and the New World Disorder*. New York: Harper Collins

Jeanneney, J.-M. (1978) *Pour un nouvel protectionnisme*. Paris: Seuil

Jobert, B. (ed.) (1994) *Le Tournant Néoliberal en Europe*. Paris: L'Harmattan

Lindberg, L. and Scheingold, S. (1970) *Europe's Would-Be Polity*. Englewood Cliffs, N.J.: Prentice Hall

Marjolin, R. (1986) *Architect of European Unity: Memoires, 1911–1986.* London: Weidenfeld and Nicolson

Milward, A. (1992) *The European Rescue of the Nation-State.* London: Routledge

Milward, A. (1983) *The Reconstruction of Western Europe, 1945–1952.* London: Methuen

Minc, A. (1990) *La Grande Illusion.* Paris: Grasset

Monnier, L. (1996) 'Politique économique et raison communautaire', in Cartelier, L., Fournière, J. and Monnier, L. (eds) *Critique de la raison communautaire: utilité publique et concurrence dans l'Union Europeénne.* Paris: Economica

Moravcsik, A. (1993) 'Preferences and Power in the EC: A Liberal Inter-governmental Approach', *J. of Common Market Studies*, 31: 473–524

Neunreither, K. (1972) 'Transformation of a Political Role: Reconsider-ing the Case of the Commission of the European Communities', *J. of Common Market Studies*, 10: 233–48.

Newhouse, J. (1967) *Collision in Brussels: The Common Market Crisis of 30 June 1965.* London: Faber and Faber

Overbeek, H. (ed.) (1993) *Restructuring Hegemony in the Global Political Economy: The Rise of Transnational Neo-Liberalism in the 1980s.* London: Routledge

Padoa-Schioppa, T. (1994) *The Road to Monetary Union in Europe: The Emperor, the Kings and the Genies.* Oxford: Clarendon

Percheron, A. (1991) 'Les Français et l'Europe: acquiescement de facade ou adhesion véritable', *Revue française de science politique*, 41: 382–406

Pinder, J. (1969) 'Problems of European Integration', in Denton, G.R. (ed.) *Economic Integration in Europe*, London: Weidenfeld and Nicolson

Prate, A. (1995) *La France en Europe.* Paris: Economica

Porter, M. (1990) *The Competitive Advantage of Nations.* New York: Col-lier Macmillan

Rand Smith, W. (1995) 'Industrial Crisis and the Left: Adjustment Strat-egies in Socialist France and Spain', *Comparative Politics*, 28: 1–24

Ross, G. (1993) 'Social Policy in the New Europe', *Studies in Political Economy*, 40: 61–73

Saint-Martin, O. (1996) 'L'Anti-Politique industrielle de l'U.E.' in Cartelier, L., Fournière, J. and Monnier, L. (eds) *Critique de la raison commu-nautaire: utilité publique et concurrence dans l'Union Europeénne.* Paris: Economica

Scott, A. (1993) 'Financing the Community: The Delors II Package', in Lodge, J. (ed.) *The European Community and the Challenge of the Fu-ture.* London: Pinter

Sharp, M. (1993) 'The Community and New Technologies', in Lodge, J. (ed.) *The European Community and the Challenge of the Future.* Lon-don: Pinter

Strange, S. (1995) 'Defective State', *Daedalus*, no. 124: 55–74

Streeck, W. (1996) 'Public Power Beyond the Nation-State: The Law of the European Community', in Boyer, R. and Drache, D. *States against Markets: The Limits of Globalization.* London: Routledge

Tinbergen, J. (1965) *International Economic Integration.* Amsterdam: Elsevier

Todd, E. (1995) 'Aux Origines du malaise politique français: les classes sociales et leurs représentations', *Le Débat*, nos. 83–85: 98–120

Verdun, A. (1996) 'An "Asymmetrical" Economic and Monetary Union in the EU: Perceptions of Monetary Authorities and Social Partners', *Journal of European Integration*, 20: 59–81

Verdun, A. (1997) 'The Democratic Deficit of the EMU', in *European Forum*, Florence: European University Institute

Wade, R. (1996) 'Globalization and its Limits: Reports of the Death of the National Economy Are Greatly Exaggerated' in Berger, S. and Dore, R. (eds) *National Diversity and Global Capitalism*. London: Cornell U.P.

Wallace, W. (1994) 'Rescue or Retreat? The Nation-State in Western Europe, 1945–93', *Political Studies*, 42: 52–76

Weiler, J. (1995) 'The State "uber alles": Demos, Telos and the German Maastricht Decision', Working Paper 6/95, Harvard Law School, Cambridge, Mass.

Zinn, K.G. (1978) 'The "Social Market" in Crisis', in Holland, S. (ed.) *Beyond Capitalist Planning*. Oxford: Basil Blackwell

Zuleeg, M. (1997) 'The European Constitution under Constitutional Constraints: The German Scenario', *European Law Review*, 22: 19–34

Part I

National Perspectives

2 Economic Consequences of EMU for Britain

Jonathan Michie

This chapter is structured as follows: following the introductory section, Section 2.2 considers the experience of the ERM. Section 2.3 then analyses the Maastricht treaty while Section 2.4 sets out the economics of a single currency. The EU's policies for jobs are discussed in Section 2.5 and Section 2.6 concludes.

2.1 INTRODUCTION

Europe seems locked into high levels of unemployment into the 21st century, with all the economic and social misery which goes with that. The blame is put on the 'world recession', or on trade unions, or on new technology, or on immigrants: almost anywhere except on government economic policy. Yet the governments of the European Union have been deliberately pursuing deflationary, low growth, high unemployment policies under the auspices of the Maastricht[1] convergence criteria.[2]

The resulting unemployment should come as no surprise. Similar policies were pursued in Britain under the gold standard[3] of the 1920s, with parallel results in terms of deflationary government economic policies and the creation of mass unemployment (Kitson and Michie, 1994). It seems that nothing has been learned. The world economy only managed to pull itself out of the Great Depression[4] in the 1930s by abandoning fixed exchange rates, cutting interest rates and boosting growth. Yet when similar policies were advocated prior to 16 September 1992, when Britain was forced out of the ERM against its will by the currency speculators, such policies were denounced as 'anti-European'. But it does our European partners no favours to have our economy in recession, any more than we are currently being helped by our EU partners pursuing restrictive policies.

Unless current European economic policy is reorientated towards the objective of full employment, embracing an active industrial and regional policy, rather than being stuck on the myopic concern with zero inflation, the route forward must once again be based on independent national growth strategies which would not only allow countries to help themselves, but in doing so to help each other. Competitive deflation – not competitive devaluation – was the real 'beggar my neighbour' policy of the 1990s. As the economist Joan Robinson put it: 'Of all bad-neighbourly conduct among trading nations, the worst is to go into a slump'.

2.2   THE ERM

The Exchange Rate Mechanism (ERM) of the European Monetary System (EMS) tried to bring national currencies more or less into line. Britain joined the ERM in October 1990. The pound was pegged at 2.95 Deutschmarks. This was too high a rate, making goods produced in Britain relatively expensive compared to goods produced elsewhere. This means that market share is lost abroad, and also at home as imports become more competitive against domestically produced goods. The overvalued rate at which the pound was pegged in the ERM therefore caused markets to be lost, production to be cut back, with firms going to the wall, and workers sacked.

Why then was an overvalued exchange rate chosen by the government when they entered the ERM in the first place? In part it was for the stated objective of squeezing inflation; what was not stated is the route by which it was hoped it would work, by deliberately making things hard for British firms, thereby forcing them to try to cut costs by turning on their workers, cutting wages and forcing increased work pressures. This is not the first time that governments have allowed the currency to be overvalued in this way. Winston Churchill as chancellor took Britain back onto the gold standard in the 1920s at an overvalued rate, with Keynes warning at the time, in his pamphlet *The Economic Consequences of Mr Churchill*, of the disastrous likely consequences of this policy – consequences which were to include the General Strike of 1926 (Keynes, 1925). Similarly, the first Thatcher recession of 1979–81 was exacerbated by the high exchange rate caused not only by the coming on-stream of North Sea oil, increasing the demand from overseas for sterling with which to buy that oil, but also by the high interest rates which followed from the government's monetarist policies. Thatcher's attempts to reduce money supply growth were pursued through increasing interest rates, aiming to reduce the amount people would then want, or be able, to borrow. But the high interest rates also attracted money into the country, pushing up the exchange rate (Michie, 1992).

In the inter-war period Britain was indeed forced to abandon the gold standard. And the exchange rate similarly fell after 1981, depreciating nearly 30 per cent by 1986, helping fuel the recovery. Likewise, the overvalued rate at which Chancellor Major entered the ERM meant that our membership was always doomed to failure. Yet those who pointed this out at the time were dismissed out of hand. It was said amongst other things that if sterling left the ERM then interest rates would have to rise; this proved false. The leadership of all three major political parties supported continued membership at the overvalued rate. Even if this had been a genuine option, it would have been a disastrous one. But in reality it was not even an option. It was unsustainable. As Bryan Gould has argued, Britain's ERM membership was vitiated by at least three policy mistakes:

> First, we chose a plainly over-valued parity. This was not an accident, but a deliberate attempt to use over-valuation as a means of bearing down on costs and imposing a counter-inflationary discipline. The result, of course, was so to enfeeble our productive economy that the gap between the exchange rate decreed by the ERM and the rate that could be justified by the performance of the real economy widened inexorably and eventually became unsustainable.
>
> Secondly, the obligations imposed by ERM membership were asymmetrical. The whole burden of staying within the parity bands fell upon the weaker economies who found that, in a vain attempt to maintain short-term competitiveness and to shore up their currencies, they were obliged to try to cut costs through deflationary measures like high interest rates and cuts in public investment.
>
> The Germans, on the other hand, whose appreciating D-Mark put constant pressure on the parity bands, recognised no obligation to bring their currency back into line by reflating and cutting interest rates. It was for this reason that the ERM became a deflationary engine. It was no accident that Western Europe became the world's unemployment black spot.

Thirdly, the ERM itself changed in nature. It ceased to be a 'crawling peg' arrangement – a sensible means of securing greater exchange rate stability by damping down excessive market volatility. It became instead the essential pre-condition for and means of the transition to a single currency. As a result, no adjustments could be permitted. The parities had to be set in concrete. Such inflexibility was inevitably shattered into fragments by the sheer force of economic realities and market pressures.

(Gould, 1993)

So the problems of the ERM lie deeper than just having joined at the wrong rate. It was a high unemployment mechanism, because all the pressure was on the weak economies to take action, rather than on the strong ones.[5] And worse, that action is designed more to prop up the currencies of the weak economies than to strengthen those economies' productive potential, which is the only sustainable basis for maintaining a healthy currency. Increased interest rates are ordered. These depress investment plans and leave the economy in question further weakened. Yet it is most likely the weakness of the economy which underlay the weakness of the currency in the first place. So a weak economy produces a weak currency; the ERM then requires the government in question to raise interest rates; and increased interest rates squeeze the country's economy, leaving it still weaker.[6]

2.3   THE MAASTRICHT TREATY

The three key points of the Maastricht treaty are described below.

All power to the central bankers

The Central Bank would be independent.[7] This means independent from any democratic influence, control or accountability. The electorate of Britain and of the European Union would no longer be able to decide on, or even influence, monetary policy. Indeed, such influence would be outlawed. This is fundamentally undemocratic. It is true that the Bank of England was made independent by the Labour Government elected in 1997, but the chancellor Gordon Brown has pledged that new mechanism will ensure that the Bank will nevertheless be accountable. At the time of writing (September 1997) the proof of this is yet to be seen.

Price stability

Not only would the central bankers be independent from the electorate, they would be constitutionally prevented from prioritizing full employment; their one 'primary objective' would be to achieve and maintain 'price stability' (this is referred to several times; see for example article 3a). Everything else would have to be secondary, 'without prejudice to this objective' (of price stability, same article). Why, then, did the treaty's drafters have such a mania for price stability? And should we object to this? The idea of price stability is often presented as preferable to inflation because it would be more stable, in the sense that it would be easier to hold inflation at that zero (or low) rate than it would be to hold inflation stable around a higher rate. But there is no reason why this should be so. The inflation rate is the average of thousands of price movements, some falling, like the price for personal computers at the moment, or houses (although the way house prices are dealt with in inflation indexes varies), some stable and some rising. If zero inflation is achieved it would not be because prices were stable, but because these movements happened to cancel each other out on average. And there is no reason why that average rate of inflation should remain static just because it previously was averaging at a value of zero or 1 per cent, rather than say 7 or 8 per cent. At a more practical level, the reason for the Maastricht treaty's preoccupation with the rate of inflation is because it arose from the deliberations of the Delors Committee (composed largely of bankers) before the European Union's economy slumped into its early-1990s recession. In part, then, Maastricht is just yesteryear's treaty, focusing on 1980s issues when what is needed as we approach the millenium are policies for expansion and employment. The other problem with the treaty is that the goal of stable prices is not to be pursued through positive interventionist measures, such as price controls, or the rejuvenating of industry which might allow cost increases to be absorbed by productivity increases rather than being passed on in higher prices. The way that progressive economic policies can help tackle inflation are set out in detail by Deakin *et al.* (1992), but the key point is that low inflation should be pursued on the basis of a strong economy which can absorb cost increases.[8] The treaty would instead limit the economic policy options to the free market pursuit of monetarism, plus rate capping.

National rate capping

Government borrowing in member states would be capped at 3 per cent of national income (GDP). Similarly, government debt would have to be kept below 60 per cent of GDP. But when GDP is falling – as it was in Britain throughout 1991 and 1992 – this could require debt to be cut in line, which could exacerbate the decline in national income itself. Also, the Maastricht treaty sets the debt criterion in terms of gross rather than net debt – that is, totally ignoring all assets. This is a very narrow view of the government's balance sheet. It in effect forbids governments from taking account of even their most liquid assets in setting fiscal policy. Selling assets to pay debt (for example through privatization), which in reality leaves the government no better off, since their assets will have fallen, is seen as an improvement according to the Maastricht conditions. Indeed, the situation is even worse than this, because under the Maastricht conditions the government's performance is thought to have improved even if it sells off assets for less than they are worth. The amount of money brought in from the sale, however low, is seen as pure gain in reducing 'gross debt', while the loss of the asset is totally ignored.

2.3.1   Maastricht and the alternatives

On alternatives to the Maastricht criteria, firstly, there is no reason to have any such rules on fiscal policy – the USA doesn't put any such rules on its States, and the British government never used to put such rules on its local authorities, until the Tories introduced rate capping. Secondly, on fiscal redistribution, the MacDougall Report (CEC, 1977) suggested that a Community budget equivalent to 7 per cent of GDP would be necessary just to tackle 40 per cent of existing inequalities, yet the budget at present is set at 1.27 per cent; the more ambitious proposal rejected at the 1992 Edinburgh summit was for this to rise to only 1.38 per cent.

There would be something to be said for creating a new superstate, with one government, one fiscal policy, one industrial policy and so on. One attraction would be the power to intervene in the economy to force through socially beneficial outcomes. But it is quite dishonest (or else naive) to present Maastricht as representing anything along these lines. It represents the precise opposite – an attempt to roll back the state on a European scale – to give capital free reign.

It is sometimes argued that the power of the international markets to dictate to nationally elected governments is such that no one country can any longer defend its own currency. But this is hardly new. It is true that this power has been boosted in recent years by the free-market, deregulatory policies pursued by governments. But probably the clearest example of such a process, designed to increase the power of multinational capital and financial markets, has been the programme of increased European Community/ Union integration. It is quite wrong to interpret this process as a reaction to the increased power of multinational capital. On the contrary, the Single European Market programme,[9] and now the Maastricht proposals for a single currency, have shifted the balance away from governments, in favour of private capital.

To respond effectively to the challenges of growth and employment, of social and environmental policy will require the exact opposite of everything that the Maastricht treaty represents. The current proposals for a single currency are at heart part of a political process which will prevent governments – whether at national or EU level – from pursuing policies to promote economic and social welfare. Instead, economic policy will be in the hands of unaccountable European central bankers. A single currency Europe will increase the leverage of the international markets to behave exactly as they wish, and will prevent elected governments from pursuing the policies they were elected on, unless of course these happen to coincide with the interests of those financial markets. And this is therefore likely to happen, with the policies of political parties becoming determined less and less in response to people's aspirations and more and more by what is deemed acceptable to the continued undisturbed operation of international financial markets and multinational corporations.

2.3.2 Background to Maastricht

The '1992' process required all member states to abolish exchange controls, allowing capital to flow freely across borders. (The Thatcher government had of course already abolished Britain's exchange controls in 1979.) This, the Commission argued, would increase economic welfare, since the money would be able to travel across frontiers in order to be put to more productive use. Instead the money went into speculation. Only 5 per cent of all capital flows now relate to trade in goods and services, or to money spent on holidays, or to any other real activity. The remaining 95 per cent is conducted by foreign exchange dealers trying to second guess each other to make a speculative profit.

Having proposed and successfully implemented this financial free for all, on quite spurious grounds, the European Commission then went on to argue that it was contradictory to maintain separate national currencies – the pound sterling, the franc, the deutschmark and so on. If there were no longer any restrictions on capital moving from one of those countries to the other, it was argued, then individual member states would no longer be able to pursue independent monetary policies; if they lowered interest rates below those operating in the other countries, money would just flow out. So since abolishing exchange controls had thereby removed the member states' ability to pursue their own independent monetary policies, they might as well recognize the fact and go the whole way, abandoning their separate currencies and handing monetary and interest rate policy over to a central bank. (And thereby also give up any exchange rate policy, since the countries would no longer have separate exchange rates to adjust.) An alternative would have been to reintroduce exchange controls. Instead we got Maastricht, which stipulates that exchange controls be outlawed forever and that a single currency be adopted.

Maastricht, by removing any possibility for currency realignment between member states, and by removing any possibility for lowering interest rates below those in other EU countries, would make the ERM permanent and compulsory. It is true that, with no separate currencies, the weakness of one economy would no longer be signalled by a weak currency, yet the lack of a signal would not abolish the structural problem. Instead, the lack of industrial competitiveness of that geographical area would lead to a loss of industry and jobs, leading to a downward slide into relative economic decline. As Wynne Godley has argued:

> It is thus an extraordinary fact about Maastricht that the only new institution to be created is a new independent central bank to run monetary policy. How is the rest of economic policy supposed to be run? How in particular is fiscal policy supposed to be determined? The authors of the Treaty appear to think that provided you have a central bank to conduct monetary policy, fiscal policy and every other aspect of economic policy can be resolved by laying down one or two simple rules, for instance

that countries should normally balance their budget. Now I think this is a very impoverished and inadequate proposal, and I am forced to the conclusion that it could only have been made by people who think that nothing more is needed. That is, people who follow the new consensus and are prepared to base all their recommendations on the idea that economies are basically self-righting systems. It should be remembered that the Delors Committee, which was the forerunner of Maastricht, was predominantly composed of central bankers; the proposal to place all power in the hands of the central bank should perhaps not be so surprising.

... we have been down this road before. The need for active fiscal and exchange rate policies in the 1920s came up against the orthodoxy of the day, that public spending would crowd out private investment and that currency adjustments could be effected with a fixed exchange rate systems by forcing down domestic wages and prices. Those truths were wrong then and they are wrong today.

(Godley, 1993)

2.4 THE ECONOMICS OF A SINGLE CURRENCY

There are obvious attractions to having a single currency across countries which have high levels of trade with each other. Equally, even the most ardent supporters of the single currency proposals would admit that there are potential problems; indeed, if it were not the case that there were real difficulties, then surely more countries would by now have tried to tap the benefits by merging their currencies? The more rational supporters of Maastricht will agree that there are costs and potential dangers, but argue that these need not be overwhelming. Thus, for example, individual countries at the moment have single currencies without their weak regions spiralling into decline. So surely a single currency area covering all fifteen member states could operate in the same way as individual countries do at present?

There are two key reasons why this is not the case. First, the Maastricht treaty could have been quite different, proposing for example a single currency alongside a democratically accountable central bank, a bank committed to the pursuit of economic development, and allowing national governments to tackle unemployment, and expand public services, through government borrowing. Instead of this, Maastricht lays down that the single currency would be administered by central bankers accountable to no one, committed to trying to reduce inflation to achieve 'stable prices', and imposing rate-capping on EU governments through restrictions in the form of rigid limits on national public expenditure.

The second problem is that the Maastricht treaty would not provide the sort of economic mechanisms which do limit the decline of weak areas within existing 'single currency areas'. Within a single country such as Britain, the government's revenue, in the form of income tax, VAT, company taxes and the like, is collected from all areas of the country. Similarly, the money is spent on health, education, unemployment pay, housing and other welfare benefits and so on, in all areas of the country. Now, if one area in particular suffers bad times there is an automatic transfer of resources from all the other areas of the country to that area. This helps prevent the depressed area from falling into a spiral of decline. If this one area hits hard times, then the profits of the companies operating in that area will fall, so they will pay less profits tax to the central government. If people are made unemployed they will pay no income tax. And those who remain in work may for example earn less overtime pay, and so they may also pay less income tax than before. The result is that less money flows from that particular area of the country into the Treasury coffers. And the same process works on the spending side. More people in that area will receive unemployment pay from central government. More money will go to that area in the form of housing benefit, social security and other transfers. So a higher share than before of national government spending will go to that area of the country. All this happens automatically without the government actively doing anything. It involves no decision making.

This process is referred to as 'fiscal transfers' since it refers to government spending (fiscal policy) and it results in money being transferred automatically from areas which are prospering to areas in economic difficulty. It operates through the tax and benefit system, affecting the whole country (the single currency area). No equivalent process would be in operation in Maastricht's new single currency area because the vast bulk of taxation revenue and public spending would remain locked within the existing nation states – the new regions of the European super-state. So the automatic transfer between regions would not take place. The poor would just get poorer. And this in turn would undermine the revenue base from which benefits are funded.

If a country's currency is overvalued and its goods are therefore uncompetitive both at home and abroad, then this will tend to cause bankruptcies and unemployment. This in turn usually forces a devaluation (or depreciation of the currency) to remove the specific problem. With a single currency that possibility will be removed as far as, say, the British economy goes, in relation to all the other countries within the single currency, and also possibly with the rest of the world. There is the additional problem that even if the rate at which we join a single currency is appropriate, then with Britain's continued relative economic decline,[10] after a few years it is likely that a depreciation of Britain's currency against Germany's would be required, and yet this would no longer be possible. Nicholas Kaldor always warned that in the Common Market Britain risked becoming the 'Northern Ireland of Europe'. There is no guaranteed 'European' fate which all will enjoy equally, regardless of policies, exchange rates and so on. It is quite possible to become a declining region, locked into a vicious cycle of decline.

2.4.1 Would a single currency avoid balance of payments deficits?

One argument which is sometimes put in favour of a single currency, which is simply wrong, is that if we had the same currency as do France, Germany and the other EU countries, then we would no longer have a balance of payments deficit with them. In fact, however, the deficit would still be there. More money would still be going out of Britain than was coming in. What would change is that this deficit, and this drain, would no longer be recorded. And it would no longer be seen as the duty of the government to do anything about it. So to that extent, the underlying problem would actually be made worse. This real imbalance in economic activity would have to be balanced instead by falling relative income and wealth in Britain, a process which would continue until we could no longer afford the imports which were causing the problem. People would be made poorer; jobs would be lost. However, as the economy becomes impoverished, less is bought from domestic firms as well, so some of these will be forced out of business. We thereby lose any exports those firms may have had, and some of their custom will go not to other domestic firms but to imports. Hence the slide into poverty does not just restrict imports, it also damages exports. So the actual shortfall of exports from imports will not necessarily be made good. It could even deteriorate. In that situation there remains little to prevent the declining region of the single currency area from sliding further into poverty. The one lifeline would be the fiscal transfers which in this single currency area would be missing. Emigration is then all that is left, although even that does not necessarily improve the well-being of those left behind, particularly if it is the well trained who get the job offers elsewhere.[11]

A similar process would operate with what is at present Britain's balance of payments deficit with non-EU states, which would likewise be apparently abolished, becoming one component of the EU's balance of payments with the rest of the world, in the same way as, say, Yorkshire's trade is subsumed within Britain's balance at present. This book-keeping transfer would simply disguise the fact that there was a net outflow of money from what would by then be the British component of the greater single currency area.

2.4.2 Monetary and political union

If the monetary integration of several countries into one is thought desirable, then it should be seen as the final act of economic, industrial, social and political integration. Putting it first threatens to undermine the whole process. Above all, if monetary policy is to be centralized then so must all the other aspects of government economic policy. Maastricht would in effect do away with all these other aspects, such as any scope for active taxation and public spending policies, leaving the European Union's economy engineless and rudderless.

A single currency could only be considered acceptable within an EU-wide taxation and benefit system, and with massively expanded regional transfers from rich to poor parts of the Union to ensure real economic convergence, with living standards and employment levels moving closer together throughout the Union rather than further apart. The sort of substantial increase in regional policy spending required was ruled out by the December 1992 Edinburgh Summit, and any suggestions that there should be an EU-wide tax and benefits system has been totally rejected whenever the subject has been raised. There seems no prospect that the richer countries are prepared to see very substantial income transfers to poorer regions either in the form of regional policy or through the automatic transfers of a tax and benefit system.

2.5   EU POLICIES FOR JOBS

The EU's December 1993 biannual summit was billed as the one which was to tackle unemployment. Indeed, Delors warned that the Union's unemployment total could be heading for 30 million by the late 1990s if the policies in his December 1993 White Paper were not adopted. Similar sentiments were articulated by the EU's social affairs commissioner, Padraig Flynn, who described the White Paper as a plan for creating 20 million jobs by the end of the decade. At the same time, Mitterrand was calling for a doubling of the EU's spending on infrastructure and growth projects, as was Delors who was proposing in particular a widening of the programme to include investment in labour-intensive sectors such as housing, as well as subsidizing borrowing for small and medium sized enterprises. Even these rather modest proposals were scorned by the German and British governments. Indeed, less than half the £5.6 billion earmarked for recovery projects by the European Investment Bank had been committed by the end of October 1993, with Commission officials blaming the low take-up on the lack of commercially viable investment projects – hardly surprising in a recession – and because companies were failing to provide the matching finance required from the private sector.

While the Delors White Paper (Commission of the European Communities, 1993) was therefore welcome insofar as it went some way towards shifting the focus of policy onto the problem of unemployment, it remained hopelessly compromised by its failure to break from the policy strait-jacket within which the Maastricht treaty has trapped governments.[12]

The jobs initiative debated at the EU's previous summit, in Copenhagen in June 1993, involved radical changes in the Union's tax and social security system. The Commission wanted member states to reduce employers' national insurance contributions, shifting the tax burden onto others. The rational for such policies is that non-wage costs such as firms' social security payments add far more in the EU states on average than they do in Japan or the US. Yet such non-wage costs are already down to Japanese and US levels in Britain, and employment levels in the UK are not actually very impressive; the relatively low level of recorded unemployment simply reflects the fact that the official figures no longer record most unemployed people in the UK.[13] There is not, then, any automatic link between employers' national insurance contributions and employment levels. Indeed, employment in manufacturing – which should be particularly sensitive to factors affecting competitiveness – is lower in Britain as a percentage of the population in work than it is in Germany or France, despite the far higher indirect employment costs in those countries.

An additional policy idea from the Commission has been to introduce such reductions in employer taxes on unskilled labour in particular. On the general idea of an employment subsidy, expanded public employment would be a more effective method of tackling unemployment, particularly if there are either inflation or balance of payments constraints (Glyn and Rowthorn, 1994). The specific idea of a differential subsidy for unskilled work – generally defined in these contexts as low-paid work, which raises a rather separate issue of why skills such as cooking or cleaning tend not to be recognized as skills – risks reducing firms' incentives to improve productivity and upgrade productive techniques (Michie and Wilkinson, 1995).

Behind the talk of jobs packages, therefore, lies the longer term agenda of economic and monetary union. What has been amply demonstrated in the academic and policy literature is that, measured against the criteria for being an 'optimum currency area', even the present 15 member states (never mind a Union with additional members) falls some way short, and this short-fall would have to be made up – if the process of integration is to proceed, and to do so without straining cohesion to breaking point – by active industrial and regional policies to ensure the continual (not just one-off) economic adjustments to so-called 'shocks', and more generally, to different levels and growth rates of output and productivity.

With talk today of the possibility of a 'two-speed Europe' – with Germany and the Benelux countries (with or without France) moving more rapidly to monetary union – it is worth recalling that the ill-fated gold standard did not collapse in one go in the 1930s: some countries attempted to maintain the fixed exchange rate system, thus heralding a two- (or multi-) tier system; (see Kitson and Michie, 1994). The ones who stuck with the system grew more slowly, those who left first grew fastest. Hence the 'speed' with which countries move towards fixed exchange rate systems should not be confused with the speed at which their economies will grow. In a two-speed Europe the 'slow' lane may be preferable.

Of course, one of the stock responses to any call for growth is to refer to the expansionary policies of the Mitterrand government in

1981, and the subsequent U-turn of 1983. The orthodox interpretation of this experience is that the Keynesian policies were discovered to be unsustainable because of balance of payments and exchange rate constraints and hence had to be abandoned. This is (as argued by Halimi *et al.*, 1994) simply false: these difficulties were not learned from the 1981–83 experience in France but were perfectly well understood and stated quite explicitly by amongst others the French Socialist Party before taking office. The problems which any government pursuing such expansionary policies would encounter were documented in advance as were the additional policies which would be necessary to see through the expansion – including the use of trade policies to ensure that imports grew only in line with exports.[14] The point is that no attempt was, in fact, made to actually introduce these additional, necessary policies; the Government instead chose the beggar-my-neighbour route of 'competitive disinflation'.

While coordination is preferable (as pointed out by Kalecki in 1932), there are nevertheless viable programmes for raising employment is a single country; indeed, the only way of building support for an EU-level expansion may be through the contagious impact of a successful expansion of employment in one country first. Indeed, the 'cooperative' route – of completing the internal market and pursuing economic and monetary union – has tended to increase industrial concentration and exacerbate regional disparities, and an active industrial policy is instead needed to ensure the development of industrial activity outside the European core. To consider the nature which such an interventionist strategy to bolster industrial performance might take, it is necessary to draw a distinction between the notion of a developmental state, organized and concerned to promote economic and industrial development, on the one hand, and a regulatory state on the other, concentrating instead on competition policy. A broadly conceived industrial strategy (as opposed to just a 'policy') is needed to offset the forces of cumulative causation which otherwise will increase disparities and exacerbate the underutilization of resources in backward regions in particular.

Current levels of unemployment are a reflection of the political priorities attached to different objectives of economic policy. The low demand created by monetarist and restrictive economic policies has eroded the capacity to produce: plant capacity, management structures, sales organization, skilled and experienced labour, and the number of firms have all settled down at a level consistent with high unemployment. Increased demand is therefore needed, but it would have to be sustained if capacity is to be rebuilt. This is unlikely with an independent European Central Bank dedicated to the achievement of price stability. The emphasis has to be shifted towards restoring full employment.

2.6   CONCLUSION

Unemployment in Europe is due to the interrelation between macroeconomic policy, balance of payments constraints and deindustrialization. The idea of pursuing active macroeconomic and industrial policies has given way to an adherence to monetarism, privatization and labour market deregulation. Yet the resulting growth in low pay, poverty and unemployment have, ironically, placed an increasing burden on the public purse. At the same time, productive efficiency is harmed by the resulting instability in the labour market – particularly within the increasingly low-paid sectors – and the loss of incentives for producers to upgrade the productive systems. A vicious circle of low-wage, low-productivity, low-investment activity is generated, leading to loss of competitiveness and growing unemployment, with the increasing burdens on the exchequer provoking yet further moves down the recessionary spiral (Michie and Wilkinson, 1994, 1995).

An alternative agenda would include, firstly, pushing for global expansion rather then being the most orthodox, 1920s-style block in the world. Secondly, there are a series of measures which there seems little hope of getting adopted, such as reestablishing exchange controls, but to paraphrase Keynes, just because people won't listen to sense is no excuse for talking nonsense. The fact that such policies would be an improvement on the current state of affairs should still be pointed out. And thirdly, there are things which would appear acceptable to call for even in today's free market climate, such as keeping the government responsible for monetary policy rather than handing it over to unaccountable central bankers; keeping the government responsible for fiscal policy, that is, abandoning the Maastricht treaty's restrictions on this; keeping the possibility of currency realignments in the event of one member state's output becoming uncompetitive, rather than adopting a single currency; and restoring the right to pursue interventionist industrial policies which are increasingly falling foul of free-market dictats from Brussels. In other words, member states should pursue the sort of industrial, interest rate, exchange rate and fiscal policies which some of them used to, before most of this became outlawed.

A rule could be introduced within the ERM that a country whose currency is drifting more than x per cent above the average would be required to cut its interest rates so as to bring about a decline towards the average (the opposite requirement to the present one), although this could be moderated by saying that such a country might be allowed not to respond in this way (that is, cut interest rates) if its unemployment rate was already below say 4 per cent or if its inflation rate was already above say 10 per cent.

To the extent that a country is obliged to 'defend' its currency, then it is damaging if this is done by raising interest rates above the rate which is appropriate for the domestic economy (that is, the rate which firms would face when wondering whether to invest). This was ex-UK chancellor Norman Lamont's problem when trying to stay in the ERM when he raised interest rates and announced that a further rise would follow that evening – it was just not credible that a government whose domestic economy was in the longest recession since the 1930s would raise interest rates and keep them there when what was required was to cut them. Instead, if the government wants to defend a particular exchange rate parity then exchange controls should be used.

What is wrong is the free market, *laissez faire* character of the process of European integration at present. So the basic point about what needs to be done is that European governments and the European Commission should stop introducing 1920s-style policies and rules; the countries of Europe should then pursue interventionist policies to tackle unemployment, and should cooperate internationally over it.

The power of international capitalism to dictate to nationally elected governments is not new, although it is true that it has been boosted in recent years by the free-market, deregulatory policies pursued by governments. Probably the clearest example of such a process, designed to increase the power of multinational capital and financial markets, has been the programme of increased European Community/Union integration. It is quite wrong to interpret this process as a reaction to the increased power of multinational capital; on the contrary, the Single European Market programme and now the Maastricht proposals for a single currency have themselves deliberately shifted the balance away from governments. To respond effectively to the challenges of growth, employment, social policy and so on will require the exact opposite of everything that the Maastricht treaty represents – which is a return to the *laissez faire* politics of the 1920s where any suggestion that governments could act was opposed by the Treasury using the very same arguments as now (that reflation in one country is impossible, and so on).

EMU is at heart a political process which will prevent governments – whether at national or EU level – from pursuing policies to promote economic and social welfare. Such a scenario is no more sustainable now that when it was last in place, namely in the 1920s and 1930s. It is likely to come to the same unpleasant end, with individual countries being eventually forced to take action regardless of the power of international capitalism. But with the European political elite so wedded to the *laissez faire* politics of Maastricht, any such attempt by the population to insist that they should be allowed to express political preferences risks taking ugly nationalist forms, against the 'internationalism' of the European central bankers and the entire existing political elite.

Notes

1. Maastricht is a town in Holland where the 'Maastricht Treaty' was signed by the finance and foreign ministers of the (then) 12 member states in February 1992. The official name for the Treaty is the *Treaty on European Union*. The aim of economic and monetary union is to abolish in three stages the national currencies of member states and introduce, by 1999 at the latest, one single currency to be managed by an 'independent' central bank whose prime policy aim would be 'price stability'. The aims of political union include common policies in foreign affairs and security, and to merge the Western European Union (WEU) with the EU.
2. The European Community is what was previously known as the European Economic Community (EEC), established by the Treaty of Rome in 1957, and referred to as the Common Market. Since the 1992 Maastricht Treaty it has generally been known as the European Union (EU), although technically the European Economic Community continues under the Maastricht Treaty of European Union.
3. A country is said to be on the gold standard when its Central Bank is obliged to give gold in exchange for any of its currency presented to it.
4. The 'Great Depression' refers to the global recession of 1929–32.
5. More responsibility should have been placed on the countries whose currencies were at the top of the currency range to take action, rather

than have the burden falling on those economies already in difficulty. The stronger economies could cut interest rates and boost government spending. As their economies expanded so they would be likely to import more. And as their currency is offered on the foreign exchange markets to pay for those imports, its price against other currencies would tend to decline back towards its central rate.

6. On the importance of creating industrial capacity as a progressive way of overcoming balance of payments and inflation constraints, see Michie and Grieve Smith (1996) and in particular the chapter by Kitson and Michie (and also Kitson and Michie, 1996a).

7. See for example the 'Protocol on the Statute of the European System of Central Banks and of the European Central Bank' at the end of the Treaty.

8. See also Michie and Wilkinson, 1992, 1993.

9. The Single European Market (SEM) – also known as the Internal Market or simply '1992' – consisted of a timetable of 300 measures agreed at the Milan EC summit in 1985 in preparation for 1 January 1993. Also known as the Cockfield plan after Commissioner Cockfield.

10. On which, see Kitson and Michie, 1996a.

11. The argument that balance of payments deficits do not matter, or that they would be eliminated with a single currency, are comprehensively demolished by the contributions in *The Economic Legacy* (Michie, ed., 1992) from Brian Reddaway, from Ken Coutts and Wynne Godley, and from John McCombie and Tony Thirlwall.

12. For a full critical assessment of the Delors White Paper, see Grieve Smith (1994).

13. See for example Kitson, Michie and Sutherland (1997).

14. On which, see Kitson and Michie, 1995a 1995b.

References

Commission of the European Communities (1977) *Report of the Study Group on the Role of Public Finance in European Integration*, Economic and Financial Series, no. 13, volumes I and II ('The MacDougall Report') Luxembourg: Commission of the European Communities

Commission of the European Communities (1993) *Growth, Competitiveness, Employment: The Challenges and Ways Forward into the 21st Century* ('The Delors White Paper'). Luxembourg: Commission of the European Communities

Deakin, S., Michie, J. and Wilkinson, F. (1992) *Inflation, Employment, Wage-bargaining and the Law*. London: Institute of Employment Rights

Glyn, A. and Rowthorn, B. (1994) 'European Employment Policies', Chapter 12 of Michie, J. and Grieve Smith, J. (eds), *Unemployment in Europe*. London: Academic Press

Godley, W. (1993) 'Foreword' to Kitson, M. and Michie, J. *Coordinated Deflation: The Tale of Two Recessions*. London: Full Employment Forum

Gould, B. (1993) 'Preface' to Kitson, M. and Michie, J. *Coordinated Deflation:*

The Tale of Two Recessions. London: Full Employment Forum

Grieve Smith, J. (1994) 'The Delors White Paper on Unemployment', *International Review of Applied Economics*, vol. 8, no. 3 (September), pp. 341–7

Halimi, S., Michie, J. and Milne, S. (1994) 'The Mitterrand Experience', Chapter 6 of Michie, J. and Grieve Smith, J. (eds) *Unemployment in Europe*. London: Academic Press

Kalecki, M. (1932) 'Is a Capitalist Overcoming of the Crisis Possible?' and 'On the Paper Plan', in Osiatynski, J. (ed.) *Collected Works of Michal Kalecki*. Oxford: Oxford University Press, 1990

Keynes, J.M. (1925) 'The Economic Consequences of Mr Churchill', in *The Collected Writings of John Maynard Keynes, Volume IX: Essays in Persuasion*, pp. 207–30, published for the Royal Economic Society by Macmillan, reprinted 1973

Kitson, M. and Michie, J. (1994) 'Depression and Recovery: Lessons from the Interwar Period', Chapter 5 of Michie, J. and Grieve Smith, J. (eds) *Unemployment in Europe*. London: Academic Press

Kitson, M. and Michie, J. (1995a) 'Trade and Growth: A Historical Perspective', Chapter 1 of Michie, J. and Grieve Smith, J. (eds) *Managing the Global Economy*. Oxford: Oxford University Press

Kitson, M. and Michie, J. (1995b) 'Conflict, Cooperation and Change: The Political Economy of Trade and Trade Policy', *Review of International Political Economy*, vol. 2, no. 4 (Autumn), pp. 632–57

Kitson, M. and Michie, J. (1996a) 'Britain's Industrial Performance Since 1960: Underinvestment and Relative Decline', *Economic Journal*, vol. 106, no. 434 (January), pp. 196–212

Kitson, M. and Michie, J. (1996b) 'Manufacturing Capacity, Investment, and Employment', in Michie, J. and Grieve Smith, J. (eds), *Creating Industrial Capacity: Towards Full Employment*. Oxford: Oxford University Press

Kitson, M., Michie, J. and Sutherland, H. (1997) 'The fiscal and distributional implications of job generation', *Cambridge Journal of Economics*, vol. 21, no. 1 (January), pp. 103–20

Michie, J. (ed.) (1992) *The Economic Legacy: 1979–1992*. London: Academic Press

Michie, J. and Grieve Smith, J. (eds) (1994) *Unemployment in Europe*. London: Academic Press

Michie, J. and Grieve Smith, J. (eds) (1995) *Managing the Global Economy*. Oxford: Oxford University Press

Michie, J. and Grieve Smith, J. (eds) (1996) *Creating Industrial Capacity: Towards Full Employment*. Oxford: Oxford University Press

Michie, J. and Wilkinson, F. (1992) 'Inflation Policy and the Restructuring of Labour Markets', Chapter 9 of Michie, J. (ed.), *The Economic Legacy: 1979–1992*. London: Academic Press

Michie, J. and Wilkinson, F. (1993) *Unemployment and Workers' Rights*. London: Institute of Employment Rights

Michie, J. and Wilkinson, F. (1994) 'The Growth of Unemployment in the 1980s', Chapter 1 of Michie, J. and Grieve Smith, J. (eds), *Unemployment in Europe*. London: Academic Press

Michie, J. and Wilkinson, F. (1995) 'Wages, Government Policy and Unemployment', *Review of Political Economy*, vol. 7, no. 2 (Special Issue on 'High Unemployment in Western Economies').

Robinson, J. (1966) 'The New Mercantilism', in *An Inaugural Lecture*. Cambridge: Cambridge University Press. Reprinted in *Collected Economic Papers*, vol. 4. Oxford: Blackwell, 1973

Wedderburn, W. (1990) *The Social Charter, European Company and Employment Rights*. London: Institute of Employment Rights

3 France: Economic and Monetary Union and the Social Divide

Bernard H. Moss

INTRODUCTION

France has played both a pivotal and a contrapuntal role in the development of the European Community (EC) and Economic and Monetary Union (EMU). Initiators of the European communities, the French were also the strongest dissenters from the market direction they took. With strong Gaullist and Communist parties, the French were sceptical of both the supranationalism and economic liberalism of the 1957 Treaty of Rome. European integration could only go so far as France, the dissenting partner, wanted. The turnabout of French policy under François Mitterrand in 1982–83, from nationalization and Keynesian reflation to deflation and competitive markets, provided the thrust for the completion of the European single market and creation of the single currency in 1992.

French monetary policy reflected the peculiar strength of the Communists (PCF) in the unions and working class. Until Mitterrand's U-turn, post-war governments had relied upon monetary inflation, devaluation and administered credit to sustain growth and guarantee social peace. With the exception of the period following General de Gaulle's seizure of power in 1958, there was little choice for governments faced with weak, divided and conflictual unions, a volatile work force, and a united Left threatening radical change. Where German governments responded to union challenges and the oil shock with deflation, the French expanded the money supply. The divergence of French policy from German after 1968 made European economic and monetary union impossible, despite several attempts.

By aligning the franc with the D-Mark at a high rate and reversing the course of economic policy in 1982–83, Mitterrand laid the basis for the single market initiative and EMU but his sound money policy, renewed again after 1988, caused higher unemployment and greater class inequality and opened up the crisis of representation and confidence which presidential candidate Jacques Chirac, borrowing from Emmanuel Todd,[1] called the social divide.

The social divide described the alienation from the elites not only of manual workers, the traditional revolutionaries, but of all wage-earners, white-collar, even managerial personnel, facing the new insecurities of the market place. Unlike the traditional class struggle, it was not structured by the PCF, but took a variety of forms. It appeared obscurely at first in the increase of abstentions and rise of the National Front after 1983 then more overtly in the 'no' vote in the 1992 referendum on Maastricht, support for the railway strike of November–December 1995, and finally the election in May 1997 of a Socialist-Communist government pledged to close this social divide.

All French elections since the oil shock of 1974 have been fought around the question of employment. A majority voted for Mitterrand in 1981 because he promised to raise wages and social benefits and to secure jobs, especially through nationalization. Once Mitterrand had adopted sound money and replaced socialism with Europe as his talisman, people could not help drawing the causal link between the Exchange Rate Mechanism (ERM) and budgetary austerity and unemployment. With the exception of the period 1987–90 when France benefited from an expansionary cycle, each new step toward EMU produced more unemployment, increased class inequality and growing poverty. EMU could only be seen by wage-earners as a betrayal not only of Mitterrand's promises but of French norms of market regulation that dated from 1945.[2]

POLITICAL ECONOMY: FRANCE VERSUS EC

The political economy of post-war France reflected the strength of the Left – Communists and Socialists – in the Liberation and post-war elections. The state was made responsible not only for social protection as elsewhere, but also for economic reconstruction and growth. This was to be achieved through the nationalization of energy and transport, a system of indicative planning, and administered credit. Price control, protectionism, and devaluation were other instruments of public economic policy. The expansion of the money supply, devaluation and extension of bank loans to selected firms to promote growth gave an inflationary bias to the economy despite ten price freezes over thirty years.[3] French growth in the 1950s depended on public investment and demand with a low rate of imports controlled by quotas.[4]

This political economy was threatened by the EC in many ways. The emphasis in proposals for a common market, from the Beyen Plan[5] in 1953 to the preliminary Spaak Report[6] in 1956, was on harmonizing policies and prices, guarding against inflation and devaluation, and aiming for a single currency. The treaty of Rome contained a liberal – largely German and Dutch – design for the construction of a regime for the free trade of goods, services, capital and labour and stable prices in which national economic and monetary policy would be coordinated. The concern for the 'approximation' of national policies rather than counter-cyclical intervention seemed to exclude competitive devaluations and pointed the ways to fixed exchange rates and, in the view of the Commission, to a single currency.[7]

The Common Market had originally been opposed by nearly everyone in France: by the administration, defending interventionism, and by industry, complaining of high labour and social costs. The government of Edgar Faure in 1955 showed no interest in a common market while that of the Socialist Guy Mollet, a member of Jean Monnet's Committee for the United States of Europe, made a counterproposal in 1956 for a European economy that would be highly planned and regulated, one favouring wage-earners over employers. When serious negotiations began, Mollet felt compelled by French opinion to insist on the prior upward harmonization of social benefits – equal wages for men and women, paid holidays, and standardized overtime pay – guaranteed by a French veto of the process. Few ministers took the negotiations seriously. 'Do whatever you want,' the negotiator on monetary questions was told, 'All this is fatuous and will never be applied; the French economy could not stand it.'[8] In the end it was fear of diplomatic isolation arising out of the crushing of the Hungarian revolution and failure of the Suez expedition that brought France together with Germany on the treaty. France conceded that social harmonization would have to occur primarily through the operation of market forces but obtained a protocol allowing the use of import quotas and export incentives and one on overtime pay – protocols that were never invoked. Few thought the treaty, greeted with indifference, would ever be enforced.[9]

It is said accurately that de Gaulle would never have signed the treaty and Mollet could never had enforced it. If de Gaulle was able to comply with the terms for a customs union, it was because he disposed of the instruments of a popular authoritarian regime. In the 1958 elections the Gaullist party swept the boards, practically eliminating the Left from parliament. De Gaulle opened the gates for French export and productivity growth by a 30 per cent devaluation in 1959. This competitive advantage was maintained by a government that was not afraid to cut wages in 1959 and requisition striking rail workers and miners, and by employers who were left free to refuse collective bargaining. France with its high growth rate and export performance in the 1960s became the model of modernization – even the Americans sent observers to find out what it was all about – and nobody in Brussels seemed to mind that its Byzantine system of state aids, exemptions and subsidies was in violation of the treaty.[10]

With the completion of the customs union in 1968 the Commission turned its attention towards a monetary union that was always implicit in the treaty. Until 1968 Germany and France had been growing apace with little inflation and without devaluation since 1958. On the basis of this convergence Raymond Barre, the French liberal economist and Commissioner of Economic Affairs, proposed the coordination of economic and monetary policy in 1969. This led to the Werner Commission, which recommended a ten-year plan to achieve a single currency with the formation of a central economic coordinating body responsible to the European Parliament. It rejected a French proposal for a European industrial policy.

This was enough for Georges Pompidou, the pro-European who had replaced de Gaulle as president in 1969, to say 'no'. The plan not only encroached upon French sovereignty, but it threatened the dynamics of French growth.[11] While the Germans met wage increases in 1967 with a tight money policy that induced recession, France responded to the social demands of May–June 1968, which raised the minimum wage 35 per cent and the average wage 8 per cent,[12] by increasing the money supply. Underlying Pompidou's veto was his concern for governability:

We cannot accept a brutal and unrestrained capitalism which would bring on political revolt in member states first in Italy and then France . . . Europe can only be made gradually. It is not M. Malfatti [president of the Commission] who will have to confront the wine growers of the Midi if there are troubles; it is the government that will have to send troops and if it turns nasty, it is the French government which will be overturned... If there's a new May 68, it is not M. Malfatti who will speak to the Séguy [Communist leader of the 1968 strikes] of the moment.[13]

Unlike conservatives in other countries, who were not afraid to increase unemployment,[14] the French faced a volatile work force and, after 1972, a radical Left that was gaining in electoral credibility. Blaming May–June on Gaullist austerity, Pompidou increased the money supply from 1970 to 1973, promoting growth as the key to social peace. Valéry Giscard d'Estaing, finance minister, remarked on French differences with the Germans, who literally welcomed higher unemployment and unused factory capacity in the battle against inflation.[15] France and Germany diverged sharply in response to the oil shock of 1974, the one[16] maintaining a high rate of growth at the cost of higher inflation and lower profits while the other made workers bear the cost of recession. Despite the shock, the Bank of France set money and credit targets to achieve 'full employment and maintain growth'.[17] Pressure on the franc was met with capital controls, foreign borrowing and drawing down reserves. The new president in 1974, Giscard d'Estaing, first tried to cool down the economy, but quickly switched to expansion with the first sign of rising unemployment. The neo-Gaullist prime minister Chirac, looking toward the cantonal elections of 1976, launched a stimulus package in September 1975 in the midst of recovery. On two occasions, in January 1974 and March 1976, because of expansionary policies the French were forced to devalue and leave the monetary 'snake', the remnant of the Werner Plan that tied the franc to the D-Mark.[18]

Dramatic change came with the appointment of Barre as prime minister in 1976. He instituted wage guidelines, stabilized the budget, restricted the money supply and, following a victory over the Left in March 1978, began to remove price controls. He only went half-way in the eyes of liberals because he did nothing to lighten the load of social transfers, especially unemployment insurance, or of selective aid and subsidized loans to industry. Overshooting his monetary targets in the face of the second oil shock, he allowed inflation to reach 13 per cent in 1980. With the best of intentions not even Barre could ignore the danger of a Left victory in 1981.[19]

It was in the context of liberalization that the new head of the Commission in 1977, Roy Jenkins, proposed a European monetary system. The French liked the idea because they thought it would create a haven of stability against the dollar and serve as an external discipline for internal austerity. With divergence indicators and credit facilities the ERM gave slightly more protection to currency margins than had the 'snake'. The Germans however warned that they would not prop up another currency if it threatened their price stability. Preference for responding to major imbalances was given the realignments, which would be subject to mutual consent. In the event of a crisis, members' finances would be collectively managed by the EC's Monetary Committee – as Mitterrand would discover.[20]

POLITICAL ECONOMY: TURNABOUT OF MITTERRAND

Mitterrand was elected in 1981 on a program derived from that of the Marxist *Projet socialiste* and the PCF that included the nationalization of major industrial firms and banks, an increase in wages and social benefits, and the reconquest of the domestic market though an industrial policy that would reduce imports from 23 to 20 per cent of GNP. State aid to industry was increased 240 per cent by 1985[21] at a time when the EC was trying to eliminate it entirely. Social transfers were increased by 13 per cent in 1981–82 and disposable income by 6.3 per cent. Jobs were created in the public sector and the labour supply cut by reductions in working time – to thirty-nine hours a week, five weeks paid vacation and retirement at sixty. But the fiscal stimulus was slight, only 2.3 per cent of GNP, not much more than in Chirac's expansion of 1975.[22]

Mitterrand may have implemented most of his program but his policies showed signs of hesitation and improvisation; they lacked the coherence that an industrial plan with perhaps temporary measures of trade protection would have given. Time was lost debating the extent of nationalization, the purpose and control of which was never made clear.[23] The Europeanist Jacques Delors, minister of finance, who never subscribed to the Common Program of the Left,[24] opposed both nationalizations and reflation. The international recession, with an over-valued dollar and rising interest rates, made recovery difficult. In the first two years Mitterrand maintained growth and employment, but at the cost of falling reserves and a rising trade and growing inflation deficit with Germany.

Mitterrand had decided it would not look good – to the Germans and others – to begin his term of office with a large devaluation within the ERM or to float outside it. Instead he was forced to make three smaller devaluation during 1981–83, involving collective management, largely German, of the French economy, which essentially reversed his expansionary thrust. The turning point came in Spring 1982 when prime minister Pierre Mauroy and Delors, after consulting with the Germans and the Commission, proposed a wage and price freeze to accompany devaluation. The plan, presented to Mitterrand while he was preoccupied with the Versailles summit of the seven wealthiest nations(G7), was approved by the EC Monetary Committee before it went to the French cabinet. The freeze brought about a loss of real wages and a historic reversal in distributive policy, which instead of favouring wages would henceforth, by deindexing wages from prices, raise profits. The government also undertook to keep the budget deficit under 3 per cent of GDP, the magical figure which became the criterion for EMU.[25]

To avoid a third austerity plan in March 1983 Mitterrand entertained a plan to leave the ERM and float the franc, and to bolster industry, which would benefit from lower interest rates, more state aid, trade protection and wage controls. He was tired, he said, of playing 'the dead dog floating in the stream'[26] to the Germans. He was apparently dissuaded by the opposition of Mauroy and Delors and by the head of Treasury, who cited low reserves and predicted a fall of the franc by more than 20 per cent. This time the Germans required a comprehensive austerity plan in return for their 5.5 per cent revaluation – a tax surcharge, compulsory loan based on income tax, and a restriction on foreign exchange for tourists – removing 2 per cent of GNP from consumption.[27]

Most commentators have concluded from this reversal that the outcome was dictated by international market forces and that there was no alternative. But like de Gaulle in 1958 Mitterrand might have solved the trade problem by a large devaluation or float, preferably at the outset. Olivier Blanchard and Pierre-Alain Muet showed that devaluation could still be effective in righting the trade balance and reducing unemployment.[28] Floating the currency would not have required large reserves, which were probably larger than they were made out to be by the Treasury.[29] It could have been given added credibility by the acceptance of some austerity measures, including wage controls, for the sake of investment rather than monetary stability. The EC was not a direct constraint on Mitterrand, exercising its influence only through the operation of the ERM and its partisans, especially Delors and Mauroy, within government.

What Mitterrand lacked was a political majority for the alternative. In 1982 only 39 per cent of the public favoured a radicalization of policy. Mitterrand had not received a clear mandate for socialist policies in 1981. His campaign cultivated 'artistic fuzziness'. By taking one quarter of the Communist vote on the first round he had reassured and obtained conservative votes on the second.[30] He had come to power by incorporating neoliberals[31] like Delors and Michel Rocard into his coalition under the guise of *autogestion* and breaking the back of the one party, the PCF, which could have mobilized support for his alternative. Divided and disoriented, the four PCF ministers did little to resist the turnabout.

Contrary to the standard account, it was Mitterrand who had refused to tie his hands with a renegotiated Common Program in 1977[32], the key issue being the extent and control of nationalized industry. Pursuing the politics of the free hand, Mitterrand chose to run against the PCF rather than with them. He surrounded himself with elite functionaries like Jacques Attali and Laurent Fabius whose mental agility and political elasticity were equal to his own. The Socialist Party (PS) he created was a middle-class organization with a high concentration of high school and university professors, who were not immune to the anti-statist ideas of the 'second Left'. Lacking a bread and butter working-class membership and a strong trade union partner, the PS could not resist the turn to neoliberalism.[33]

Mitterrand soon made a virtue out of vice. He took up the cause of private enterprise and complained of excessive taxes and government interference. He embraced high tech, venture and adventure capitalism – with a trip to Silicon Valley and an arm around the rogue businessman Bernard Tapie. Public opinion followed suit. From a term of opprobrium profitability became cause for emulation while nationalization fell into ill-repute. Even the normally sullen work force began in opinion polls at least to view employers with sympathy and trust.[34]

The government acted with the zeal of the newly converted. Mitterrand suddenly announced a 1 per cent lowering of taxes by 1985. Pierre Bérégovoy, a working-class minister who was dazzled by treasury officials, was not to be outdone by the British or Americans in the creation of a unified financial market with new exchanges for unlisted securities, non-voting and preferred shares, certificates of deposit, and financial futures.[35] The issuance of the shares allowed the government to sell off 70 per cent of nationalized subsidiaries by 1986.[36]

Banks were no longer to control the flow of credit to selective industries but to act as simple intermediaries between financial markets and industry on the German model.[37] The government adopted an open market system of money supply and interest rate control. State subsidized loans, amounting to 43 per cent of total business loans in 1979, were curtailed.[38] When the franc was threatened again in November 1985, Bérégovoy, resolving not to suffer another humiliation, converted to sound money.[39]

Mitterrand changed the fundamentals of the economy. Under the impact of rising unemployment and deindexation the average real wage per employee dropped 1.7 per cent between 1982 and 1988 while public employees faced a loss of 5.7 per cent in their rates of pay.[40] For the first time since the 1960s wages failed to keep up with productivity.[41] Between 1982 and 1987 the household share of value-added fell by 4.7 per cent while that of firms rose 3.0 per cent.[42] Profit margins, which had fallen to the lowest level of 13.3. per cent in 1982, were back to normal levels of 18.4 per cent by 1987.[43] The tax burden was shifted from companies to households.[44] Helped by real interest rates of 6 per cent, asset values grew from 122 per cent of household income to 179 per cent while more working-class families became indebted.[45] By 1994 the wages share of national income had fallen nine points since 1982 to 59.7 per cent, far more than in the US or Germany.[46] Mitterrand had produced significantly more, not less, income inequality.

There was nothing like a converted Left government to destabilize the labour movement and stifle protest. The Communists went from defeat in 1981 to decline as their share of the vote fell below seven per cent in the 1988 presidential elections. Trade unions, which had rebounded slightly after 1981, plumbed record lows for rates of strikes and unionization, which fell to two million or eight per cent of wage earners in the 1990s.[47] Writers talked of the disappearance of the labour movement and working class, which had lost two million jobs since 1975.[48] The number of people who identified with a social class fell from 68 per cent in 1976 to 56 per cent in 1987; half the public found the notions of Left and Right to be outdated.[49] Nearly 80 per cent of voters were content to vote for the three parties of consensus in the 1988 legislative elections. In 1989 the French celebrated the bicentennial of the Revolution as the end of a certain kind of history.[50]

Mitterrand was reelected as president in 1988 by rising above partisan concerns and appealing to the middle ground. The new Rocard government rejected devaluation in July 1988 and established the policy of 'competitive deflation'[51] whereby a strong franc, causing unemployment, would drive down wages, interest rates and costs leading to a virtuous circle of investment and export growth. The fixed exchange rates of ERM gave added credibility to this policy because it guaranteed that governments would be punished with higher real exchange rates for allowing inflation.[52] Mitterrand said there was no alternative – no more possibility of a trade-off between inflation and unemployment on the famous Philips curve.[53] Bérégovoy however called it a political choice: 'There is no majority for a competitive devaluation, nor for a little inflation or too much of a deficit'.[54] The study by Blanchard and Muet found that competitive deflation would take twenty years to achieve equilibrium.[55] France paid a stiff price for competitive deflation – rising unemployment since 1990, reaching 12.7 per cent in 1994, high real interest rates, two points above the Germans,[56] and low growth – an estimated 1 per cent of GDP lost annually.[57]

MITTERRAND: FROM SOCIALISM TO SINGLE MARKET AND CURRENCY

In 1984 Mitterrand had sought to compensate for his unpopularity at home by taking new initiatives on Europe. Europe would provide a new goal and moral justification for his domestic policy reversal.[58] 'France is my country, but Europe is my future,' he said. His conversion to monetarism had levelled policy differences between him and the British and Germans. In his shuttle diplomacy he discovered a common denominator among the major powers in the desire to complete the single market with the elimination of non-tariff barriers and the principle of the mutual recognition of goods and services. The appointment of Delors, Mitterrand's second choice, to head the Commission gave renewed impetus to the campaign to complete the single market by 1992. Mitterrand and Delors urged progress toward monetary union, but were opposed by Britain and Germany, which wanted the prior liberation of exchange controls. Mitterrand eventually agreed with the Germans on the free movement of capital by 1990 in return for a promise of fiscal harmonization that was never kept.[59] The Single European

Act (SEA) of 1987, making reference to monetary union in the preamble, combined completion of the single market with limited institutional reform.[60]

Whereas the SEA can best be explained by domestic conversion to neoliberal politics, the proposal for EMU was a rather direct byproduct of the single market operating with relatively fixed exchange rates and low inflation under the ERM. Since 1983 there had been minimal adjustment of exchange rates against the D-mark. The major states had renounced the use of monetary policy to regulate employment and growth. National monetary autonomy was in any event incompatible with the combination of free markets, capital mobility and fixed exchange rates. In the context of the EU these elements implied a single currency with an independent central bank committed to price stability and insulated from national political influences – that at least was the conclusion of the German foreign minister Hans Dietrich Genscher and the European Council of June 1988, which entrusted the Delors Committee, consisting of central bank governors, with fixing the stages for monetary union.[61]

EMU as it emerged at Maastricht was an attempt to supersede the power of the Bundesbank with its EU clone.[62] Fearful of the consequences of German reunification, Mitterrand rushed the process. Ignoring ministerial proposals, he accepted German terms for EMU in order to tie Germany to the West. The Bank of France had initially proposed a European reserve fund to maintain parities among members of the ERM and with third parties. Bérégovoy counted on the British plan for a hard ecu or common currency to block the German project, but Mitterrand told officials the Germans were their ally and that France would have more influence over the European Bank than they presently had over the D-Mark. In his rush Mitterrand abandoned proposals to complement the Bank with an economic government of finance ministers responsible for fiscal and budgetary policy and a consultative congress of national legislators.[63] Mitterrand claimed that member states would still run the Bank. The treaty gave the Council of Ministers power to set internal parities and the external rate of the euro as well as guidelines for national economic policy, but the council had no powers of enforcement or coordination with the bank and it had to act without prejudice to the aim of price stability and in accordance with competitive market principles.[64]

MONETARISM AND THE SOCIAL DIVIDE

The single currency incorporated certain assumptions not only of economics but of society and politics. In France it was based upon a political consensus and social disequilibrium that could not last forever. Like SEA the single currency contravened traditional French notions of national sovereignty and state interventionism. How could Mitterrand have disappointed the hopes he had fostered in the people of the Left and betrayed these principles without causing some backlash?

Before long voices would be raised to challenge the monetarist consensus known as the *pensée unique*, the official doctrine. The backlash was not perceived at first because it took the form of abstentions and votes for the anti-immigrant National Front,[65] especially among unskilled workers faced with job loss. Voters for the Front were seen at first as racists rather than victims of unemployment and ruined communities. A record 34 per cent of registered voters abstained in the 1988 presidential elections in which the two main candidates eluded the employment issue of concern to most.[66] In the regional elections of 1992 the three consensus parties received the support of only one-third of registered voters.[67] The legislative elections of 1993 confirmed the disenchantment, with 31 per cent abstentions and a record 5 per cent spoiled ballots. With less than 3 per cent more than they had received in 1986, the Right swept to the largest majority that any party had obtained under the French Republic – more out of disgust with the Socialist record on employment than any enthusiasm for the Right.[68] The disillusionment underlying this vote was made obvious in the European elections of June 1994 when the government list obtained only 25.6 per cent and the Socialist Rocard a dismal 14.5 per cent with only 22 per cent of workers voting for a consensus party![69]

In the 1995 presidential contest Jean-Marie Le Pen, candidate of the Front, obtained a majority among workers, 30 per cent, with 34 per cent among voters who felt *défavorisés*, hard done by. Coming from deindustrialized regions of the Left in the North, East and Midi, these voters were the *deçus* of Mitterrand, workers who still shared the values of the Left – the belief in state intervention and the defense of wage-earners – but who felt betrayed by it.[70]

But the most pronounced manifestation of the social divide was the 1992 referendum on Maastricht. Mitterrand had expected easy approval for the treaty. Not only did the 'no' vote nearly win, but it drew its largest percentages from the people of the Left who had elected Mitterrand in 1981, blue and white-collar workers and peasants coming from Left regions – from the urban Seine Saint-Denis to the rural Limousin. Nowhere else in Europe was the disillusionment with the EC so great.[71] This was not a nationalist vote but a class vote of protest by those who associated sound money and the single currency with unemployment. Sixty-four per cent of workers voted 'no'. Only one-third of voters thought Maastricht would be favourable to employment. Significantly, two thirds of the managerial and professional class voted 'yes', signifying their confidence in the wider European market. The result, if formally favourable to Maastricht, signified class division over the single currency.[72]

The working class had not disappeared; it turned up in odd places. It had fallen from 39 to 27 per cent of the population due to job loss, but almost all the losses came from the unskilled.[73] The relative professionalization of workers brought them closer in status, situation and earnings to those of the so-called salariat – white-collar workers and technicians – who were growing in numbers. Treating lower-paid clerical staff as workers meant that over half of French households were still working-class, by far the largest bloc in society. Workers as such faced an unemployment rate of 18 per cent in 1995. The new element of the 1990s was the spread of fear of unemployment to the middle classes, including managerial personnel, whose jobs were no longer secure. Over half of male voters feared unemployment in 1992; over a quarter of French families had been recently affected by it in 1996. Moreover, 1.7 million of those employed in 1995 held temporary contracts that were part and parcel of the 'hire and fire' economy.[74]

Parallel dissatisfaction with the government and the EC followed the rising curve of unemployment during the recession of 1991–92.[75] Seventy per cent of voters cited unemployment as the reason for the defeat of the Socialists in 1993. Gone was the optimism of the mid-1980s, especially among young people, who now said they distrusted private employers and felt they would live more poorly than their parents.[76] Relying on precarious jobs and family handouts, young people under 25 had sunk to the poverty level of 1950.[77] There was a general loss of faith in business and demand for more state intervention and social protection.[78] Distrust of the governing class was high: 61 per cent thought it showed little concern for the public interest and 49 per cent that it put European construction ahead of France.[79]

Chirac knew that in order to win the presidency against his fellow neo-Gaullist Edouard Balladur, the comfortable bourgeois, he had to tap this discontent. A survey had shown that 74 per cent of the middle class wanted the change from financial orthodoxy that was demanded by the anti-Maastricht Gaullist Philippe Séguin.[80] A master juggler of contradictions. Chirac pledged to put finance in the service of the economy while vowing to respect the convergence criteria. He portrayed himself as the candidate of change focusing on wages, unemployment and exclusion and what he called the *fracture sociale* or social divide between the people and the elites. The discontented provided him the margin of victory over Balladur on the first round and over Lionel Jospin on the second.[81]

He chose a government headed by Alain Juppé that reflected the orthodox views of the majority. Juppé started out without any clear direction, worrying the Germans about his largesse without earning popular favour. On 26 October 1995, after conferring with Kohl, Chirac announced that henceforth the government would give priority to budget cutting in conformity with its Maastricht commitment. Opinion saw this turn as a betrayal of Chirac's pledges to tackle unemployment and the social divide. The consequences of the shift were seen on 15 November 1995 when Juppé suddenly announced a reform of the social security system by the fast-track procedure of the *ordonnance*. Social security was by far the largest ticket item in the national budget with a widening deficit caused by unemployment. If the government was to reduce the national deficit below the 3 per cent required by Maastricht, measures had to be taken to balance contributions and benefits.[82]

POPULAR RESISTANCE: 1995 TRANSPORT STRIKE

Juppé proposed a comprehensive reform that angered nearly everyone. It imposed new taxes while putting a cap on spending, transferred control from unions to the state, and eliminated special regimes for public sector workers. The government gambled that outcries from vested interests would neutralize each other and that unions would be divided and powerless. The reform met with the approval of the leader of the CFDT, the formerly Christian-Democratic union, which since the 1980s had become the collaborative partner. It enraged the social-democratic FO union, which administered the health scheme and which went all the way, calling a general strike with its Cold-War enemy, the Communist-led CGT union, to defeat the plan.[83]

The government came up against the resistance of the railway workers, who, led by CGT, were one of the last bastions of militancy and solidarity in the work force. They were protesting not only against the elimination of their special regime, which meant retirement at 50 for engineers, but also against government plans to cut jobs further, shut down lines and sub-contract services.[84] They also feared application of the EU directive on competition would lead to privatization. The paralysis of the trains and Parisian transport was total. Other public service workers joined sporadically – postal and energy workers and teachers – and student strikes for better conditions in universities, which had begun earlier, spread across the country.

Demonstrations of support were particularly large, larger than in 1968 in the provinces, especially in the west and southwest. Most supporters came from the public rather than private sector where fear of unemployment weighed heavily. Juppé had said that he would resign if two million people hit the streets. On 12 December 1995 that figure was probably reached. Unlike May–June 1968 when students had taken the lead, railway workers led marches with students straggling in the rear. The crowds joined the CGT and FO in demanding the withdrawal of the Juppé plan. Attempts to turn people inconvenienced by the strike against it failed miserably. A majority of the public supported the strike, an estimated 57 per cent including 45 per cent of professional and managerial personnel.[85]

The strike disclosed demands and resentments that were normally repressed. In their meetings strikers complained of being asked to tighten their belts by successive governments only to see casual employees replace full timers; they decried the market ideology that pervaded the public sector with pressures for speed-up and productivity.[86] The jobs crisis affected people at the two extremities of working life from students looking for first time jobs to workers who had contracted for early retirement.[87] The strike evoked general fear of unemployment and social regression for the younger generation. The defense of employment and public service resonated with the wider public.

By 12 December 1995 it was obvious that the movement had reached its crest and could only subside for lack of a political alternative. The strike had caught the PS and PCF, who never asked for Juppé's resignation, unprepared for power. The PCF, whose union led the strike, treated it as a social and not a political movement. What that meant was that they were too weak and the PS too unreconstructed to formulate a credible alternative. What they did not say was that they were themselves divided – between working-class traditionalists strong in the North and Val du Marne and *refondateur* modernizers popular with intellectuals – and rudderless. Like the PS they had abandoned socialism as their goal; for Robert Hue,[88] secretary-general, as for Eduard Bernstein, the first socialist revisionist, the movement was everything and the goal nothing. Traumatized by the collapse of the Common Program in 1977, they had also repudiated the notion of a transitional or common program for either an intermediate regime or a transition to socialism.[89] They could do little but accompany the popular movement.

The government, unable to sabotage the strike and unwilling to call new elections, decided to compromise on the immediate demands of rail workers.[90] Juppé told them he would maintain the special regime, adjourn plans to restructure the railway and consult with unions about social security and jobs. This was enough for the CFDT and moderate unions to begin the return to work. Workers were coming up to Christmas and had no prospect of changing the government. The government went ahead with the Juppé plan without consultation. Public sector wages were frozen, France-Télécom was semi-privatized and EDF-GDF, the gas and electricity board, prepared for commercialization under a EU directive. As the Juppé plan was put in place, lower growth (1.3 per cent) and higher unemployment than expected reduced payroll taxes in 1996 and made the 3 per cent deficit target even more unattainable.[91] Since moderate reforms only increased deficits, Chirac said he was prepared to take more Draconian measures, but hesitated before the deterioration of the political situation.

END OF *PENSÉE UNIQUE*: POLITICS SHIFTS TO LEFT

The strikes and rallies of December 1995 had the effect of hardening and strengthening the Left and shifting the positions of all parties on Maastricht. Chirac placed the question of public service and employment on the EU agenda and argued at the G7 meeting for a socially responsible 'third way'. Séguin, conceding it was impractical to renegotiate Maastricht, called for a Franco-German initiative on employment. Even the arch-European Giscard d'Estaing demanded a more liberal interpretation of the criteria. The PS progressed in a by-election in the Var and the PCF at Gardanne in the Bouches-du-Rhône. Opinion polls in 1996 showed the Left obtaining a parliamentary majority despite scepticism regarding their ability to perform any better than the government on employment.

The social divide deepened, but despite calls by the CGT there was no repetition of the December 1995 strikes. Instead, strikes remained local and sectional, rarely involving blue-collar workers, and often taking physical forms. These were the strikes of truckers, interns, bankers at the Crédit foncier, posties, and auxiliary teachers, using occupations, confinements of directors, and road-blocks, and the mass Parisian rally against anti-immigrant legislation.[92] In the face of increasing unemployment the public mood darkened and confidence in the government sank to historic lows.[93] As the strikes had shown, there was a spontaneous resurgence of anti-capitalist sentiment that had no apparent connection with the PCF. A BVA survey conducted on the eve of the election found that unemployment overshadowed all other issues.[94] From this survey Serge Marti detected in *Le Monde* (22 Apr.) a shift of Left ideology from the centrist Catholic notion of the *exclus*, which assumes a satisfied middle-class majority, [95] to the traditional socialist opposition between a majority of exploited and minority of privileged. The depoliticization of the 1980s was over; 90 per cent of people identified themselves with either Right or Left, but not with any one party within these families. They were engaged politically, but sceptical of parties and politicians.[96]

As in 1968, the strikes of December 1995 had their greatest impact on the PS. The Socialist Left of the party won a motion to return to administrative approval for collective dismissals, an emotionally-charged emblematic issue, and obtained 40 per cent on a motion to renegotiate Maastricht. The party, including Laurent Fabius and Martine Aubry, daughter of Delors, conceded the failure of EU social policy and conditioned their approval of EMU upon inclusive membership, a competitive rate for the euro, and the creation of a European economic government to control the central bank and launch a Keynesian reflation. The party moreover adopted a range of reforms for youth employment, the thirty-five hour week without loss of pay, and wage reflation that could only blow out inflation and government deficits contrary to the requirements of Maastricht.[97]

In response to the public mood the Socialists had moved closer to an alliance with the Communists, which was concluded for the surprise election called by Chirac in April 1997. The joint PS-PCF election declaration called for the creation of 700 000 new jobs, the thirty-five hour week without reduction in pay, an end to privatization, reducing sales taxes and increasing the wealth tax, wage increases, new rights for workers, and a rejection of the Maastricht criteria.[98] The Socialist electoral program issued on 2 May basically ratified these choices with the reaffirmation by Jospin of the goals of reducing unemployment and social inequality and the stipulation that implementation would be gradual, participatory and controlled.[99] Jospin told *Le Monde* (21 May 1997) that he would not be bound by the EU Pact of Stability perpetuating the Maastricht criteria negotiated at Dublin and that the decision about the privatization of France Télécom would belong to its employees, who were opposed. An important feature of the program was its critical attitude toward the Mitterrand legacy. One wondered how the party could reconcile it with its ideological *aggiornamento* in 1990.

The contradiction was even more blatant in the case of the PCF. While claiming – with some regret – to be working within the system, the PCF was as maximalist as ever, demanding an increase of the minimum wage by 3500fr and of minimum income support, the RMI, by 1500fr, the taxation of financial profits for social security, the suspensive power of works councils over dismissals, the creation of one and a half million new jobs, the reintroduction of sectoral plans, taxing runaway shops, and the renegotiation of Maastricht.[100] The contradiction between demands and doctrine masked the division between working-class traditionalists and middle-class modernizers, which had a European dimension. The division prevented the party from carrying out its petition campaign for a referendum on Maastricht. Debate over participation in the government nearly tore the party apart, but even the traditionalists realized that 10 per cent was not enough for them to wage any effective opposition to Jospin and that it could not resist the popular elan for unity. Gone was the semblance of party unity shattered into overlapping currents. The thirty-four Communist deputies in parliament, divided into at least three tendencies, were free to vote as they pleased.

Chirac's decision to call for an early election on behalf of Europe, approved by Majority leaders, was not unreasonable. He needed a vote of confidence for drastic social cuts, the Juppé plan having proven insufficient to reduce the deficit.[101] He faced the possibility of a deteriorating political situation that would interfere with final decisions about the euro in 1998. He hoped to catch the Socialists and Communists off-guard, divided within and without. The Socialist vote was soft and sceptical on immigration and employment, peaking far below 30 per cent. This was the best moment for Chirac to renew his mandate.

What Chirac failed to gauge was the depth of the social divide, which would repudiate his government even in the absence of a coherent Left, a movement so profound that it would make the alternative credible. The alienation affected not only young and working-class people who had voted for Chirac in 1995 and who switched to the Left, but also traditional middle-class supporters, *cadres* who stayed home, and shopkeepers and artisans, who voted for the Front.[102] The campaign of the Right lacked focus; the liberal kite flown by Alain Madelin was quickly hauled down. The resignation of Juppé, squabbling among factions, and baroque leadership combinations – Séguin and Madelin – did nothing to help the Right on the second round. The doctrinal *aggiornamento* of the Left meant that the Right could no longer brandish the red menace.

Europe, which was the sub-text for policy differences, was barely mentioned. After justifying the dissolution by reference to Europe, Chirac and the Right dropped the theme. Nobody wanted to defend Maastricht yet only the National Front dared to be anti-European. Coming from different directions, Socialists and Communists converged in their criticism of Maastricht. Juppé joined Jospin in calling for an economic government for Europe.[103] The new consensus described as pro-European was not however what other Europeans had in mind.

The main result was not the victory of the Left, which barely advanced its natural score – 1993 being an anomalous disaster for the Socialists – but the strength of the National Front and collapse of the Right. On the decisive round the Left barely edged out the Right with 47.7 per cent to 46.2 per cent, down from 55.1 per cent in 1981.[104] Under a proportional system the National Front with 15 per cent would have held the balance of power. The Left was preferred because of its concern for social justice and equality, jobs and wages. But remembering the Mitterrand experience, people did not think the Socialists any better able to solve the employment problem than the Right.[105]

JOSPIN VERSUS EMU: CONTRADICTIONS OF SOCIAL DEMOCRACY

The new government named by Jospin was small, compact and very much his own instrument. Gone were representatives of party factions, Delors and the elephants Fabius and Rocard, too compromised by the Mitterrand experience. Jospin was a man of the Left in the old fashioned sense, an earnest Protestant son of a working-class father who belonged to the old guard socialists, the SFIO., an official who gave up a diplomatic career to teach economics in a technical college, a Mitterrand Socialist who had passed through the school of orthodox Trotskyism.[106] 'The Center in France,' he has said, 'is like the Bermuda triangle – anyone who approaches it disappears.'[107] As leader of the party under Mitterrand in the first term and a Keynesian economist with a Marxian twist, Jospin was always a discreet critic of the *franc fort*.[108] In 1992 he had called for a 'no' to the vote against Maastricht rather than an affirmative vote for it. His finance minister, Dominique Strauss-Kahn, another critic, who had advocated industrial policy, was of similar tendency. His advisor, Muet, was author of the study that demonstrated the ineffectiveness of competitive disinflation.[109] The anti-Maastricht striker Jean-Pierre Chevènement was responsible for public order at Interior. The minister of environment was Dominique Voynet, leader of the ecologists, who had also opposed Maastricht. On the other hand, the Europeanists Hubert Védrine, Matine Aubry and Elizabeth Guigou were at Foreign Affairs, Employment and Justice. The priority of all ministers, whatever their backgrounds, was employment.

In his policy declaration before parliament on 19 June 1997 Jospin invoked the Jacobin discourse of civic morality to justify a republican pact from which Europe was conspicuously absent.[110] The axis of his program was a gradual and controlled reflation that would be based on increasing returns to labour. The minimal 4 per cent raise of the minimum wage, which disappointed the PCF and unions, and the convening of a conference on wages, employment and working time were emblematic of his gradualism. The reduction of the working week from thirty-nine to thirty-five hours without loss of pay was to be achieved through negotiations between unions and employers within the terms of a framework law over the five-year duration of the legislature during which time 750 000 new jobs for young people in private and public sectors would also be created.

Employment would be given priority within existing spending limits waived only for the ministry of employment. Increased expenditure would be funded by new taxes on corporate profits and savings. Public services and employment would be defended. The aims of fuller employment and greater equality would be attained slowly but surely without confrontation and crisis.

Critics argued that Jospin with his moderation would fall far short of his goals and would be forced in any event by market forces and international pressures to reverse course like Mitterrand before him.[111] For Mitterrand had given away those instruments of national economic policy like nationalization, exchange and price control and administered credit that could be used to tame and resist those pressures. Some costs of the Jospin program could be absorbed by business in the rising trade cycle that was expected. But however gradually applied the program for a thirty-five hour week paid thirty-nine and for subsidized job creation would impose new taxes and wage bills on industry that in an unregulated market could lead to disinvestment – layoffs, plant closures and capital flight – nullifying the effect of the reforms.

This prognosis, shared by financial markets and most observers, reckoned however without the social divide. The French love to cry 'wolf' about crisis but this one was deeply felt. Popular exigencies transcending the parties weighed heavily on the government. Five regimes in the previous seventeen years had promised and failed to deal with unemployment. There was a feeling that this was the last chance, an awareness that if the government did not fulfil its pledges to reduce joblessness and inequality, 'ça va pêter' – all hell would break loose – by which was meant a loss of faith in democracy, a turn to the Front, anomic violence, the breakdown of law and order. Alternatively, there was hope that if the government, which disposed of enormous good will across the electorate, kept its commitments and rebuilt public confidence that it might be able to overcome the formidable market and international constraints it faced.

Reflecting popular mood, parliament would not allow power to be confiscated by the executive or high functionaries[112] as occurred under Mitterrand. The parliamentary and cabinet majority, like the social movement itself, were pluralistic with the PCF holding the balance of power. Though numerically weaker and less coherent than they had been in 1981 the Communists may have disposed of greater leverage because they were not bound by any discipline of loyalty and could thus in their diversity be more responsive to popular opinion. Jospin adopted a method of reform through consultation with unions that led by the CGT would not tolerate pauses but would press for reforms such as the thirty-five hour week that could break spending and inflation limits. On the other hand, the election did not bring any rush into the unions or surge of strikes. So long as popular pressure remained low, the government could string out its reforms and avoid confrontation with business. If the recovery were to stall and opinion turn sour, however, it might have to consider a radicalization of policy in which the state took back some of the instruments it gave away under Mitterrand.

Much depended on the outcome of EMU, which was not compatible with Jospin's domestic program. In principle the government wanted both the single currency and the program. The PS thought it could have both by transforming EMU into an intergovernmental instrument of reflation and job creation. This project required alteration of the Stability Pact, which proved impossible under the astringent conditions of the EU summit in Amsterdam in June 1997. Two weeks after assuming power Jospin was in no position to provoke both a constitutional and European crisis over the pact, vigorously upheld by both Chirac and the Germans. Instead, he was forced to accept a resolution, inspired by Tony Blair, that made employment a goal but only by way of encouraging more flexible labour markets, essentially poorer wages and conditions, which was the contrary of French intentions.

Facing strict application of the Maastricht criteria, Jospin suggested that the French would have to choose between meeting them and employment.[113] He was elected on the pledge that he would never invoke austerity to meet them. The rising trade cycle might permit him to satisfy them without austerity, but the stability criteria would remain a permanent constraint upon public spending and employment policy especially in the event of a new downturn in the French economy. Sooner or later, the French Left would have to choose between EMU and healing the social divide.

Notes

1. Todd, 1995.
2. Keeler and Schain, 1996, pp. 3–9, and Cameron, 1996b.
3. Loriaux, 1991, pp. 136–63.
4. Asselain, 1989, pp. 123–35.
5. Milward, 1992, pp. 186–191.
6. Comité, 1956, pp. 16, 72, 96.
7. Treaty of Rome, articles 2, 103, 104, 107. Dyson, 1994, pp. 67–8.
8. Prate, 1991, p. 54.
9. Elgey, 1992, pp. 575–620. Marjolin, 1986, pp. 280–303. Kusters, 1990, pp. 110–293, 334–57. Prate, 1991, pp. 56–63. Guillen, 1988. Low-level negotiators may have accepted the principle of a common market before Suez as Milward (1992, p. 212) finds, but final decisions, which were eminently political, belonged to the government. Mollet never thought France would be bound in detail by the treaty (Holland, 1980, p. 64, n. 23).
10. Prate, 1991, p. 86.
11. Loriaux, 1991, pp. 191–3.
12. Lecointe *et al*, 1989, p. 144.
13. Cited in Association, 1995, pp. 352–3.
14. Hibbs, 1977.
15. Dumez and Jeunemaître, 1990, 141.
16. Lecointe *et al*, 1989, pp. 138–43.
17. Goodman, 1992, p. 111.
18. *Ibid.*, pp. 116–8.
19. Sachs and Wyplosz, 1986, pp. 268–9. Goodman, 1992, pp. 118–25.
20. Goodman, 1992, p. 132. Dyson, 1994, pp. 106–11.
21. Stoffaes, 1989, p. 85.
22. Halimi *et al*, 1994, pp. 101–3.
23. Rand Smith, 1990.
24. Interview with Delors, 15 June 1977.
25. Giesbert, 1990, pp. 150–4. Bauchard, 1986, pp. 98–103. Favier and Martin-Roland, 1990, pp. 45–7.
26. Cited in July, 1986, p. 96.
27. The surcharge was substituted for the higher social security taxes demanded by the Germans (Bauchard, 1986, pp. 144–7). Giesbert, 1990, pp. 169–82. Attali, 1993, I, p. 417.
28. Blanchard and Muet, 1993, pp. 38–41.
29. Cameron, 1996a, p. 81, n. 62.
30. Grunberg, 1986, pp. 23, 27, 61–2.
31. Cf. Jobert, ed., 1994. French neoliberalism did not preclude union negotiations or a public sector run on market principles.
32. Moss, 1990.
33. Portelli, 1980, pp. 122–200. Christofferson, 1991, pp. 11–64. Cf. Rand Smith, 1995, p. 19.
34. Schmidt, 1996, pp. 123–5. Christofferson, 1991, p. 223.
35. Virard, 1993, pp. 102–12.
36. Rand Smith, 1990, p. 85.

37. Loriaux, 1991, pp. 223–7.
38. Cerny, 1989, p. 187.
39. Virard, 1993, pp. 228–9.
40. Lecointe *et al*, 1989, pp. 146–8. Centre, 1989, pp. 20, 43.
41. Blanchard and Muet, 1993, p. 49.
42. Lecointe *et al*, 1989, p. 142.
43. *Ibid.*, p. 157.
44. Gélédan, ed., 1993, pp. 78, 156, 223.
45. Virard, 1993, pp. 234–6.
46. Fitoussi, 1995, p. 117. *Le Monde*, 21 June 1996.
47. Jefferys, 1996a, p. 515 (table 1).
48. Gorz, 1980, Touraine *et al*, 1984, Rosanvallon, 1988.
49. Kesselman, 1989, pp. 71, 74.
50. Cf. Fukuyama, 1992, and Kaplan, 1995.
51. The term originated with Jean-Baptiste de Foucault, an advisor to Delors, and was propagated as official doctrine by Hervé Hannoun, Bérégovoy's *chef de cabinet* (Aeschimann and Riché, 1996, pp. 59, 83).
52. Giavazzi and Pagano, 1988.
53. Virard, 1993, p. 237.
54. Gélédan, ed., 1993, p. 153.
55. Blanchard and Muet, 1993.
56. Fitoussi, 1995, pp. 17, 71.
57. Interview with Jean-Paul Fitoussi of the OFCE, 3 April 1996.
58. Ross, 1996, pp. 39–40.
59. Bérégovoy wanted to make fiscal harmonization a condition for the free movement of capital (Aeschimann and Riché, 1996, p. 48).
60. Moravcsik, 1991.
61. Padoa-Schioppa, 1994, pp. 4–7. Dyson, 1994, pp. 126–8, 154–8.
62. Dyson, 1994, pp. 154–8. Cameron, 1996b, pp. 340–5.
63. Italianer, 1993, p. 69. 'Projet sur l'union monétaire et financière', *Notes bleues*, 28 January 1991. Aeschimann and Riché, 1996, pp. 88–92.
64. Articles 3a, 105, 109j.
65. Todd, 1995, pp. 106–9. Schain, 1996, pp. 176–9. Jaffré, 1986.
66. Raymond, 1994.
67. Habert *et al*, eds, 1992.
68. Jaffré, 1993, pp. 250–65.
69. Todd, 1995, pp. 103–6. Dupoirier and Grunberg, 1995, p. 154.
70. Perrineau, 1995, pp. 247–8. N. Mayer, *Le Monde*, 29 November 1996, p. 15, 5 June 1997, p. 10. G. Grunberg and P. Perrineau, *Libération*, 3 June 1997, pp. 10–11.
71. Cameron, 1995, pp. 148–9, and 1996b, p. 353–7.
72. *Politis*, 1 October 1992. Denni, 1993, p. 95. E. Todd, *Nouvel Observateur*, 24 September 1992, pp. 30–1, and Todd, 1995, pp. 100–1, 106–9.
73. Todd, 1995, pp. 102–3.
74. *Ibid.*, pp. 103–6, 113–16. Mossuz-Lavau, 1994, pp. 349–51. *Le Monde*, 8 May, 11 June 1996.
75. Cameron, 1996b, pp. 348–9, 353. *Le Monde*, 15 June 1996, graph p. 6.
76. *Le Monde*, 28 October 1995.

77. *Le Monde*, 26 September 1996.
78. Dupoirier and Grunberg, 1995, pp. 152–4.
79. *Le Monde*, 25 October, 7 December 1995.
80. Todd, 1995, p. 113.
81. Gerstlé, 1995.
82. *Le Monde*, 26 October, 17 November 1996.
83. *Ibid.*, 17, 23 November 1996.
84. Le Goff and Caillé, 1996, pp. 43–8, 69–70. Interviews with CGT and CFDT leaders, 4 and 6 January 1996.
85. *Le Monde*, 26, 30 November, 6, 13 December 1995, 5 January 1996. Jefferys, 1996b, p. 15.
86. D. Le Guilledoux, 'Les Paroles des grévistes', *Le Monde*, 5 December 1995, p. 14.
87. J.-P. Fitoussi, *Le Monde*, 5 December 1995.
88. Hue, 1995, pp. 309–42.
89. Martelli, 1995, pp. 65–81. Moss, 1990.
90. *Le Monde*, 12 December 1995.
91. Cameron, 1996b, pp. 366–8.
92. *Le Monde*, 18 February 1997.
93. *Ibid.*, 11 October, 2 November 1996.
94. *Passages*, May–June 1997, pp. 66–7.
95. Cf. Delors, 1994, p. 74, and Rosanvallon *et al*, 1986.
96. A. Muxel, *Le Monde*, 5 June 1997, p. 12.
97. *Le Monde*, 2 July, 14 November 1996.
98. *Ibid.*, 2 May 1997.
99. *Ibid.*, 3 May 1997.
100. *5 axes d'initiatives: propositions soumises á la reflexion et au vote des Français par le Parti Communiste Français.*
101. Juppé memo, *Le Monde*, 11 July 1997.
102. N. Mayer and J. Jaffré, *Le Monde*, 29 May 1997, pp. 10–11, and A. Muxel, *Le Monde*, 5 June 1997, p. 12.
103. *Le Monde*, 20 May 1997.
104. J. Jaffré, *Le Monde*, 5 June 1997, p. 10.
105. G. Grunberg and P. Perrineau, *Libération*, 3 June 1997, pp. 10–11.
106. *Le Monde*, 4 July 1997, p. 13.
107. Cited by F. Lewis, *International Herald Tribune*, 10 June 1997, p. 8.
108. *Le Monde*, 3 June 1997.
109. Blanchard and Muet, 1993, pp. 38–41.
110. *Le Monde*, 21 June 1997.
111. *Ibid.*, also *Time*, 16 June 1997.
112. Aeschimann and Riché, 1996.
113. *Le Monde*, 5 July 1997, p. 6.

References

Aeschimann, E. and Riché, P. (1996) *La Guerre de sept ans: histoire secréte du franc fort, 1989–1996*. Paris: Calmann-Lévy

Asselain, J. (1989) 'La Réinsertion de l'économie française dans les échanges internationales (1950–1960)', in Lesourne, J. (ed.) *L'Urgence du futur*. Paris: Economica

Association Georges Pompidou (1995) *Georges Pompidou et l'Europe*. Paris: Editions complexe

Attali, J. (1993) *Verbatim*. Paris: Fayard

Bauchard, P. (1986) *La Guerre des deux roses: du rêve á la réalité, 1981–1985*. Paris: Grasset

Blanchard, O. and Muet, P.-A. (1993) 'Competitiveness Through Disinflation: An Assessment of French Economic Strategy', *Economic Policy*, no. 16: 12–56

Cameron, D. (1995) 'From Barre to Balladur: Economic Policy in the Era of the EMS', in G. Flynn (ed.), *Remaking the Hexagon: The New France in the New Europe*. Boulder, Col.: Westview

Cameron, D. (1996a) 'Exchange Rate Politics in France, 1981–1983: The Regime-defining Choices of the Mitterrand Presidency', in Daley, A. (ed.) *The Mitterrand Era: Policy Alternatives and Political Mobilization in France*. New York: Macmillan

Cameron, D. (1996b) 'National Interest, the Dilemmas of European Integration and Malaise', in Keeler, J. and Schain, M. (eds) *Chirac's Challenge: Liberalization, Europeanization and Malaise in France*. New York: St. Martin's Press

Centre d'étude des revenus et des coûts (1989) *Les Français et leurs revenus: le tournant des années 80*. Paris: Editions La Découverte

Cerny, P. (1989) 'The "Little Big Bang" in Paris: Financial Market Deregulation in a *Dirigiste* System', *European Journal of Political Research*, 17: 169–92

Christofferson, T. (1991) *The Socialists in Power, 1981–1986: From Autogestion to Cohabitation*. London: Associated University Press

Comité intergouvernemental créé par la conférence de Messine (1956) *Rapport des chefs de délégation aux ministres des affaires étrangéres*

Delors, J. (1994) *L'Unité d'un homme*. Paris: Odile Jacob

Denni, B. (1993) 'Du référendum du 20 septembre 1992 aux élections législatives de mars 1993', in Perrineau, P. and Ysmal, C. (eds) *Le Vote sanction: les élections législatives des 21 et 28 mars 1993*. Paris: Presses de la FNSP

Dumez, H. and Jeunemaître, A. (1990) 'A Style of Economic Regulation, France 1969–86: A Comparison between France and West Germany', *Government and Policy*, 8: 139–48

Dupoirier, E. and Grunberg, G. (1995) 'La Déchirure sociale', *Pouvoirs*, no. 73, pp. 143–58

Dyson, K. (1994) *Elusive Union: The Process of Economic and Monetary Union in Europe*. London: Longman

Elgey, G. (1991) *Histoire de la IV République 3. La République des tourmentes*. Paris: Fayard

Favier, P. and Martin-Roland, M. (1990) *La Décennie Mitterrand: Les Ruptures (1981–1984)*. Paris: Seuil

Featherstone, K. (1994) 'Jean Monnet and the "Democratic Deficit" in the European Union', *J. of Common Market Studies*, 32: 149–70

Fitoussi, J.-P. (1995) *Le Débat interdit: monnaie, Europe, pauvreté*. Paris: Arléa

Fukuyama, F. (1992) *The End of History and the Last Man*. London: Hamish Hamilton

Gélédan, A. (ed.) (1993) *Le Bilan économique des années Mitterrand, 1981–1994*. Paris: Le Monde-Editions

Gerstlé, J. (1995) 'La Dynamique sélective d'une campagne décisive' in Perrineau, P. and Ysmal, C. (eds) *Le Vote de crise l'élection présidentielle de 1995*. Paris: Presses de la FNSP

Giavazzi, F. and Pagano, M. (1988) 'The Advantage of "Tying One's Hands": EMS Discipline and Central Bank Credibility', *European Economic Review*, 32: 1055–82

Giesbert, F.-O. (1990) *Le Président*. Paris: Seuil

Goodman, J. (1992) *Monetary Sovereignty: The Politics of Central Banking in Western Europe*. London: Cornell U.P.

Gorz, A. (1980) *Adieux au prolétariat*. Paris: Editions Galilée

Grunberg, G. (1986) 'Causes et fragilités de la victoire socialiste de 1981', in Lancelot, A. (ed.) *1981: Les Elections de l'alternative*. Paris: Presses de la FNSP

Guillen, P. (1988) 'L'Europe-remède á l'impuissance française? le gouvernement Guy Mollet et la négotiation des traités de Rome, 1955–57', *Revue d'histoire diplomatique*, 102: 319–35

Habert, P., Perrineau, P. and Ysmal, C. (eds) (1992) *Le Vote éclaté: les élections régionales et cantonales des 22 et 29 mars 1992*. Paris: Presses de la FNSP

Halimi, S., Michie, J. and Milne, S. (1994) 'The Mitterrand Experience', in Michie, J. and Grieve Smith, J. (eds) *Unemployment in Europe*. London: Academic Press

Hibbs, Jr., D. (1977) 'Political Parties and Macro-economic Policy', *American Political Science Review*, 71: 1467–87

Holland, S. (1980) *The Uncommon Market*. London: Macmillan

Hue, R. (1995) *Communisme: la mutation*. Paris: Stock

Italianer, A. (1993) 'Mastering Maastricht: EMU Issues and How They Were Settled', in Gretschmann, K. (ed.) *Economic and Monetary Union: Implications for National Policy-Makers*. Dordecht: M. Nijhoff

Jaffré, J. (1986) 'Front National: la relève protestataire', in Dupoirier, E. and Grunberg, G. (eds) *Mars 1986: la drôle de défaite de la gauche*. Paris: P.U.F.

Jaffré, J. (1993) 'Les Grandes Vagues électorales sous la Cinquième République', in Perrineau, P. and Ysmal, C. (eds) *Le Vote sanction; les élections législatives des 21 et 28 Mars 1993*. Paris: Presses de la FNSP

Jeffreys, S. (1996a) 'Down But Not Out: French Unions after Chirac', *Work, Employment and Society*, 10: 509–27

Jeffreys, S. (1996b) 'France 1995: The Backward March of Labour Halted?', *Capital and Class*, no. 57, pp. 7–21

Jobert, B., (ed.) (1994) *Tournant néoliberal en Europe*. Paris: L'Harmattan

July, S. (1986) *Les Années Mitterrand*. Paris: Bernard Grasset

Kaplan, S. (1995) *Farewell Revolution: The Historians' Feud, France, 1789/ 1989*. London: Cornell U.P.

Keeler, J. and Schain, M. (1996) 'Mitterrand's Legacy, Chirac's Challenge', in Keeler, J. and Schain, M. (eds) *Chirac's Challenge*. New York: St. Martin's Press

Kesselman, M. (1989) 'La Nouvelle Cuisine en politique: la fin de l'exceptionnalité française' in Mény, Y. (ed.), *Idéologies, partis politiques et groupes sociaux*. Paris: Presses de la FNSP

Kusters, H. (1990) *Fondements de la Communauté économique européenne*. Paris: Editions Labor

Le Goff, J.-P. and Caillé, A. (1996) *Le Tournant de décembre*. Paris: La Découverte

Lecointe, F., Przedborski, V. and Sterdyniak, H. (1989) 'Salaires, prix et répartition' in Jeanneney, J.-M. (ed.) *L'Economie française depuis 1967: la traversée des turbulences mondiales*. Paris: Seuil

Loriaux, M. (1991) *France after Hegemony: International Change and Financial Reform*. London: Cornell U.P.

Marjolin, R. (1986) *Le Travail d'une vie: mémoires, 1911–1986*. Paris: Robert Laffont

Martelli, R. (1995) *Le Rouge et le bleu: essai sur le Communisme dans l'histoire française*. Paris: Editions ouvrières

Milward, A. (1992) *European Rescue of the Nation-State*. London: Routledge

Moravcsik, A. (1991) 'Negotiating the Single European Act: National Interests and Conventional Statecraft in the European Community', *International Organization*, 45: 19–56

Moss, B. (1990) 'Workers and the Common Program (1968–1978): The Failure of French Communism', *Science & Society*, 54: 42–66

Mossuz-Lavau, J. (1994) *Les Français et la politique: enquête sur une crise*. Paris: Odile Jacob

Padoa-Schioppa, T. (1994) *The Road to Monetary Union in Europe*. Oxford: Clarendon

Perrineau, P. (1995) 'Dynamique du vote Le Pen: le poids du "gaucho-lepenisme"', in Perrineau, P. and Ysmal, C. (eds) *Vote de Crise*. Paris: Presses de la FNSP

Portelli, H. (1980) *Le Socialisme français tel qu'il est*. Paris: P.U.F.

Prate, A. (1991) *Quelle Europe?* Paris: Commentaire Julliard

Rand Smith, W. (1995) 'Industrial Crisis and the Left: Adjustment Strategies in Socialist France and Spain', *Comparative Politics*, 28: 1–24

Rand Smith, W. (1990) 'Nationalization for What? Capitalist Power and Public Enterprise in Mitterrand's France', *Politics and Society*, 18: 75–100

Raymond, G. (1994) 'The Decline of the Established Parties', in Raymond, G. (ed.) *France during the Socialist Years*. Aldershot: Dartmouth

Rosanvallon, P. (1988) *La Question syndicale*. Paris: Hachette

Rosanvallon, P., Julliard, J. and Furet, F. (1986) *La République du centre*. Paris: Calmann-Lévy

Ross, G. (1996) 'The Limits of Political Economy: Mitterrand and the Crisis of the French Left', in Daley, A. (ed.) *The Mitterrand Era*. New York: Macmillan

Sachs, J. and Wyplosz, C. (1986) 'The Economic Consequences of President Mitterrand', *Economic Policy*, no. 2, pp. 261–306

Schain, M. (1996) 'The Immigration Debate and the National Front', in Keeler, J. and Schain, M. (eds) *Chirac's Challenge*. New York: St. Martin's Press

Schmidt, V. (1996) 'An End to French Exceptionalism? The Transformation of Business under Mitterrand', in Daley, A. (ed.) *The Mitterrand Era*. New York: Macmillan

Stoffaes, C. (1989) 'La Modernisation de l'appareil de production et son financement', in Lesourne, J. (ed.) *L'Urgence du futur*. Paris: Economica

Todd, E. (1995) 'Aux Origines du malaise politique français: les classes sociales et leurs représentations', *Le Débat*, nos. 83–85, pp. 98–120

Touraine, A., Wieviorka, M. and Dubet, F. (1984) *Le Mouvement ouvrier*. Paris: Fayard

Virard, M.-P. (1993) *Comment Mitterrand a découvert l'économie*. Paris: Albin Michel

4 Hoist with its Own Petard: Consequences of the Single Currency for Germany

Jörg Huffschmid

4.1 INTRODUCTION: THE GERMAN ROLE IN THE DESIGN OF EMU

The design of Economic and Monetary Union (EMU), as it was conceived and decided at the Intergovernmental Conference in December 1991 and laid down in the Treaty of Maastricht, is the result of two tendencies in the European Community. In both Germany played a prominent role.

The first tendency was the political desire to advance from the European common market to a political union. It was partly motivated by the aim to play a greater role as a regional bloc in the world. A common economic policy and currency was to strengthen the European position in a more internationalized economy. And a common foreign and security policy was to enhance European weight in international affairs. Both objectives were reinforced by the collapse of eastern European socialism and the ensuing uncertainty about the new structures and axes after the Cold War. The decisive thrust for more political unification in Europe, however, was developed as a reaction to the events in Germany. It should be remembered that all major governments of the EC were initially either sceptical or opposed to German unification and endorsed it only after it had became obvious that it could not be prevented. But this made it all the more imperative for the EC members, particularly for France, to integrate the larger and supposedly more powerful Germany into a common European policy structure with joint decision making and control. Germany, and especially chancellor Kohl, were only too willing to accept this price for unification.[1]

In this sense the EMU design of Maastricht was similar to the early years of European integration in the 1950s. It appeared necessary to form a regional bloc against communism (and in the eyes of some western European countries as a counterweight to US dominance) and to bind Germany into a tight political and economic European structure to prevent new military adventures. The German government seized the opportunity for transition from a defeated enemy to a strong partner. However, and this is another similarity between the two periods, the forces urging a European union were not strong enough to overcome traditional national and nationalist forces and concepts of national sovereignty. Thus, just as the European Defense and Political Community failed in the early 1950s, the European Political Union was not realized in Maastricht. In both cases political unification was substituted by economic integration: the European Coal and Steel Community (ECSC), the European Economic Community (EEC) and the European Atomic Energy Community (Euratom) in the 1950s and the three-stage Economic and Monetary Union (EMU) in 1991 respectively.

The second basic tendency in the EMU design of Maastricht was the result of a far-reaching shift in the economic policy paradigm which had prevailed throughout Western Europe for three decades after the war. In the Maastricht treaty the free market was given absolute priority: neoliberalism, a controversial economic and social doctrine, achieved the status of supranationally binding rules for economic and monetary policy in the EU. The narrow concentration of monetary policy on disinflation and of fiscal policy on deficit reduction marked a victory of fundamentalist economic essentialism over a more complex multi-objective and multi-level conception of the economy and its political control that emphasizes full employment, welfare, and international monetary cooperation. Under the pressure of increased international competition after the collapse of the Bretton Woods system this conception was successfully challenged by the neoliberal and monetarist counter-revolution in economic theory and policy. The strongest spearhead of this policy shift in the EC was Germany and especially the Deutsche Bundesbank. The model of the European Central Bank (ECB) is strongly shaped after the Bundesbank, its legal task is even more strictly confined to preserving price stability and its political independence even greater than that of the Bundesbank. In the Maastricht negotiations the German representatives introduced such large amount of strictly anti-inflationary and austerity conditions –

known as the convergence criteria – that other governments suspected that Germany did not want monetary union, a view which was probably realistic for the Bundesbank and a strong fraction of German politicians and enterprises. In order to prevent a failure of the conference Germany agreed 'in the final hours of the intergovernmental conference' to the reassuring provision of article 109j section 4 that monetary union (more precisely the third stage of EMU) should begin in any case not later than on 1 January 1999 and that 'Germany will not be able to opt out'.[2] Both the convergence criteria and the ultimate date for the beginning of the third stage resulted in enormous pressure upon member countries. The recently negotiated 'pact for stability and growth' even reinforces this pressure.

The result of these two tendencies is an 'ever closer union' (Article A of the Treaty on European Union) with a strongly austerity-prone and deflationary economic policy program. It is argued elsewhere in this book that such a program will lead to stagnation, unemployment, and social polarization in the EU as a whole and that it will undermine social coherence and solidarity. This chapter discusses whether, to what extent, and in which forms these effects will apply to Germany, in terms of macroeconomic performance as well as of basic social and industrial relations. Section 4.2 sketches the German starting point for EMU in explaining the main structural and economic policy elements which allowed Germany to achieve a hegemonic position in the EU. The subsequent Section 4.3 analyses the likely macroeconomic consequences of EMU for the German economy: the generalized tendency to stagnation and persistently high unemployment will also prevail in Germany. With regard to the social tissue of the German 'social market economy', it is argued in Section 4.4 that although tendencies to transform the German economy and society into a kind of American- or UK-style casino capitalism will be reinforced, the cooperative downsizing of living conditions under persistently high unemployment is also possible. The final Section 4.5 concludes with the argument that, just as German strategies were decisive for the enforcement of neoliberalism in the Treaty of Maastricht and the EU, a shift in German economic policy direction would also be helpful for the EU.

4.2 AUSTERITY-BASED HEGEMONY: GERMAN ECONOMIC STRATEGY BEFORE EMU

From the end of the 1950s, Germany has been the strongest economy in Western Europe. German economic policy conceptions had a great influence on the structure and strategy of European integration from the start of the European Economic Community. But it was only in the 1980s that the German economy and economic policy rose to a clearly hegemonic position in the EC. This position was written into the Maastricht treaty and it was upheld even when the severe problems of the new Bundesländer affected the overall performance of the German economy.

German economic hegemony in Europe is not only the result of the size and productivity of the country. It was established, and has been consolidated since the mid 1970s, through a neomercantilist economic strategy of strong export promotion and conquest of international markets, particularly at the expense of other EU members. The domestic basis for this policy was the victory of the Bundesbank conception of economic policy, with exclusive priority for price stability as a springboard for international competitiveness.

Strong export orientation is not new for the German economy, and it is essentially based on its specific sectoral structure, with a high share and a broad range of manufacturing industry.[3] One of the great pushes for German reconstruction in the early 1950s was the export boom induced by the Korean war. In the 1960s and 1970s Germany already had the second highest export share in GNP of all big industrial nations (after the UK, see Table 4.1).

The most decisive development, however, occurred in the 1980s. Whereas the export share in the other large countries rose only modestly or remained constant, that of West Germany made a big leap forward, from 24 per cent of GDP in the 1970s to 30 per cent in the 1980s and to 33 per cent in the first half of the 1990s, although German unification and a complete collapse of eastern German exports brought a sharp fall in overall German export share. But even so Germany is today the second largest export nation in the world (after the USA), with the world's highest per capita exports, a world market share of around 10 per cent and a trade surplus of about 100 bn DM in 1996.

The different export development of Germany and the other G7 countries during the last decade suggests that German success occurred at the expense of the latter. This is indeed reflected in

Table 4.1 Export shares of GDP for four leading EC members, the USA and Japan

Country	1961–70**	1971–80**	1981–90**	1990–95**
West Germany	19.3	24.2	30.3	33.0
Germany*				22.8
France	13.5	19.5	22.3	22.7
Italy	14.6	20.8	21.4	23.2
United Kingdom	20.5	26.5	25.9	25.2
USA	5.3	8.0	8.6	10.7
Japan	9.9	12.2	12.6	9.7

* including former GDR
** average of yearly shares

Source: *European Economy*, Nr. 61, 1996, Statistical Appendix, Table 38

Table 4.2 Trade balances of four leading EC members in the 1970s, 1980s and 1990s, cumulated $bn

Country	1970s*	1980s*	1990s*
Germany**	142.7	399.0	271.4
France	−9.3	−83.35	4.8
Italy	−12.6	−44.46	116.7
UK	−48.4	−112.2	−129.8

* cumulated trade surpluses or deficits (–) in bn $, 1970–79, 1980–89, 1990–95
** 1990s including former GDR

Source: OECD, *Economic Outlook*

the development of the trade balances of the four big EC members (see Table 4.2).

As can be seen in Table 4.2 Germany had already realized a considerable trade surplus during the 1970s, whereas France and Italy had a moderate, and Great Britain a considerable, deficit. In the subsequent decade – when the European Monetary System (EMS) was already in place – the disparities in the development on international trade exploded, leading to an enormous surplus in Germany and very problematic deficits in the other three countries.

This absolute and relative improvement of the German trade position with regard to her European partners was to a large extent the result of an economic strategy, which the German government and especially the German Bundesbank could enforce domestically and impose upon the rest of Europe. It has rightly been called a neomercantilist strategy of permanent undervaluation of the increasingly stronger DM, which at the same time became the second important reserve medium of the world.[4] The main elements of this strategy can be described as follows.[5]

After the economic crises of 1975 and 1981, and even more so after the take-over of the government by the conservative coalition, the hour of the Bundesbank arrived. From then on economic policy meant mostly restrictive money supply and reduction of government expenditures, primarily in the welfare sector of the economy. The multiobjective, multilevel and multitool approach of the social democratic government, which had – not in theory but in practice – also been the general guideline for conservative governments during the 1950s and 1960s, was more and more abandoned and replaced by the exclusive fixation on price stability, austerity and deregulation. Economic stability was increasingly defined as price stability, disregarding the alarming increase of unemployment, income inequality, and social instability.

The monetarist fixation on internal price stability led to conflicts with the task of external currency stabilization in a regime of fixed exchange rates. The Bundesbank openly opposed the Bretton Woods System and welcomed its abandonment in the first half of the 1970s, and was from the beginning sceptical or even hostile to the introduction of a regional exchange rate regime like the EMS, introduced in 1978.[6] One might think that if, in cases of parity imbalances between two countries, the central banks of both countries are obliged to intervene in the currency market in order to restore equilibrium, this would force the Bundesbank to compromise between internal price stabilization and exchange rate stabilization, thus accepting a part of the adjustment burden. This was – or could have been – the spirit of solidarity behind the EMS.[7] But this was not the understanding of the Bundesbank, nor that of the majority of the German scientific community at the time. The Bundesbank made it quite clear from the beginning of the EMS that it was not willing to follow the obligation of unlimited intervention if that would endanger its primary concern about price stability. What is more, if the report of Emminger is correct, the Bundesbank got the assurance of the German government that it would be released from the obligation of intervention if necessary and that it could

even decide whether it was necessary or not.[8] When it did intervene in exchange markets, or took measures to like effect, the
Bundesbank regularly accompanied these measures by sterilizing
measures on the German money market, usually through restrictive open market operations. This policy did not only generate sharply
falling inflation rates in Germany. It also maintained the competitive advantage over the weaker countries and thus the superior
German trade position. Persistent inflation differentials made the
DM a permanently undervalued currency – in spite of more than a
dozen realignments with appreciation of the DM against one, several or all EMS currencies.

German unification in 1990 brought a dramatic change into the
German economic situation without a corresponding change in
economic policy. For the first time in more than two decades the
German export boom stopped, the trade surplus fell sharply from
75 bn US$ in 1989 to 18 bn US$ in 1991[9] and the current account
balance showed a deficit for the first time. After unification, imports into the new Länder from West Germany exploded, mainly
financed through transfers from the west, which in turn were financed
through a sharp rise in public deficits. Thus the government invol-
untarily triggered off a unification boom with growth rates for West
Germany of 5.7 per cent in 1990 and 4.5 per cent in 1991; similar
rates had last been reached in the 1970s. This boom, which generated spillover effects for the relevant trading partners of Germany[10]
was brought to an abrupt end by the obsessive policy of the
Bundesbank which raised the discount rate five times in 18 months
from 6.0 per cent to 8.75 per cent between November 1990 and
June 1992 as a pre-emptive strike against supposed inflation dangers. This contractionary policy generated devastating consequences
for the EC, exacerbating recessionary tendencies and exposing partner
currencies to speculative pressures which led to the currency crisis
in 1992 and in the end to the practical abandonment of the ERM
in 1993. Thus shortly before the introduction of the single currency in the EU we have the strange situation that Europe has
returned to a floating rate regime instead of – as one would expect
in the run-up to monetary union – consolidating a system with ever
narrower fluctuation bands.

The German government and the Bundesbank seem determined
to continue the twin strategies of domestic austerity and external
mercantilism. This strategy had imposed slow growth, high unemployment and severe cuts in the domestic welfare system in Germany

long before Maastricht. On the other hand it has generated increased profits for German business and a remarkable redistribution of income and wealth towards the rich: from 1980 to 1993 gross profits rose by 185 per cent against a 63 per cent rise in gross wages. Tax policy exacerbated the disparity: the increase in net profits was 251 per cent, five times the rise in net wages (52 per cent).[11]

With Maastricht, German economic policy has been imposed upon the EU as a whole. The question is whether this strategy will be viable and what repercussions it will have upon the German model.

4.3 MACROECONOMIC CONSEQUENCES OF THE SINGLE CURRENCY FOR GERMANY

In this section it is assumed that in the third stage of EMU the course of a very restrictive interpretation of the already restrictive rules of the Maastricht treaty will continue: monetary policy concentrates exclusively on disinflationary measures, the main objective of fiscal policy is the reduction of public deficits via expenditure cuts and employment policy is confined to deregulation and the 'loosening' of labour market rigidities. The overall consequences of this policy are obvious and have already been felt during the last five years after the signing of the Maastricht treaty. Under the austerity regime of Maastricht the economy of the EU will remain trapped in a downward spiral with low growth or stagnation, high and rising levels of unemployment, increasing inequality of income distribution and an erosion of the financial basis for all social security and welfare systems. The European domestic components of final effective demand – private consumption and government expenditure – will develop only sluggishly, stagnate or even fall because of low wages and a further erosion of the tax base which is under way in Germany, France and in other EC countries in a wave of competitive tax reductions. Therefore the prospects for private investment as intermediate demand are not brilliant either.

Germany, which has since the 1980s pushed the EU into this contractionary policy trap, will of course also be affected by its consequences. The negative effects will be even stronger than before because the European economic landscape has become more uniform and more generally stagnant. A beggar-my-neighbour policy becomes increasingly difficult, and its success less likely, when the neighbour has fewer resources.

Despite these depressing prospects two possibilities remain for a more positive outlook – an improvement in competitiveness of European firms in general, or German firms in particular. Firstly, the EU could – under the leadership of Germany and France – try as a whole during the next decade or two to play the same role with regard to the rest of the world – mainly the two other capitalist centres – which Germany had played towards the rest of the EU during the 1980s: compensating low domestic demand by enhanced exports and foreign direct investment (FDI), thus maintaining a rather high and increasing level of business activity and rate of profit in a stagnant domestic environment. This seems to be the policy line the EU is following: to accomplish through a policy of strict austerity competitive price advantages on world markets and thus expand the export share in EU-GDP (which is at present about the same size as that of the USA and Japan, around 10 per cent). If this strategy is successful, it would still not – or only marginally – contribute to the creation of new jobs in the EU, but it would create positive profit perspectives for the leading firms of the EU – to a large extent German, French and British firms.

However, it is very questionable whether a neo-mercantilistic strategy of the EU towards the rest of the world can succeed. The success of Germany in the 1980s was not only based on an undervalued DM and comparatively high productivity but also on German political power to enforce such a merchantilistic policy against the rest of Europe without triggering off retaliations from the most affected countries. This will not be possible for the EU as a whole against the other two centres of the capitalist world. The economic circumstances and power relations on the world market in the 1990s are quite different from the relationships within the EC during the 1970s and 1980s. Without the structural and size advantages of Germany in the EC, the combined economies of the EU have no superior productivity and are not even larger than those of the two other regional blocs, the NAFTA and the Asian Pacific area. Therefore the intensity of competition between the three centres will increase with an uncertain outcome. It is improbable that the EU as a whole is capable of reaching such considerable and persistent competitive advantages over the rest of the world as would be sufficient to compensate for a chronic weakness of domestic demand – in the EU as well as in Germany. On the other hand, the intensified competition will enhance economic insecurity in the world economy. This could lead to a further increase in the level of interest rates, impeding real growth and promoting financial investment. Unless a new form of international economic cooperation is developed during the next years – including managed trade, FDI rules and mechanisms of international monetary balancing and control – the result will be increasingly hot economic wars, including competitive austerity and devaluation strategies.

If an improvement of the German economic situation cannot be expected from a generally stronger position of the EU in the world with particular spillovers to Germany, the second possibility must be explored. Are there specific competitive advantages which will allow a better performance of German firms than of businesses from other EU members? There are three specific fields in which such advantages could occur:

- First, in a single currency regime the possibility of weaker countries improving their competitive position through devaluation no longer exists. This could strengthen the German position on the European market. On the other hand, the particular German advantage during the 1980s was based on high inflation differentials. The real exchange rate was lower, and therefore German commodities cheaper even if the nominal price for the DM rose through appreciation. In a Maastricht style monetary union inflation differentials as a basis for Germany's competitive advantage have largely disappeared, and it is questionable whether the remaining differentials will really induce a shift of demand toward German suppliers.
- Second, relative economic advantages can possibly be realized through a more than average increase in foreign direct investment or in mergers and acquisition activity of German firms in other EU countries, partly substituting exports by foreign production, partly extending export opportunities through enhanced presence and repair and maintenance facilities for domestic products. But there is no empirical evidence for such a German advantage: the total amount of FDI outflows from 1990 to 1995 was 131 bn US$ for Germany, 143 bn US$ for the United Kingdom and 151 bn US$ for France.[12] The same is true for mergers and acquisitions. German firms acted as buyers in only 14.4 per cent of all international mergers with EU participation from 1990 to 1995, a percentage far below Germany's 25 per cent share in EU GDP. French firms were buyers in 18.5 per cent of all cases corresponding to France's 17.7 per cent of GNP. Great Britain

on the other hand was active as buyer in more than a quarter (26.5 per cent) of all acquisitions, with a GNP share of 14.4 per cent.[13] Out of the 20 largest mergers with EU participation, in only three cases German corporations (Hoechst, Deutsche Bank and Allianz Holding) acted as buyers, as against ten UK firms.[14] It is undoubtedly true that German firms have acquired a strong position on European markets during the last ten years,[15] but it cannot be said that their competitive position has improved recently or that it is likely to improve in the near future with regard to the two major European competitors, France and Great Britain.

– Third, a particular domain of German is the 'emerging markets' of eastern Europe. About a quarter of foreign trade of the Commonwealth of Independent States (CIS) and 43 per cent of trade of the ten Central and Eastern European Countries (CEEC) with the OECD countries is trade with Germany.[16] The share of German exports going to the Czech Republic has risen from roughly 2 per cent to 8.3 per cent in the 1990s. German foreign direct investment in the transition countries rose from 2.2 bn DM to 9.0 bn DM which is still not more than 0.8 per cent and 2.6 per cent of all German foreign investment.[17] Although the overall amount and share of German FDI in transition countries is not very impressive, leading German firms have established strategic positions particularly in Poland, Hungary and the Czech republic.[18] With respect to eastern Europe it can be assumed that Germany will further extend her influence and market share. The problem is that the eastern markets have not yet really taken off. Therefore the compensation for lack of domestic demand has so far remained weak. But this could change within the next decade and then Germany would probably be in a considerably stronger position with regard to other European competitors.

On balance the particular specificities of the German economy will not enable it to escape the general depressive consequences of the competitive austerity course laid down in the Maastricht treaty and reinforced in the Stability Pact (SP). Within this environment of stagnation and high unemployment, leading German firms are not likely to realize comparative trade or investment advantages with regard to French or British competitors. Their better starting position in eastern Europe has as yet not paid off substantially, but it may do so in the future. But this will neither offset the generally weak outlook for EMU nor establish a long-term and stable general superiority of the German economy. From an economic perspective the benefits from German hegemony in Europe appear to be exhausted, which does not in itself indicate the near end of this hegemony.

Slow growth, high unemployment, falling incomes and growing public deficits as the general economic perspectives for Germany in a single currency regime à la Maastricht will also mean that the deep divide between the former West Germany and the former GDR will not be dampened but exacerbated with ensuing budgetary and political problems. The only realistic chance for a convergence between the old and the new German Länder is strong macroeconomic growth which makes room for catch-up processes in the east and creates the public resources which are still, and for the foreseeable future, necessary in order to stimulate more than average productivity and production increases in the five new Länder. Stagnation or low growth will on the other hand affect these Länder particularly strongly because the largest part of eastern firms have been taken over by western groups and are usually the first ones to be closed down in a recession.

4.4 SYSTEMIC CHANGE OR COOPERATIVE DOWNSIZING: THE FUTURE OF THE GERMAN 'SOCIAL MARKET ECONOMY' IN EMU

The stagnationary implications of the Maastricht regime will also affect the system of social and industrial relations in Germany. The specific German construction of a social market economy ('soziale Marktwirtschaft') which has already come under attack under the austerity policy of the 1980s will be further eroded and undermined up to a point where its functioning is at risk. Its structure was established in the post-war reconstruction period under the influence of the Cold War on the one hand, and rapidly rising production and real incomes on the other. It consisted of four basic elements: market ideology, social correctives and welfare systems, pragmatic interventions in the reconstruction period and critical sectors, and a tight system of cooperation between labour and capital. This labour – capital cooperation – with a strong bias in favour of capital – within a free market system is the specific difference of the German post-war order from other countries where the market orientation was less accentuated and socialist forces had a certain influence. The structure of the social market economy was maintained – under a somewhat more Keynesian terminology – even when the Social Democrats took over the government in 1966. The 'Economic Stability and Growth Promotion Act' of 1967 is perhaps the best expression of this orientation. It obliged the government to pursue 'within the framework of a market economy' four equally important economic objectives: steady and appropriate economic growth, price stability, a high level of employment, and balanced international economic relations.

This model has come under increasing pressure since the beginning of the low growth period in the mid-1970s. The balance of the four objectives was given up and replaced by the almost exclusive orientation towards price stability as a lever for enhancing international competitiveness. The level of the social security and welfare system has since been reduced continuously, the primacy of the market in the economy being given increased effect. With German unity in 1990 and the ensuing financial pressures, the thrust of social cuts was enhanced and the neoliberal fundamentalism of free markets, deregulation and redistribution in favour of profits advanced further, leading to even more unemployment, social polarization and exclusion. At the same time not only the Social Democratic government, but also the conservatives who came to office in 1982, tried to maintain the cooperative basis of the system. And they have been successful until now: in spite of drastic social cuts and more and more bitter conflicts the tissue of the social market economy has not been destroyed, although it has been damaged and eroded in several places.

Recently strong forces from German industry has explicitly rejected the existing system of the social market economy as obsolete and demanded its abolition. Several attempts undertaken by the unions to negotiate more jobs for moderation in wage and working time claims have been rejected brusquely by the Federation of German Industry and talks under mediation of the government have failed. More deregulation of social protection, privatization of social security and public services and flexibilization of the labour market – these are the battle cries of strong parts of business and government and the American and the British pattern of development are recommended as a model for Germany, too. The Maastricht treaty has made this tendency the main economic policy orientation in Europe and given its supranational validity. This has of course repercussions for Germany and strengthens the forces aiming at the complete destruction of the social market economy. In the government the Ministry of Economic Affairs is the strongest advocate for this perspective of 'systems change' in Germany and the Liberal Democrats (the FDP) are the party flagship of this line.

On the other hand there are still strong forces, within the conservative government and in business circles, who are opposed to an outright break-up of the social market economy. In their view social cooperation is the basis of social peace, which they regard as the most important factor in the success story of the German economy. They want to preserve the generally cooperative social climate and achieve the necessary measures to enhance German competitiveness – wage reductions, tax reductions, welfare reductions – within the existing institutional framework. The Federal Association of German Employers Associations is more inclined to follow this line, as is the Ministry for Labour and Social Order in the federal government.

The difference between the two perspectives for the social pattern of German development under the Maastricht rule can clearly be seen in the recent discussion about the system of old age and retirement insurance. There was broad agreement that because of long lasting unemployment and demographic changes the financial basis of the system would not be viable in the future and that employers' contributions to old age insurance could under no circumstances be increased. To improve the financial perspective the chief of government in Saxony, Kurt Biedenkopf, proposed to largely abolish the system of intergenerational transfers and replace it by private pension funds as in the US and UK. The proposal was supported by large parts of the business community and rather enthusiastically welcomed by the big banks and their investment branches. Nevertheless, after a short and passionate discussion within the government it was clearly rejected. Instead the proposal from the Ministry of Labour and Social Order to reduce the level of old age payments considerably, from a maximum of 70 per cent to 63 per cent of previous income was accepted. The idea of abolishing federal welfare programs altogether, as in the USA, has so far not emerged in Germany and it would not have a chance of realization in the foreseeable future.

There are two equally undesirable alternatives for the German structure of social and industrial relations. Either the cooperative and highly regulated structure of the system is abandoned altogether and replaced by an American-style system of social paralysis, particularization, polarization and survival of the fittest, where the strong state appears mostly in the form of the police and military forces. Or the basic structure is maintained and utilized as a basis for a further 'cooperative' reduction of income, welfare and social protection with strong and increasingly authoritarian public regulation. The economic and social effects of the two versions are very similar; in both cases it is persistently high unemployment, falling real incomes and welfare benefits, strong redistribution of income and wealth in favour of profits and the rich, and therefore a further polarization of society. The difference between the two alternatives concerns the political process of implementation and the perception of those affected by it. It is quite conceivable that the strong cooperative spirit in the trade unions, together with the relative advantages of Germany in a generally stagnant environment, could lead to a situation where the drastic reduction in living standards of the majority is perceived as unavoidable under conditions of globalization and could be implemented in an orderly and cooperative way.

4.5   THE GERMAN ROLE FOR FULL EMPLOYMENT IN THE EU

Strong export interests and the narrow monetary fixation of the Bundesbank have, since the mid-1970s, led to the austerity-backed neomercantilist strategy of Germany in Europe. The success of this policy had the effect of transforming Germany's economy into a hegemonic one with the DM becoming the European anchor currency. The generalization of German austerity for the EU through the Treaty of Maastricht will lead to a further slow-down of growth and persistently high unemployment, as there is little chance of overcoming stagnation through higher world market shares at the expense of America or Japan. Because the chances to profit permanently from her hegemonic position become smaller with the generalization of stagnation the German economy will also be severely affected by the repercussions of austerity.

A way out of this perspective requires a change of economic policy in the EU.[19] Monetary policy must be relaxed to give room from a tightly coordinated expansionary fiscal policy with primary emphasis on the stimulation of growth and employment. The promotion of European unity and cohesion requires additional transfers from the richer to the poorer countries and the establishment of a larger European budget to fulfil central economic stabilization and redistribution tasks. To protect such a policy turnaround against capital flight and speculative attacks the EU should introduce adequate measures like a foreign exchange transaction tax. And it should make use of the possibilities of temporary capital controls in emergency cases.

German economic policy can play a paramount role in initiating and implementing such a change of economic policy orientation. The present strictly monetarist course has been enforced in the EU by Germany against the objections and resistance of other countries who are even more affected by the negative consequences of this course than Germany. Therefore, if Germany did start to change its strictly monetarist attitude, this change would certainly not have to be imposed on other countries but would be welcomed by them.

To change economic policy in Germany one must criticize the monetary and fiscal policy provisions of the Maastricht treaty. They have been inserted into the treaty under the influence and pressure of the Bundesbank, and they are presently instrumentalized in Germany as an external constraint, which must be accepted for the sake of European unity. For a long time the unions have accepted the rules of Maastricht because they were sold as necessary elements of such unity and critics of Maastricht were denounced as anti-European. But this argument is losing its force. Austerity is more and more perceived not as a price for unity but as the road to division and polarization in Europe. In Germany, too, opposition grows against the policy of income and welfare cuts and comprehensive downsizing, legitimized by allegedly European imperatives. This criticism could and should be supported and reinforced by the elaboration of realistic and positive alternatives for European economic development from which Germany would benefit greatly. Under the given circumstances the way to fuller employment requires mobilization and political pressure from below.

Notes

1. See the joint letter of 18 April 1990 of former French president François Mitterrand and German chancellor Kohl to the participants of the EC summit in Dublin in which they proposed to complement Economic and Monetary Union by a Political Union, which would come into effect at the beginning of 1993 (cf. Europa-Archiv, 1990, D283).
2. Kenen, 1995, p. 26.

3. Germany is the country with the highest share of employment in manu-facturing in the EU. In 1983–85 it was 33.6 per cent for Germany against 27.3 per cent for the EU average and until 1990–92 this share had only decreased marginally to 32.4 per cent against a much stronger reduction of the EU average to 24.9 per cent; see European Commission, 1996, pp. 52–3.

4. The share of the DM in world currency reserves rose from 10.2 per cent in 1981 to 20.8 per cent in 1990, see Deutsche Bundesbank, *Annual Report*, 1982, p. 69 and 1990, p. 67. In 1996 it had fallen to 14.1 per cent, still remaining the second largest reserve medium behind the US $ (62.7 per cent) and before the yen (7.0 per cent), see Deutsche Bundesbank, 1997, p. 29.

5. Huffschmid, 1994, vol. 2, ch. 2.

6. See the memoirs of the former president of the Bundesbank, Otmar Emminger (Emminger, 1986, pp. 228–51) where he describes very frankly and even proudly the decisive role of the Bundesbank in the abolition of the fixed parity system of Bretton Woods.

7. 'The intervention rules and credit arrangements of the EMS had been designed to guarantee that countries with weak and strong currencies would bear joint and symmetric responsibility for the defense of the system. Whenever a country's currency reached the edge of its band *vis-à-vis* one of its partners' currencies, the partner was supposed to inter-vene unstintingly to keep the exchange rate from leaving the band ... In effect the system was meant to protect a weak-currency country from exhausting its reserves and being forced to devalue'. Kenen, 1995, p. 162.

8. Emminger, 1986, p. 362.

9. Measured in DM the fall was even steeper, from 135 bn DM to 22 bn DM; see Sachverständigenrat, 1996, p. 418.

10. European Commission, 1996a, p. 40.

11. Schäfer, 1996, pp. 598–9.

12. UNCTAD, 1996, p. 233.

13. European Commission, 1996a, p. 6.

14. *Ibid.*, p. 11.

15. Huffschmid, 1994, vol. 2, ch. 1.

16. DIW, 1996, p. 558.

17. Deutsche Bundesbank, 1996b, pp. 32, 34.

18. Huffschmid, 1994, vol. 2, ch. 5.

19. European Economists, 1997.

References

Deutsche Bundesbank (1996a) 'Neuere Tendenzen in den wirtschaftlichen Beziehungen zwischen Deutschland und den mittel und osteuropäischen Reformländern', *Monatsbericht*, July pp. 31–47

Deutsche Bundesbank (1996b) 'Kapitalverflechtung mit dem Ausland,' *Statistische Sonderveröffentlichung*, 10, Frankfurt

Deutsche Bundesbank (1997) 'Die Rolle der D-Mark als internationale Anlage- und Reservewährung', *Monatsberichte*, April, pp. 17–30

Deutsches Institut für Wirtschaftsforshung (DIW) (1996) 'Mehr Beschäftigung in der EU durch Außenhandel mit den Transformationsländern', *Wochenbericht*, 34, pp. 557–65

Eichengreen, B. and Wyplosz, C. (1993) 'The Unstable EMS', *Brookings Papers on Economic Activity*, pp. 51–124

Emminger, O. (1986) *D–Mark, Dollar, Währungskrisen. Erinnerungen eines ehemaligen Bundesbankpräsidenten.* Stuttgart: Deutsche Verlagsanstalt

European Commission (1996a) *Mergers and Acquisitions, European Economy, Supplement A: Economic Analyses*, no. 7, pp. 1–15

European Commission (1996b) *Economic Evaluation of the Internal Market*, Reports and Studies, no. 4. Luxembourg: Office for Official Publications of the European Communities

European Economists (1997) *Full Employment, Social Cohesion and Equity for Europe – Alternatives to Competitive Austerity. A Declaration and a Memorandum of European Economists.* Bremen: Manuscript

Herr, H. (1991) 'Der Merkantilismus der Bundesrepublik in der Weltwirtschaft' in Voy, K., Polster, W. and Thomasberger, C. (eds) *Marktwirtschaft...*, pp. 227–61

Huffschmid, J. (1994) *Wem gehört Europa? Wirtschaftspolitik und Kapitalstrategien in der EG. Band 1: Wirtschaftspolitik in der EG.* Heilbronn: Distel

Kenen, P.B. (1995) *Economic and Monetary Union in Europe. Moving Beyond Maastricht.* Cambridge: Cambridge University Press

Polster, W. and Voy, K. (1991) 'Von der politischen Regulierung zur Selbstregulierung der Märkte – Die Entwicklung von Wirtschafts–und Ordnungspolitik in der Bundesrepublik' in Voy, K., Polster, W. and Thomasberger, C. (eds) *Marktwirtschaft...*, pp. 169–226

Sachverständigenrat zur Begutchtung der gesamtwirtschaftlichen Entwicklung (1996) *Jahresgutachten 1996/97.* Bonn: Bundestagsdrucksache 13/6200

Schäfer, C. (1996) 'Mit falschen Verteilungs – "Götzen" zu echten Standortproblemen – Zur Entwicklung der Verteilung in 1995 und den Vorjahren', *WSI-Mitteilungen*, 49, pp. 597–616

United Nations Conference on Trade and Development (UNCTAD) (1996) *World Investment Report 1996. Investment, Trade and International Policy Arrangements.* New York and Geneva: United Nations

Voy, K., Polster, W. and Thomasberger, C. (eds) (1991) *Marktwirtschaft und politische Regulierung. Beiträge zur Wirtschafts- und Gesellschaftsgeschichte der Bundesrepublik Deutschland (1949–1989).* Marburg: Metropolis

5 Italy Towards European Monetary Union (and Domestic Disunion)

Annamaria Simonazzi and
Fernando Vianello[1]

The prospects for monetary union are fraught with uncertainty. Prestigious politicians, authoritative Eurocrats and austere central bankers debate whether the deficit of a given country amounts to 3.2 or 3.0 per cent of the GDP when the GDP measure itself is so vague an estimate as to make such calculations dubious. The construction of Europe has indeed been transformed into 'a sort of parody of an accountant's nightmare' (Keynes, 1982, p. 241). In order to understand why things have taken this turn – and whether they are likely to get better in the future – reference must be made to the interests of those who rule the roost. This is why our chapter begins with Germany (Section 5.1). Sections 5.2 to 5.5 then discuss the long history of Italy's wobbling public finances and their over-hasty redressment – imposed by the Maastricht criteria – which has aggravated the country's inveterate problems, paved the way for new ones and made the political transition Italy is going through tougher and more hazardous. In particular, the deepening of the north–south and east–west economic and social divide has set in motion centrifugal forces in the richer parts of the country while creating an explosive situation in the poorer. What is at stake is indeed the very idea of a common Italian destiny.

The chances of Italy emerging from its difficulties will depend on its capacity to produce income and employment, and thus also on how its productive structure will respond to the new conditions created by the deepening and widening of the EU (Section 5.6). Both the productive and the financial problems will in turn be affected by the EU's macroeconomic stance and exchange rate policy (Section 5.7). On this front the Stability Pact represents a most alarming sign.

5.1

The German economic model, as we knew it before reunifaction, was based on the accumulation of current account surpluses, which strengthened the D-Mark, attracted capital inflows and enabled Germany to finance a huge flow of commercial credits and direct investments to Communist and Third World countries. After reunification, the flow of investments and social transfers to the eastern regions turned the current account surplus into a deficit (from +48.3 billion dollars in 1990 to −18.7 billion in 1991). At the same time the fall of the Communist regimes in the Central and Eastern European (CEE) countries generated new opportunities for economic penetration and productive integration, while also making it more urgent than ever to favour growth in those countries, not least in order to stem the east–west migratory flood. Closer productive integration with Eastern Europe and the prospective enlargement to it of the EU also represent an important part of the German response to the challenge of world-wide decentralization of production and the formation of large trading blocs. Delocalization to low labour-cost areas makes it possible, in fact, to preserve the competitiveness of national industry in the 'sensitive' sectors, more vulnerable to a strong currency policy, and this may ease the traditional conflict between industry (and government) on the one hand and finance (and the Bundesbank) on the other on exchange rate policy. It is this – and not just the Germans' notorious obsession with inflation – that makes a strong currency policy so appealing to Germany: it must be able to attract massive inflows of low cost capital to divert into the CEE and Third World countries.

Acceptance of the single currency was the price Germany had to pay for France's consent to German reunification and future enlargement of the EU to the CEE countries, a prospect that should make the rebirth of the German giant less disquieting for those countries. However, Germany succeeded in obtaining guarantees that the strength of the euro would not be jeopardized by the participation of countries with hefty public debts and scant credibility in their determination to reduce them. Otherwise the difficulties that, say, the Italian government might face in tackling the public debt could generate expectations of intervention by the European Central Bank, thus making the strong currency policy more costly in terms of interest rates. Higher interest rates would in turn exacerbate the difficulties of the government in question. If this were to threaten a crisis of confidence and new lows in that government's securities, the European Central Bank would come up against the alternatives of either intervening or exposing investors to serious losses – and the government in question to risk of insolvency.

Thus we can appreciate the toughness of the Maastricht criteria. They respond to Germany's need to make a strong currency of the euro, even at the cost of keeping some countries out. We can also see why the criteria were not revised, as one might have expected, with the slowing down of European growth. The result was that all the countries reacted to the falling fiscal revenues with further deflationary measures, disregarding the cumulative effects such measures were bound to produce when adopted simultaneously. Thus all wished to be virtuous, and none could. Not even Germany.

At this point – with the 'virtue gap' between Italy and Germany close to zero in terms of deficit to GDP ratio (the debt to GDP criterion has never, up to now, been taken quite as seriously) – the rules have been changed. What mattered was no longer formal respect for the criteria (though all countries were, and still are, engaged in 'creative accounting' to this end) but the long run 'sustainability' of the results obtained. And for the future, criteria yet more rigorous than those of the Maastricht treaty were agreed upon in the Stability Pact, together with financial sanctions for defaulters.

5.2

Italy is an obvious target for Maastricht watchers. Yet to appraise its present record of precarious virtue, one must rehearse its past history of profligacy. Here there are two important points to bear in mind. In the first place, owing to Italy's peculiar situation in the immediate post-war period – as a country with a strong Communist Party and, moreover, in a strategic geopolitical location – the capacity to hold together a vast anti-Communist social bloc was made the main goal, and the ultimate source of legitimation, of government action. The second point is that the concentration of industrial development in the northern regions required measures of income support in a large part of the country – also in order to prevent social tensions from getting out of hand. The priority accorded to these aims meant (a) creating and perpetuating a flow of public expenditure to the southern regions, 'thus giving rise to a ruling class dissociated from production, interested solely in continuing and increasing public subsidies' (Graziani, 1972, p. 95); (b) hiring, paying, organizing and retiring public employees according to the canons of patronage and consensus rather than efficiency; (c) granting fiscal privileges and turning a blind eye to the tax evasion of large sections of the middle class, which stood as bastions of social stability and support for the parties in government. Two factors prevented a fiscal problem from appearing: the cancelling-out of the public debt as a result of wartime and post-war inflation and the rapid growth of the economy.

In the late 1960s and early 1970s Italy was rocked by waves of working class protest and a more general social and political unrest, matched by radical changes in life-styles and customs. The problem of consensus took on important new aspects and new burdens were piled on to the public budget. Important and costly reforms were introduced: at last Italy had its own national health service and the pensions system was overhauled. Public employees saw their pay hiked while generous support was given to industrial restructuring and above all to restoring the profitability of firms, particularly through cuts in social security contributions. The new demands could have been met by diverting resources from other ends, but this would have meant hitting social groups – and forgoing flows of expenditure – that had been and remained essential to the general design of consensus. And so the idea, which had been suggested, was rapidly abandoned, and the new costs added to the old. If this did not totally wreck Italy's public finance it was thanks mainly to inflation, which curbed the growth of the public debt in real terms while at the same time causing a hefty fiscal drag that hit hardest at employee incomes. The state was actually taking money from workers (and security holders) with one hand and giving it to firms with the other, thus helping the latter foot their rising wage bills,[2] aggravated by the fuller wage indexation agreed upon in early 1975. This mechanism effectively complemented the policy of currency depreciation and inflationary profit recovery which provided the basis for the flexible approach to social conflict prompted by the change in industrial relations.

The policy of currency depreciation, started in early 1973, predated by several months the oil crisis, which caught the Italian economy in a phase of steeply rising prices and vigorously growing investments. Rapidly worsening current accounts, accelerating inflation, stern warnings from the IMF and the adoption of deflationary measures were the preclude and theme music to the first government of 'national solidarity', which followed upon the impressive electoral gains made by the Communist Party in 1976. Austerity and sacrifices were the watchwords of this government, which – with the help of governor Baffi's shrewd policy of letting the lira drop against the mark while rising against the dollar – could take the credit for a spectacular improvement in the current account of the balance of payments. The reason why the Communist Party gave its support to this policy is to be found not only in its attempt to obtain full legitimation, but also in the political culture of a party which has always regarded itself as the bearer of 'national' (rather than 'class') interests.

On the other hand, this episode confirmed a constant rule in Italian politics, according to which the Left is coopted into government, or its whereabouts, to secure consensus to deflationary policies. As noted by A. Ginzburg, in Italy phases of expanding demand and intensive capital accumulation are marked by governments supported by conservative political coalitions. The rapid rise in imports caused by Italy's incomplete productive structure – and, not infrequently, capital flight – trigger a balance of payments crisis, which is met with a monetary squeeze. In the subsequent phase of recession we find governments supported by more or less left-leaning coalitions, which exhaust their function as soon as conditions for a new phase of expansion are created.[3]

Mystery still wraps the circumstances of the kidnapping, long imprisonment and assassination of the Christian Democrat Party president Aldo Moro in 1978, though not the ultimate reasons. Participation of the Communist Party in the government of the country, for which Moro had been the major advocate, did not really seem compatible with an international situation resting largely on the maintenance of the status quo in Europe. Shortly after, the Christian Democrats drove a wedge into the government coalition by insisting on Italy's immediate participation in the EMS when domestic conditions – with inflation at 20 per cent – advised postponement. The defeat of the Communist Party in the 1979 election sanctioned the end of the 'national solidarity' policy.

The second oil shock, which came that year, did not stop the government from launching into an expansionary policy out of phase with the world cycle, squandering the foreign currency reserves so painstakingly amassed during the period of 'national solidarity'. The measures adopted (increased tax allowances, pension rises, and fuller indexation of public employees' salaries) are eloquent evidence of a calculated operation to consolidate the social ground for the new political course.

The Bank of Italy's annual Reports suggest that by the early 1980s inflation was being curbed, thanks largely to a non-fully-accommodating exchange rate policy (that is, by devaluing the lira by less than the inflation differential).[4] However, the high industrial profit margins pointed up in the same Reports[5] suggest that more decisive here than a tough exchange rate policy was the crumbling of the labour front, especially after the emblematic defeat of the FIAT workers' militant wing in October 1980. This marked a breakthrough in industrial relations, which paved the way both for intensive industrial restructuring, leading to a dramatic drop in employment and thus wearing down the workers' resistance even more, and to progressive reduction of wage indexation. The tightening of monetary policy in turn helped consolidate the new pattern of power relations and bring about disinflation – with the help of the falling prices of raw materials plus, since the mid-1980s, dollar depreciation and the oil counter-shock.

In this period severe demands were made on the state coffers to support the wave of industrial restructuring and rationalization – particularly with massive recourse to early retirement schemes and transfer payments to workers temporarily laid off or working shorter hours – and to create new jobs in the public sector. At the same time interest payments were growing as a result of rising international rates (although the effect was tempered by capital controls) and a growing public debt. A further contribution to the rise in interest payments came from the so-called 'divorce' between the Bank of Italy and the Treasury in 1981, which relieved the former from the obligation to finance the public deficit. This was the first manifestation of a conflict that – as we shall soon see – was to grow increasingly harsh. As for the receipts, the effects of the fiscal drag came to be increasingly replaced by the raising of tax rates and the levying of new taxes (but not by a substantial reduction of tax evasion). By the mid-1980s public expenditure and fiscal revenues amounted roughly to 50 and 40 per cent of the GDP respectively, each being 10 points higher than a decade earlier.

In 1984 a decree partially suspending wage indexation came in for stiff opposition from the Communist Party, but the referendum they launched to abrogate it met with defeat. With the ensuing political isolation of the Communist Party and the more combative wing of the unions, the cycle of political and social restoration that had begun in 1978 with the assassination of Aldo Moro may be said to have come to its conclusion. And with order restored in the factories and in society a decade and a half of government action inspired almost solely by a flexible approach to social conflict, and the desire to stop the country slipping any further left, may also be said to have reached its term.

5.3

While up to this point Italy's shaky public finances can be seen as the price to be paid for a long, complex political operation, the persistence of primary deficits in the 1980s was mainly the fault of a corrupt, irresponsible political class squandering public money, seeing in public expenditure a means of self-enrichment as well as the cement to reinforce their systems of patronage and to create new, arrogant potentates. This political class accepted with reckless nonchalance the Draconian conditions of the Maastricht treaty as the deficit reached 10 per cent of the GDP while the public debt soared past the 100 per cent mark.

The party-led grabs system called CAF (from the names of two premiers, Craxi and Andreotti, and Christian Democrat Party secretary, Forlani) found its antagonist in the Bank of Italy, which took the leadership of what we shall term the 'Party for Europe'. The distinctive features of the 'Party for Europe' are, on the one hand, the conviction – by no means new in the history of Italian political thinking – that civil progress in the country cannot rely solely on internal energies, but needs a discipline imposed from without and, on the other hand, an ingenuous confidence that things will naturally take their own positive turn once the discipline is imposed[6] – and that external conditioning, always underpinned by the interests of those applying it, and not of those subjected to it, cannot itself become a further, possibly huge, obstacle.

Between 1987 and 1992 the role of external constraint was attributed to stable intra-European exchange rates, presented by the Bank of Italy and its allies as a stage in the transition to monetary union, to be made on the basis of existing parities. The need to defend the exchange rate, while no longer relying on capital controls, abolished in 1990, offered something of an 'objective' justification for high interest rates and the refusal of the Bank of Italy to finance the public deficit. High interest rates would – they calculated – confront the government with the choice between converting to a policy of financial rigour or being overwhelmed by the exponential growth of both public and foreign debt. The public money in support of industrial restructuring and laid-off workers would have to be diverted from other ends or drawn from new sources. Thus the backing of industrial firms and unions alike would be obtained for the design to stem the flow of public money into the patronage system and crack down on tax evasion. At the same time, firms would find themselves compelled not only to stand out against demands for pay rises but also to step up productivity and innovation, and move to products with a lower price elasticity of demand. In short, the simplistic view of the 'Party for Europe' was that stable exchange and high interest rates would together knit a straitjacket that the economy, society and politicians would eventually adjust to.

The strong currency policy may not have lived up to expectations in terms of technological advance and upgrading of production, but it did spur firms on to renew their plant in advance, with consequent sharp rises in productivity, and to cut costs by reorienting the decentralization of production towards low labour-cost countries, in particular in the former Communist and Maghreb areas. From a political point of view, its consequences were not unequivocal. On the one hand, it managed to drive a wedge into the party-led grabs system, causing a struggle to develop within it over the control of a reduced flow of resources. On the other hand, massive inflows of short-term capital, attracted by the high interest rates and the hope of capital gains accruing from their reduction in the near future, made it possible for the lira to occupy a comfortable position in the 'narrow band' it had entered in January 1990 and this, paradoxically, made it less urgent to redress public finance and easier for the government to put off the day of reckoning.

This came in September 1992, when the relentless growth of the current account deficit – feeding, and being fed by, the growth of the foreign debt in an endless spiral – reached its inevitable outcome, currency crisis. This was obviously not the result expected from the stable exchange rate policy (in spite of a persistent inflation differential) and high interest rates. We can only suppose, therefore, that the Bank of Italy was counting on the joint commitment of the EC countries to defend existing parties up to monetary union. No such commitment had ever been entered upon, however, and the Bundesbank in particular made no secret of its impatience with fixed exchange rates, especially after Germany's request for unilateral revaluation of the mark on reunification had been turned down by the other countries. International speculation could only respond accordingly.[7]

5.4

After the currency crisis the CAF promptly declared its candidacy to succeed itself in the new role of financial redresser. The Draconian emergency measures taken by the Amato government confirmed the rule according to which financial redressment is more easily undertaken in the aftermath of a currency crisis than in the attempt to prevent it. But by then the final rout of the CAF was already under way: on the one hand, the fall of the Communist regimes had made international support to corrupt national governments less necessary and less defensible; on the other hand, endless extortion, lack of fixed rules and the complexity and slowness of the division-of-spoils procedures had resulted in widespread hostility towards the party-led grabs system, whose domestic and international isolation obstructed its customary response of nipping any judicial action in the bud. The enquiries of a courageous group of magistrates uncovered so much – and such deeply rooted – corruption, not to speak of the connections certain eminent politicians had with the Mafia and Camorra, that even Italy's traditionally cynical, disenchanted public opinion was shaken to the core.

A first sign that public opinion was becoming thoroughly sickened with the way the country was governed came with the referendum of 9 June 1991 on the preference vote, which aimed at stamping out gerrymandering, but was in fact to pave the way to abandonment of the proportional system. Voters ignored Socialist party secretary Bettino Craxi's arrogant invitation to spend the day at the seaside and the single preference proposal won over 95 per cent of the votes. At the time Craxi was still dreaming of exploiting the crisis in the Communist Party – which had in the meantime become the Democratic Party of the Left – to invert power relations between Socialists and (former) Communists as Mitterrand had in France. Two years later he was to abandon his office as party secretary and one more year was enough to make of him a fugitive from justice – or, as he prefers to put it, an exile.

A second, significant sign came with the resounding success of the Northern League in the 1992 general election. The League – which has now advanced from its initial federalism to out-and-out separatism – was and remains above all a movement of fiscal revolt and protest against the inefficiency and corruption of the central government. What it calls into question is the north–south pact mentioned in Section 5.2 above: on the one hand, an industrial base concentrated in the north and, on the other hand, consensus in the south organized through patronage-based public spending.

In the last two decades the centre of gravity of the Italian industrial system has moved from the north-western regions forming what used to be called the 'industrial triangle' to the north-eastern regions,[8] which form presently an economic area closely integrated with Germany on the one hand and with the CEE countries on the other (see Section 5.6 below). With a high share of their production going to foreign markets, the firms in this part of Italy are less interested in what becomes of the rest of the country than was that old protagonist of economic development in Italy, the industry of the north-west, for which public spending in the south represented an important source of demand, both directly and through its multiplier effects. Moreover, the small and medium-size firms making up most of the north-eastern industrial network chafe at the exasperating slowness and inefficiency of the public administration, which the large firms find various ways of getting round, and are more exposed to the oppression of petty politicians and corrupt government officials than the big companies. On top of all this, despite large-scale evasion the tax burden has steadily grown, and the reaction is to attribute this to the need to finance public spending in the south and provide a living for layabout officials and dishonest 'Roman' politicians (although Lombardy and Veneto traditionally provided their fair share of the latter). An apt setting is thus created not only for the success of the Northern League, but also – and above all – for the sense of being estranged from the national community and for the subversive potential lurking in one of the richest and most dynamic parts of the country.

In 1993 political crisis and economic emergency carried to government the governor of the Bank of Italy Carlo A. Ciampi, a living symbol of the 'Party for Europe'. His government brought in authoritative 'technicians' from outside the political arena and gained the support of the Democratic Party of the Left (PDS). Ciampi's programme focused on a policy of disinflation and financial redressment negotiated with the unions. The big industry of the north-west, controlling most of the so-called independent press, made up the third party in this 'neo-corporative' pact.

Shortly before the 1992 currency crisis wage indexation had been done away with. A more comperehensive labour cost agreement was promoted by the Ciampi government in July 1993. Together with depressed internal demand and intensified competition in the distribution sector, wage restraint made it possible – at the cost of a fall in real wages – to combine sharp currency depreciation (and impressive growth in profit margins) with only moderate inflation. Exports grew steadily with domestic demand in the doldrums. Benefiting from this situation were the areas where the exporting industries are most concentrated while others, notably in the south, went on losing ground. At the same time fiscal discipline provided a justification for a severe downsizing of the state-owned industry, mostly located in the south, while the southern economy was also hard hit by the crisis of the construction sector. Moreover, after forty years the so-called 'extraordinary intervention' in the south was brought to an end. Execrable as its past management might have been, this was no justification for the idea that one need only halt the flow of public spending for the energies of the south to stir from their long, aid-induced slumber and find their own way to productive ends. A more constructive response would have been to divert spending in the south from the mortifying system of personal subordination it had created to one favouring autonomy, initiative and industriousness. The EU initiative, not sufficiently resisted by the Italian government, went in exactly the opposite direction, depriving southern industry of the important advantage of tax-benefited social security contributions, one of the few incentives that had eluded control by the patronage system (and its not infrequent criminal connections).

5.5

Falling real wages and salaries, cuts in social expenditure, increasing unemployment and the impoverishment of the south, but also the fears of tax dodgers, the heavy fiscal burden placed on honest tax-payers, or those unable to evade taxes, and the malaise of the small entrepreneurs in the north-east: all this underpinned the success of Silvio Berlusconi. In the space of a few months this television tycoon, who had risen under the aegis of Craxi, set up a new political force, Forza Italia, headed a coalition including the Northern League and the ex-fascists of Alleanza Nazionale and won the 1994 election by promising sweeping tax cuts and the creation of 'one million jobs'. Berlusconi's populism collected together those excluded from the 'neo-corporative' pact, shaped the protest of rich and poor alike and easily took possession of the space left empty by rigour without design.

This is not the place to rehearse the story of the Berlusconi government, nor the crumbling of its majority, which led to the subsequent government led by Lamberto Dini, nor, lastly, the sea-changes undergone by the latter: from minister in the Berlusconi government to head of a non-party 'technical' government to slippery ally of the Left. Both governments were advantaged by a phase of economic recovery, by virtue of which they managed to preserve the primary surpluses achieved by the previous governments. However, neither the Berlusconi government at its very beginnings, up to the new currency crisis of July 1994, nor the Dini government immediately prior to the 1996 elections, were immune to the seductions of profligacy. This rendered all the more difficult the task the Prodi government set itself in the subsequent recessionary phase, namely, to bring down the deficit-to-GDP ratio in 1997 to 3 per cent in order to enter the EMU in the first wave.

A dispassionate assessment of this decision cannot disregard the way in which the relations will likely be governed between the countries entering the EMU from its inception ('ins') and those remaining outside ('outs'). As far as one can see, these relations will be based on a system of pegged exchange rates along the lines of the EMS, now reentered by Italy after its exit in 1992, but with a fluctuation band that cannot be as wide as the current 15 per cent band. A system of this kind seems acceptable (indeed, offers considerable advantages) provided that 'ins' and 'outs' alike commit themselves to defending the currencies under attack and controls on capital movements are reintroduced. But in the current climate of thought this latter proposal appears almost provocative. And, as regards the task of defending the currencies under attack, the well-known reluctance of the Bundesbank to shoulder such a burden – which will no doubt be inherited by the European Central Bank – combines with the punitive (and self-punitive) tenet according to which, since the 'outs' are the cause of their own ills, it is up to them to defend their currency with every device they have available and without flinching before the worst social costs.

Experience shows that an exchange rate agreement built on such foundations can be toppled by speculation at any moment. And that, in any case, the need to defend their currencies would constrain the 'outs' to a policy of high interest rates. This would be disastrous for a country like Italy that in 1996 had to devote more than 10 per cent of its GDP to servicing its public debt and whose primary surplus can scarcely be maintained for long at the level of 4.4 per cent reached in 1996 (not to speak of the record level of 6.7 per cent expected for 1997). Hence the Italian government's decision to do everything it can to be among the first to enter the EMU and to slim the deficit-to-GDP ratio to 3 per cent by use of temporary measures like the one-off 'Europe tax', while waiting for the fall in interest rates following the adoption of the single currency to bring more lasting relief to the budget. Note that what the adoption of the single currency actually entails is a reduction in the interest differential between Italy and Germany. Whether, and to what extent, this will translate itself into a reduction in the absolute level of the Italian rates will depend on the policy of the European Central Bank (and the US Federal Reserve). If, however, interest rates are destined to diminish, reducing the public deficit to 3 per cent of GDP now by non-temporary measures would be tantamount to taking on a sacrifice that would subsequently turn out to have been excessive.

The adoption of temporary measures would give the government time and scope to tackle the two burdensome problems of public expenditure and taxation, which are both problems of composition rather than of quantity. Non-interest public expenditure is lower in Italy (at 42.3 per cent of GDP in 1996) than the European average (over 45 per cent for the EU excluding Italy). Social expenditure is roughly in line with the European average, and lower than in France and in Germany. What it needs is not to be reduced, but to be made more effective and to be redirected towards those categories of citizens who, by income and age, are more seriously in need of public support. Pursuit of the first of these two aims, effectiveness, is hampered by the appalling inefficiency of the public administration, perhaps the biggest single stumbling block in the way of progress; that of the second, equity, by the very high tax evasion which makes near nonsense of any attempt to determine who has the right to what on the basis of tax returns. This effect of evasion is even more disruptive than its consequences on the fiscal revenue, as it makes any serious reform of the welfare state impossible. What is certain is that discipline imposed from without – and so often invoked from within – is not helping in this direction. By shifting the emphasis onto the 'sustainability' of financial healing (see Section 5.1 above), the EU has not only undermined the argument for recourse to temporary measures, but it has also called for further, and less temporary, deflationary measures, thus shaking the government's credibility, making cohesion more difficult for the government coalition and paving the way to social and political instability.

5.6

The deepening and eastward widening of the EU will accelerate the process of regional restructuring unleashed by the Single Market. Moreover it will take place in a context of increasing globalization, and without the help (as we argued in Section 5.1 above) of an accommodating European exchange rate policy. Will this exact prohibitive social and economic costs of adjustment from the weaker members of the Union? The answer for Italy depends very much on an appraisal of the characteristics of Italian industry and of the process of structural change which it has undergone. We can distinguish two main approaches.

The studies aiming to explain a country's trade performance and specialization by using a sectoral taxonomy based on the characteristics of the innovation process[9] agree in giving a description of the European productive structure as weaker than the Japanese and US ones in 'science based' sectors, especially in microelectronics and information technologies, and highly dualistic, divided between a northern core, specialized in technologically 'advanced' sectors and a southern periphery, specialized in 'traditional' sectors. This way of looking at the matter has led some authors to the conclusion that the rich northern countries, with a revealed comparative advantage in investment goods, will get the most out of a fully-fledged Single Market and the opening of the new eastern markets. On the other hand, the industrial structure of the southern members of the Union will have to face the direct competition of the products of the CEE countries. Thus, both the deepening and the eastward widening of the Union are likely to produce an asymmetric distribution of benefits and costs, leading to an increased polarization between core and periphery.[10]

According to this view, Italy's strong and increasing advantage in 'specialized suppliers', basically engineering, does not make up for her basic weaknesses – marked specialization in 'traditional' sectors, disadvantage in 'science based' sectors and a continuous loss of competitiveness in 'scale intensive' sectors – so that the country runs a serious risk of deindustrialization. Italy is at a disadvantage in relation to the challenges confronting the European countries from three different points of view: (a) the small size of its firms and its weakness in oligopolistic, high technology sectors prevents it from taking advantage of the scale economies triggered by the Single Market and participating in the rush for the creation of 'European champions'; (b) the single currency, which entails the loss of the exchange rate as a tool to defend price competitiveness (and compensate for losses in non-price competitiveness), will put in jeopardy a whole array of industries with a high price-elasticity of demand;[11] (c) the eastward enlargement will bring in new low-cost competitors in the very products of Italy's comparative advantage and specialization.

The approach we have just described is based on a concept of competitiveness which refers to sectors, rather than firms or systems of firms, and on a concept of innovation based on 'codified' knowledge, which is what the number of patents or the amount of R&D expenditure attempt to quantify. This kind of knowledge, however, represents only the first stage in the process of innovation. The competitiveness of productive systems depends quite as much, or in fact even more, upon the nature, quality and quantity of 'tacit' knowledge, that is the ability and experience in 'doing', which is basically relational and develops from the sedimentation of productive practices, personal relations and cooperative attitudes embedded in a socioeconomic and institutional environment. The way in which 'codified', or abstract, knowledge combines with the layers of the locally-embedded 'tacit', or practical, knowledge has necessarily a territorial dimension.[12] In this perspective – of a continuous flow of incremental innovations in products, processes, organization, sourcing and marketing – there are no 'traditional' or 'advanced' sectors, but more or less innovative productive systems.[13]

When we look at the matter from the point of view of the Italian productive systems, we reach somewhat different conclusions from those suggested by the studies referred to previously. The most dynamic productive systems have grown in close complementarity with the German economy, either conquering or filling the space left by the process of decentralization and upgrading of the German industry. The impelling forces were paramount in the north-east (see Section 5.4 above), which has gone through a rapid process of growth in those sectors which represent the backbone of the Italian pattern of specialization – not only textiles, clothing, footwear and furniture, but also plastics and a wide range of machinery and parts. This model of production, based on a network of small and medium-size firms, often organized in 'industrial districts', has then spread south – mainly through sub-contracting – along the eastern (Adriatic) coast.

As we mentioned in Section 5.3 above, in the strong currency period of 1987–92 the most dynamic firms in the 'traditional' sectors began to imitate the German pattern of subcontracting, reorienting decentralization from domestic to foreign low labour-cost areas, particularly in the Mediterranean and CEE countries. From this point of view the enlargement of the EU to the CEE countries may represent an opportunity rather than a threat. Furthermore, owing to their marked specialization in consumer durables and investment goods, Italian firms are in a position to take advantage of the prospective expansion of the eastern markets. Although the eastward enlargement is still very much a German business, Italian firms have been increasing their trade with the CEE countries; in 1994, Italy ranked second after Germany, though at a huge distance, among the EU(12) exporters to the CEE countries.[14]

The real problem for Italy seems, indeed, to rest in the geographical division not only between north and south, but also in both parts of the country between a dynamic east and a declining or underdeveloped west. A closer integration with northern and eastern Europe will tend to exacerbate this division – if only by the diversion of subcontracting from the southern regions of Italy to the low-cost areas of eastern Europe. As for the north-east itself, the rapid growth of exports (and profits) following the 1992 devaluation shows that exchange rate changes may still play an important role. Monetary unification may indeed entail the risk that a too rapid process of delocalization of production can lead to an excessive contraction of the productive network and to impoverished social-economic relations, ultimately weakening the intrinsic strength of the local productive systems.[15]

5.7

While domestic firms can, in principle, maintain and increase their competitiveness and market shares through world-wide sourcing (though long-run competitiveness is made up by more than simply low labour costs), a nation can prove unable to endure the long-lasting unemployment and shrinking productive base which such a pattern of development is bound to bring about, if not duly supplemented by the creation of new industries and new jobs to replace those destroyed by industrial restructuring and decentralization. And this is a goal that monetary union, if properly geared to growth, could contribute to. The advantage of monetary union lies in the fact that the constraint to growth represented for each country by the recording of intra-European balances of payments falls away. Geared as it was to accumulating robust current accounts surpluses, Germany's traditional neomercantilist policy has made this constraint very severe for the other European countries since their growth was (of necessity) conditioned by German growth, and this in turn was (by choice) conditioned by growth in German exports. This applies in particular to Italy, whose dependence on imports in the investment and food sectors has meant that phases of rapid capital accumulation have systematically been cut short by balance of payments crises and the consequent need to adopt deflationary measures (see Section 5.2). The situation is even worse now, with German deflation spreading to the other countries not only through the trade balance (thanks to stable exchange rates) but also through the public budget (thanks to the common effort to meet the Maastricht parameters). With exports to the rest of the world left as the only dynamic component of demand, Europe has been transformed into a vast export-led growth area. Once intra-European balances of payments are no longer recorded, growth will no longer be limited by the increase it induces in the net imports of each single member country of the EU, no small part of which comes from the other member countries, but by the increase in the net imports of the European Union, or in other words of an area whose propensity to import is even lower than that of the United States. Monetary union, thus, could entail the creation of an economic entity able both to sustain domestic-led growth – taking care of its depressed areas and launching large-scale projects to modernize transport and telecommunications – and to finance a massive flow of commercial credit, direct investment and aid to CEE, Mitterranean and developing countries.

Exports of capital goods to these countries will, of course, have to be matched by a growing flow of imports from them, to make room for which labour and entrepreneurial flair will have to be shifted to other types of production. However, with full employment reasonably widespread – and secured by policies targeted to the areas negatively affected – the process could go ahead without any serious damage. An accommodating exchange rate policy could also help make the necessary adjustments less painful.

A great opportunity has evidently arisen. At the present moment, however, there are few signs that it will be taken up. Even if the EMU is not nipped in the bud by a rise in German interest rates, the 'Stability Pact' points in the direction of an extension of the traditional German economic model to the whole European Union, with the complicity of an economic theory fully worthy of the two epithets Keynes applied to the version ruling in his days – 'misleading and disastrous' as a guide for action.[16] This means that credit, direct investments and aid are to be 'paid for' not out of increased income and savings, but by stepping up fiscal pressure, cutting social spending and reducing transfers to the depressed areas, while the limitations imposed to the national budgets will make transfers to areas hit by an asymmetric shock impossible without resorting to new taxes. The construction of Europe will, thus, come up against staunch resistance from the more negatively affected, to the great advantage of resurgent nationalism and localism.

Deprived of the exchange rate tool and, at the same time, of control over monetary and fiscal policy – and confronted with growing unemployment – countries disinclined to endure events passively will have few tools to fall back on. Among these, worthy of mention in virtue of the massive use already made of them are: (a) deregulation of the labour market, creating opportunities to reduce monetary wages and worsen labour conditions; (b) reductions in social contributions, usually financed with cuts in public expenditure; (c) lavish tax inducements for investors (bringing a growing part of the fiscal burden to bear on employee income). Some countries are thus able to enhance their competitiveness and, as in the case of Ireland, attract a massive inflow of foreign investments. If all the countries join in the game – and sooner or later they would have no choice – these advantages must inevitably dry up. What will remain is the cost all must bear for having adopted a new, more unjust social model.

Notes

1. We thank Claudio De Vincenti, Bernard H. Moss, and Margherita Russo for helpful comments.
2. Giavazzi and Spaventa, 1989.
3. Ginzburg, 1986.
4. Bank of Italy's Report for 1986, pp. 129–31.
5. Bank of Italy's Report for 1986, p. 104, Fig. B9, and Bank of Italy's Report for 1987, p. 114.
6. Ginzburg, 1995.
7. The capital inflow into weak currency countries has been interpreted as evidence of the 'credibility' of the 'new EMS' policy of rigidly fixed exchange rates. For a critique see Simonazzi and Vianello, 1996.
8. According to the official definition, north-eastern Italy includes the regions of Emilia, Friuli-Venezia Giulia, Veneto and Trentino-Alto Adige. Economic integration with Germany is also strong in a part of Lombardy. The Northern League has its strongholds in Lombardy and Veneto.
9. This taxonomy, originally suggested for firms (see Pavitt, 1984), was subsequently extended to sectors and supplemented with indicators of the innovative capacity of a nation's industry, such as patents and expenditure on R&D, or of its strength *vis-à-vis* foreign competitors, such as direct investment, mergers and acquisitions.
10. For a critical survey of the studies aiming at evaluating the costs and benefits of EU enlargement see Grabbe and Hughes, 1997.
11. The ability of exchange rate depreciation to make up, even in the short run, for the cumulative non-price competitive disadvantages of the Italian industrial system is however increasingly questioned. See for instance Rossi, 1996.
12. This view of innovation and competitiveness has been propounded by students of the Italian districts. See, in particular, Brusco, 1982, Becattini, 1991 and Russo, 1996.
13. For an application to a typically 'traditional' sector, textiles and clothing, see Ginzburg and Simonazzi, 1995.
14. In 1994 the German share of total EU(12) exports to the CEE countries was 57 per cent (42.2 per cent in 1989), as against 13.5 per cent for Italy and 7 per cent for France. See Grabbe and Hughes, 1997, p. 29.
15. See on this point Conti and Menghinello, 1996, p. 294.
16. Keynes, 1973, p. 3.

References

Becattini, G. (1991) 'The Industrial District as a Creative Milieu', in Benko, G. and Dunford, M. (eds), *Industrial Change and Regional Development*. London: Belhaven Press
Brusco, S. (1982) 'The Emilian Model: Productive Decentralization and Social Integration', *Cambridge Journal of Economics*, VI: 167–84

Conti, G. and Menghinello, S. (1996) 'Territorio e competitività: l'importanza dei sistemi locali per le esportazioni italiane di manufatti. Un'analisi per province (1985–94)', in Istituto Nazionale per il Commercio Estero, *Rapporto sul commercio estero*. Roma

Giavazzi, F. and Spaventa, L. (1989) 'Italia: gli effetti reali dell'inflazione e della disinflazione', *Rivista di politica economica*, LXXIX: 5–49

Ginzburg, A. (1986) 'Dependency and the Political Solution of Balance of Payments Crises: The Italian Case', in Foxley, A., McPherson, M.S. and O'Donnel, G. (eds) *Development, Democracy and the Art of Trespassing. Essays in Honor of Albert O. Hirschman*. Notre Dame: University of Notre Dame Press

Ginzburg, A. (1995) 'Nazionalismi ed economia: un rapporto complicato', *Passato e presente*, XIII: 113–22

Ginzburg, A. and Simonazzi, A. (1995) 'Patterns of Production and Distribution in Europe: The Case of the Textile and Clothing Sector', in Schiattarella, R. (ed.) *New Challenges for European and International Business*. Roma

Grabbe, H. and Hughes, K. (1997) *Eastward Enlargement of the European Union*. London: Royal Institute of International Affairs

Graziani, A. (1972) 'Introduzione', in Graziani, A. (ed.), *L'economia italiana: 1945–70*. Bologna: Mulino

Keynes, J.M. (1973) 'The General Theory of Employment, Interest and Money', in *The Collected Writings of John Maynard Keynes*, vol. VII. London: Macmillan

Keynes, J.M. (1982) 'National Self-Sufficiency (1933)', in *The Collected Writings of John Maynard Keynes*, vol. XXI. London: Macmillan

Pavitt, K. (1984) 'Sectoral Patterns of Technical Change: Towards a Taxonomy and a Theory', *Research Policy*, XIII: 343–73

Rossi, S. (1996) 'Due episodi a confronto di riequilibrio dell'interscambio commerciale italiano: 1975–78 e 1992–95', in Istituto Nazionale per il Commercio Estero, *Rapporto sul commercio estero*. Roma

Russo, M. (1996) *Cambiamento tecnico e relazioni tra imprese*. Torino: Rosenberg & Sellier

Simonazzi, A. and Vianello, F. (1996) 'Credibility or "Exit Speed"? Reflections Prompted by the 1992 EMS Crisis', *Rivista Italiana di Economia*, no. 1, pp. 5–24

6 State Intervention and the Question of European Integration in Spain

Miguel Martinez Lucio

European integration and the impact of the Maastricht Treaty raise a range of issues. The emergence of a coordinated economic and political space in Europe continues to depend on the political calculations and strategies that exist at the level of the nation state. In Spain, economic and social regulation in the last two decades has depended crucially on the utilization and reinterpretation of European policy developments. Maastricht not only provides a range of policy constraints but also provides a key point of reference for the development of economic and social regulation. Hence, there are ideological and political mechanisms that need to be explained if the actual impact and politics of Maastricht, along with the broader issue of integration, are to be fully comprehended. This chapter first of all outlines the broader framework of Spanish engagement with the EU. The quest for further integration and the concept of 'Europeanization' are explained from the point of view of Spanish developments. The chapter then points to the difficulties that have arisen as a consequence of the emerging European discourse of deregulation within the Spanish system, which has evolved in a complex manner and lacks the stability and coherence of northern European systems of regulation.

HISTORICAL BACKGROUND AND ECONOMIC ACHIEVEMENTS

Spain's membership of the EC in 1985 under the Socialist government of the PSOE (*Partido Socialista Obrero Español*) was a key development in the country's history. It was essential that the emerging democracy within Spain be integrated politically and further stabilized after the attempted coup d'état of 1981. In fact, membership

125

confirmed the reentry into 'Europe' of a country that had been at its margins since the eighteenth century. One should not underestimate the symbolic significance of this event and its representation within Spain; the country was now on board the 'train of history'. Very much as in Germany in the 1950s the political benefits of membership were seen as paramount to the institutional consolidation of the country. The Socialist government in the decade after Spain's entry in 1985 accepted many of the key political proposals for further unification even though this meant curbing its traditional industries and sectors. The Spanish government supported European integration and then the Maastricht criteria throughout the course of negotiations. And there has been relatively little criticism of EMU in Spain due to the desire to benefit from more stable currency structures.

It was also felt in the mid-1980s that integration meant that the country would get access to the markets of the Community, which would assist Spain's economic development. It would encourage inward investors to transfer production and capital to the country. Spain's economic development since the 1970s had been based not just on state intervention and the mixed economy but also on a competitive edge in labour costs and, more importantly, on high levels of inward investment.[1] Increasingly, the key players in Spanish manufacturing have been foreign multinationals. Multinationals were locating in Spain with a view to pushing their products into the EU. The growing internationalization of the Spanish economy and its insertion within the global circuit of capital made membership appear essential.

More specifically, it was felt that insertion into the European economy would integrate the Spanish economy technologically.[2] The belief that new technology was central to future economic and industrial development had permeated many policy circles, especially those of the Socialists with their project for a 'post-industrial' Spain. Exhibitions of robotics in arts centres, forums and discussions on the development of post-industrial society, and the development within universities of courses covering information technology were central to the preparation of the country in terms of external technological and economic integration. The 1980s in Spain were a strange combination of modernist progress with technological development and post-modern irony, a questioning of traditional state roles and the support of consumerist trends within the culture. The evolution of a new soft/portable culture and the increasing way in which new consumerist trends were based on the consumption of imported technological products and transnational capital, were represented and used as a distancing from the Francoist years with their closed, paternalist and protected economy.[3] The European dimension was presented as a feature of this move away from 'traditional' state economic forms. On the other hand, Spain increasingly exported through its tourist and cultural industries stereotypical images of the country and its culture – pliable images that focused on exotic/erotic representations of Spain. This is reflected even within the alternative cinema of the last ten years, especially in the films of Almodovar and Luna. Membership was perceived within a various quarters as a necessity not only for the future development of the Spanish economy and political system, but also for its new cultural discourse and evolving middle classes.

Measuring the effects of economic integration is not easy. One can evaluate growth but isolating the causes of success can be difficult. Alternatively, one can try to view the degree of political stability and the level of protest as indicators of how integration is being received and evaluated. During the initial phases of membership the country continued to experience high levels of inward investment and external trade.[4] In terms of growth rates the average for 1985 to 1990 was 5 per cent which could have been attributable to a range of factors such as declining oil prices.[5] Between 1985 and 1992 the average GDP per capita increased by 27 per cent in real terms and job creation was extensive due to the massive increase in demand. Spain was also a net recipient of EC funds during this period. Politically, the country went through a bout of confidence based on the stability of the PSOE regime until the early 1990s and the high profile gained from the Barcelona Olympics and Seville's Expo92.

How much of this was due to integration in the EC is uncertain, although integration certainly permitted these developments to continue. The threat of public sector debt destabilization and high inflation rates, which had been the bane of the 1970s, was clearly receding in the light of EU membership in the 1980s and early 1990s. Spain has not found any serious difficulties in adapting itself to the social and industrial relations framework of the continent in the form of the social dimension of the EC. In terms of areas such as health and safety, employment rights and other social issues the Spanish state has managed to consolidate certain formal rights for workers. Social policy integration has not been a major dilemma – although this may actually say more about the lack of substantive content within the social dimension itself and the tendency to articulate a social political project based on the common, perhaps lowest common, denominator within the continent.[6] Threlfall[7] argues that on the question of working conditions the Socialist government was very supportive of developments whilst on questions related to employment rights issues, such as sexual equality, there was some considerable catching up. However, on questions related to social and welfare expenditure the government was much more reluctant to support new measures. The policy of the Socialist Government from the mid-1980s onwards was much more concerned with constraining the growth of the state.[8]

Membership also provided policy-making elites in Spain with a legitimation for industrial restructuring and for 'measured' (that is, limited) growth in terms of social intervention. The government used integration to avoid extensive state intervention, to curtail the expansion of key traditional sectors, and to promote market values and deregulation. In many respects the Socialist government (1982–96) would have found it much more difficult to execute its market socialist programme without the EU dimension. Europeanization – the final modernization of Spain – was linked ideologically to questions of stability and certainly to key economic indicators such as inflation, state expenditure and debt. During the mid to late 1990s, indicators were clearly beginning to show positive improvements within the country confirming for some the claims that Maastricht was 'organizing' the Spanish economy and constraining some of its 'bureaucratic features'. The whole project of Europeanization became reduced within certain governing circles to the question of 'taming' the economy and the state: modernization became moderation. With this came a new language of governance and political procedure, which is discussed below. That is not to say that the Spanish public was convinced by the question of integration and in particular the Maastricht agreement. Yet the question of institutional legitimacy was tied by elites to the whole issue of Europeanization and financial 'stability'. Alternative readings of Europe as a social Europe and welfare-oriented Europe were downplayed and marginalized by such elite discourses.

EUROPEAN INTEGRATION AND REGULATION

There is a tendency within the debate on European integration and national economic policy to see developments in terms of a zero-sum analysis of the relation between the two tiers. The European dimension is seen as an imposition on the role of the nation state in economic terms. However, we need to be aware that the effects of integration depend on the national context, on the way integration interfaces with national projects. How is integration referenced and used within national political discourse and action by governments? Governments entered into the process of integration very clear about the *quid pro quo* of such an exchange. The language and criteria of the Single European Market and Maastricht then became the subject of national projects that utilized these languages and criteria to restructure and deregulate. This interactive feature of European integration is usually bypassed in much of the traditional analysis which assumes a centralized and uniformly imposed system of supranational governance. The point is that European projects are the product of certain national economic discourses, projects which are in turn used to reconfigure the role of the state and the pattern of economic and social regulation. That is not to say that the author agrees with the thesis of nation state decline in the face of globalization. As has been put clearly by Panitch,[9] the nation state finds new roles and mediates many of these global economic developments.

The Spanish government was a firm supporter of European integration and the Maastricht agreement even if this meant a constriction of national economic policy.[10] The question of national autonomy and sovereignty was never a key issue for the political elites of the Spanish state or amongst the country's financial and industrial interest groups. The Communist-Left coalition – Izquierda Unida – was virtually alone in voicing concerns about European integration. The reasons for this lack of concern were varied but the concern with instability within Spain and the view of the EU as a form of economic stabilization was critical. Constriction of national economic policy was also favoured because of the lack of faith in the stability of the peseta. Hence the adage familiar to the PSOE and now the Conservative government of the *Partido Populare* that 'there is no choice'.

A period of extensive public deficits and inflation in the 1970s left an indelible mark on the policy-making elites of Spain – the fear of 'Latin Americanization'. The fear of being pushed, by the social and political pressures of a post-dictatorial situation, into extensive state expenditure led to the character of corporatist policy making in Spain, limiting the inclusion of social partners, unions and employers' organizations within decision making.[11] Corporatist developments tended to be limited and ritualistic, dealing with the implementation of policy rather than policy making.[12] The informality of corporatist arrangements gave the government considerable flexibility, allowing it to convene negotiations at some junctures and to keep its distance from them at others. This strategy has been called 'strategic displacement' in political decision making and this has been a central feature of economic policy in democratic Spain.[13]

Maastricht allows the economic centre-right policy framework to be further 'guarded' from social intervention and priorities, thus reinforcing the soft Thatcherite character of the social-democratic left in Spain. This was seen with the reluctance shown to the social dimension discussed above and the Spanish government's uneven responses to the social and welfare aspects of the EU's social politics.[14] Governability is further reinforced via this external reference point; the external 'fits' a specific internal concern. A whole discourse of political legitimacy evolved in Spain founded on whether a government achieved or was close to the Maastricht criteria. The criteria became, by the mid-1990s, a test of government ability; the PSOE was seen to be failing this test whilst the following 1996 Conservative government established its credibility by its ability to 'tame the public sector' and behave in a 'European manner'.

The European dimension and the obsession with minimizing the economic cost of the public sector has other uses as well in terms of the labour market and the 'cost of labour'. The cult of labour competition and the cost of labour market regulation are expressed in terms of the historic issues of the cost of dismissal. The questioning of redundancy costs for temporary contracted workers who form one third of the workforce, the growth of the submerged economy, and the constant use of individual dismissal procedures that circumvent legal procedures and limit the role of unions[15] have not appeased this obsession with the employer's burden. In many ways the question of labour cost is another dimension of this myth of Europe as being free from bureaucratic procedure. In fact the Maastricht treaty has been used to further the national political project that had evolved since the early 1980s, which has had as its objective the development of a modern state limited in its social and interventionist character. The Maastricht treaty fitted the advancement of this project.

ALTERNATIVE ECONOMIC OUTCOMES

It is possible to offer an alternative evaluation of the effects of market integration on Spain. As a result of this market integration, the Spanish state did not take advantage of certain economic opportunities. Public policies were oriented towards monetary integration at the expense of industrial policy. In terms of inward investment there has been a move to indirect, portfolio investment at the expense of direct investment.[16] Spanish companies are increasingly being taken over and this does not always lead to any subsequent improvement in their technological base. Spanish production processes are being integrated within Europe by transnational corporations in a partial and uneven manner.

The structure of production and employment has been gradually approaching that of the 'advanced' European economies. The total working population in 1994 was 15 468 000. Of these, 9 652 400 were men and 5 815 000 were women, out of a population of approximately 40 million. Agriculture accounted for 1 150 000, which is high compared to the EU average. Services accounted for 7 046 000, industry and construction for 2 473 000 and 1 058 000 respectively. Public administration has been a major area of expansion. The long-delayed development of a welfare state and the creation of new state structures in the autonomous regions or *autonomías* set up under the 1978 constitution resulted in the increase of public employment as a proportion of the total by more than 50 per cent.

However, the working population is small in comparison to other countries. The participation rate was 63.3 per cent in 1995 for men but only 36.2 per cent of women were economically active (although this figure had been steadily increasing from less than a quarter at the beginning of the 1970s). The overall unemployment rate in 1995 was 22.9 per cent; since 1985 it has been twice the average of the EU. Women suffered a much higher unemployment rate than men, peaking at 30.6 per cent according to the Ministry of Labour.[17] Another feature, especially significant given the salience of the issue of mass unemployment in political debate since the early 1980s, is the poor coverage of state unemployment benefit. The unemployed receive direct benefits for a maximum of two years only, which must be seen in the light of some of the highest rates of long-term unemployment in Europe. The extent of youth unemployment has seriously restricted young people's experience of liberal-democratic industrial relations and of jointly regulated workplaces; the highly absorbing education system, in terms of time and the continuing role of family structures, has 'cushioned' the political and labour market impact of what are high levels of youth unemployment. In 1995 42.5 per cent of citizens aged 16–24 and 50 per cent of women were unemployed. Whilst some have argued that the cost of redundancy in Spain has been excessive, the reality is that almost a third of the workforce is on temporary contracts. In fact, in 1995, two million people lost their jobs and 63 per cent of these received no compensation due to their contract status (*Gaceta Sindical*, September–October 1996).

In human resource and employment terms the tale of integration is somewhat different from the optimistic readings outlined above. This is reflected in the standard-of-living statistics. In the last twenty years there has been no convergence between European standards of living and those of Spain in real terms. In 1995 the average income per capita was 76.1 per cent of the EU's average which, whilst an improvement of 1985's 67.7 per cent, was still below the 77.9 per cent of the mid-1970s. In fact, there remains a marked difference from other members of the EU, a difference which has concerned many public bodies (see the publications of the Economic and Social Council in Spain, Consejo Economico y Social).[18]

Another problem is the continuing nature of technological dependency. Technology is in great part imported: the internal production and development of technological products has not been a major feature of recent developments. In this respect the types of integration assumed in the earlier phase of membership have not been realized. Inward investment in the last few years has tended to be located in low-technology sectors, and when the investment has been directed towards manufacturing this has mainly been in the final assembly line process which are already established as opposed to high technology manufacturing and production.

A major problem has been that the need to integrate Spain into the European monetary systems of the EU has led to an obsessive focusing on monetary policy and currency stabilization within the broad framework of economic policy. Such an obsession has undermined the evolution of proactive labour market polices, training strategies and, more importantly, industrial policy. The lack of a consistent industrial and technology policy has been continuously lamented by employers and trade unions.

European monetary policy in the form of EMU and the attempt to work within specified criteria has imposed a series of constraints on the Spanish state. The Maastricht criteria for convergence, in terms of public debt and deficit ratios, have forced the Spanish state to constrain its economic and social intervention over the last four years. The effect of such constraints on public expenditure, imposed through Maastricht, must be measured in terms of the national economic context. Countries such as Germany and Holland have a legitimized and stable regulatory tradition; they also have established forms of public intervention whether they are restructuring features of the economy or not. They have an established economic and political structure of strong institutionalism[19] which they can defend, at the moment, *vis-à-vis* external Maastricht-type criteria without it having extremely adverse effects on their systems of regulation. The case of countries such as Spain is different. They are having to deregulate and having to constrain the role of the state at a time when effective – not to be confused with bureaucratic – state intervention has not been appropriately established and when economically they are working from a more unevenly developed economic context.

Here is the problem, the dilemma of the 'double transition' in southern European countries such as Spain: constructing an organized and regulated economy in the context of global 'restructuring' and reorganization. Reaching convergence criteria means withholding expenditure in areas that have been more dependent on it and with fewer alternatives than would otherwise be the case. Spain has evolved as a successful democracy but regulatory processes and traditions need time to establish themselves.

Monetarism has meant that economic policy has not been focused on restructuring Spanish industry in such a way that it can overcome its historic problems of being fragmented and dominated by relatively small companies with unevenly skilled employees. Industrial policy has been driven mainly by a focus on redundancy and downsizing.[20] Not only has industrial policy been undermined by the obsession with monetary policy, but the attempt to maintain a high level for the peseta at certain points during Spain's EU membership, due to the need for monetary integration and the attraction of foreign capital, has also meant that interest rates have been on average exceedingly high, which has had a negative effect on Spanish business concerns during much of the last decade.[21]

The new Conservative government has been trying to appease the unions by agreeing to long-term stability in the areas of pensions and agrarian payments, for example, but the reality is that cutbacks in the area of public sector pay and in health led to a wave of demonstrations and public sector strikes in the mid-1990s. Throughout Europe the Maastricht criteria have tended to give rise to industrial and popular conflict within the public sector and Spain is emerging as a prime example of this. The question is how the process of economic modernization, consistent and effective regulation of the economy, and real value-added growth as opposed to growth based on the increasing casualization of labour and employment will be possible within the framework of EMU. For countries such as Spain what is an apparent success in relative political terms may prove to undermine their real economic basis in the longer term.

CONCLUSION

The record presented above shows that regardless of stable economic measures and the steady yet uneven convergence with Maastricht criteria from 1995 to 1997, the broader economic context within which the Spanish nation exists is such that further weakening and fragmentation in regulation means that key actors may not be able to cope with what are deep-seated structural problems. The structure of regulation and the role of the state in Europe varies enormously in areas such as labour markets and industrial policy.[22] High valued-added economies tend to have very regulated systems of governance. The role of regulation and its character is key to economic success.[23] Stable currencies and public expenditure ratios are only one aspect of the totality of state roles and objectives. Economically and ideologically, Maastricht legitimates a vision of economic development which may constrain those wider functions of regulation which have led to value-added, technologically intensive, and high-skill-based economic processes. The Maastricht Treaty fits a New Right logic emerging within parts of the European political spectrum based on limiting the role of the state and privileging monetary concerns and the question of inflation within economic policy.

The aim of this chapter has been to illustrate the complex political interplay that constitutes the new European politics. Alternatives are limited not by a series of simple supranational 'impositions' but by complex linkages between national projects and supranational developments. In addition, the chapter points to the way 'constriction' leads to 'fragmentation' in national economic and social policy, even when circumstances may actually be improving in economic terms. This outcome is not inevitable; it emerges because of the general questioning of welfare and economic intervention amongst the Centre and the Right and the way 'Europeanization' is constructed around a whole new project based on viewing governance as economic restraint. The supranational is still subject to the mediating role of the national, as is beginning to be argued with reference to globalization.[24] However, this mediation may occur in such a manner that it undermines the participative spheres of state action, the role of democratic processes within the state and the space to discuss alternative projects.[25] The European project as developed in Spain pushes the state and economy towards a 'defensive' orientation as opposed to an 'offensive' one, one based on short-termism, cost-based strategies and a general market-led disorganization of the economy as has been seen in Britain.[26] 'Convergence' within Europe in such cases is more likely to be nominal than real for countries such as Spain.[27]

Notes

1. Buckley and Artisien, 1987.
2. Castells *et al*, 1986.
3. Alonso and Conde, 1984.
4. Salmon, 1991.
5. Tovias, 1995.
6. Rhodes, 1991.
7. Threlfall, 1997.
8. Navarro, 1997.
9. Panitch, 1995.
10. García Añoveros, 1994.
11. Roca, 1983.
12. Martínez Lucio, 1997.
13. Martínez Lucio, 1983; Foweraker, 1989.
14. Threlfall, 1997.
15. Bilbao, 1991.
16. Salmon, 1995.

17. Ministry of Labour and Social Affairs, 1996.
18. Consejo Economico y Social, 1996.
19. Streeck, 1991.
20. Aragón Medina, 1993.
21. Arasa Medina, 1992.
22. Boyer, 1988.
23. See Williams and Haslam, 1993; Nolan and O'Donnell, 1991; Leborgne and Lipietz, 1990; and Boyer, 1988.
24. Panitch, 1995.
25. Bromley, 1997.
26. Lash and Urry, 1987.
27. See Martin and Velazquez, 1996; and Arasa Medina, 1992.

References

Alonso, L.E. and Conde, F. (1984) *Historia del Consumo en España*. Madrid: Debate
Aragón Medina, J. (1993) 'Crisis economica y reformas laborales', *Economistas*, pp. 22–31
Arasa Medina, C. (1992) '1982–1992: diez años de política económica en España', *Revista de Económica Aplicada e Historia Económica*, 2: 77–120
Bilbao, A. (1991) 'Trabajadores, gestión económica y crisis sindical', in Miguélez, F. and Prieto, C. (eds) *Las Relaciones Laborales en España*. Madrid: Siglo veinteuno
Boyer, R. (1988) *The Search for Flexibility*. Oxford: Clarendon Press
Bromley, S. (1997) 'Globalization?', *Radical Philosophy*, no. 80 Nov/Dec, pp. 2–5
Buckley, P. and Artisien, P. (1987) 'Policy Issues of Intra-EC Investment', *Journal of Common Market Studies*, December, pp. 105–28
Castells, M. *et al* (1986) *El Desafia tecnologico: España y las nuevas tecnologias*. Madrid: Editorial Alianza
Comin, F. (1995) 'La dificil convergencia de la economía española: un problema historico', *Papeles de Economia Espanola*, 66: 78–91
Consejo Economico y Social (1996) *Memoria 1996*. Madrid: CES
Foweraker, J. (1989) *Making Democracy in Spain*. Cambridge: Cambridge University Press
García Añoveros, J. (1996) 'España y la Union Europea', *El Pais Annuario*. Madrid
Jessop, B. (1990) *State Theory*. Oxford: Polity Press
Lash, S. and Urry, S. (1987) *The End of Organised Capitalism*. Oxford: Polity Press
Leborgne, D. and Lipietz, A. (1990) 'How to Avoid a Two Tier Europe', *Labor and Society*, 15(2): 177–99
Martin, C. and Velazquez, F.J. (1996) 'Una estimacion de la presencia de capital extranjera en al economia espanola y de algunas de sus consecuencias', *Papeles de Economia Espanola*, 66: 160–175

Martínez Lucio, M. (1983) *Corporatism and Political Transition*, MA Thesis. Colchester: University of Essex

Martínez Lucio, M. (1997) 'Spain: Constructing Actors and Institutions in a Context of Change' in Ferner, A. and Hyman, R. (eds) *Industrial Relations in the New Europe*. Oxford: Basil Blackwell (second edition)

Ministry of Labour and Social Affairs (1996) *Annuario de Estadisticas Laborales y Asuntos Sociales 1995*. Madrid

Navarro, V. (1997) 'The Decline of Spanish Social Democracy', *The Socialist Register*. London: Merlin

Nolan, P. and O'Donnell, K. (1991) 'Flexible Specialisation and the Failure of British Manufacturing: A Critique of Hirst and Zeitlin', *Political Quarterly*, 62(1): 106–25.

Olson, M. (1965) *The Logic of Collective Action*. Harvard: Harvard University Press

Panitch, L. (1995) 'Globalisation and the State', *The Socialist Register*. London: Merlin

Ramsay, H. (1990) *1992 – The Year of the Multinational?*, Warwick Papers in Industrial Relations. Warwick: Warwick University Press

Rhodes, M. (1991) 'The Social Dimension of the Single Market', *European Journal of Political Research*, 19: 245–80

Roca, J. (1983) 'Economic Analysis and Neo-Corporatism', paper presented at European University Institute

Salmon, K. (1991) *The Modern Spanish Economy*. London: Pinter

Salmon, K. (1995) 'Spain in the World Economy', in Gillespie, R., Rodrigo, F. and Story, J. (eds) *Democratic Spain*. London: Routledge

Streeck, W. (1991) 'On the Institutional Conditions of Diversified Quality Production', in Streeck, W. *Social Institutions and Economic Performance*. London: Sage

Threlfall, M. (1997) 'Spanish Government Responses to EU Policy' forthcoming in *South European Society and Politics*

Torfing, J. (1991) 'A Hegemony Approach to Capitalist Regulation', in Bertramsen, R.B., Thomsen, J.P.F., and Torfing, J. (eds) *State, Economy and Society*. London: Unwin Hyman

Tovias, A. (1995) 'Spain in the European Community', in Gillespie, R., Rodrigo, F. and Story, J. (eds) *Democratic Spain*. London: Routledge

Williams, K. and Haslam, C. (1993) 'Beyond Management: Problems of the Average Car Company', paper for the *Lean Production and Labor Conference*, Wayne State University

Part II

Europe in Crisis?

7 Is the European Community Politically Neutral? The Free Market Agenda

Bernard H. Moss

INTRODUCTION: LIBERAL ORIGINS

The European Community (EC) is usually discussed as a supranational project without reference to political orientation and purpose. The claim is made for its political neutrality as between liberals and socialists in the European tradition. Its foremost constitutional authority stresses the primacy of the free market principles, but notes that article 222 of the Treaty of Rome authorizes public ownership and suggests scope for a high degree of public intervention and indicative planning.[1] Most analysts, treating the EC as either politically neutral or completely adaptable, assume that it merely reflects the preferences of its constituents, the existing balance of political and economic forces within it.[2] They do not believe that it constitutes in itself, apart from the influence that the international environment may exercise on any country, a barrier to market intervention in member states. Theirs is a reflective view of base and superstructure that neglects the powerful autonomous role that EC principles, institutions and practices have had on the evolution of national economies, social coalitions and internal politics.

Alan Milward, the historian who has investigated the commercial origins of the Treaty of Rome, sees it as a product of mixed economies, of nation states that were pursuing welfarist, mercantilist and redistributive objectives.[3] Obviously, the success of such policies required growth, which was linked with trade. But why did the states conclude a treaty that, in the words of the former French premier Pierre Mendés-France, was 'based on the classical liberalism of the nineteenth century, which holds that competition pure and simple resolves all problems'?[4] Milward, like others,[5] exaggerates

141

the extent to which post-war European states were dedicated to income redistribution. As he admits, Keynesian demand management was used only erratically in France, more to subsidize business than increase consumer demand, and not at all in Germany, Italy and Belgium.[6] Wage levels remained low in the 1950s, below that of 1938 in France until 1955; the age of mass consumption was yet to drawn.[7] Unions were weak and divided in France and Italy where collective bargaining was practically unknown. The two most important factors in post-war growth were the exploitation of cheap labour reserves, which allowed wage increases to lag behind those of productivity,[8] and the expansion of trade among the six that was consolidated by the EC.

The neomercantilist and welfarist tendencies of which Milward speaks were much more evident in the prologue to Rome: in the European Coal and Steel Community (ECSC), preliminary discussions of the common market begun in 1953, and the Spaak Report, which laid the groundwork for the Treaty of Rome. The ECSC had provisions for the reconversion of industry and retraining of workers displaced by competition and for emergency powers to fix prices and quotas. Since the Common Market was first proposed by the Dutch banker Johann Beyen in 1953, the partners had assumed that the removal of tariffs would be accompanied by common policies on wages, employment and social policy.[9] The Spaak Report, which recognized the inequalities that market competition can generate, also featured funds for reconversation and retraining. The French memorandum to the negotiators of April 1956 was frankly socialist. It insisted upon the prior harmonization of social policy and wages, restrictions on labour mobility, national planning and a redistribution of income to wages.[10]

Yet in the end the French, out of fear of economic and diplomatic isolation, capitulated and signed a treaty reflecting the liberal orientation of the Dutch and Germans. The turning point came when they conceded that social reforms would have to come primarily from the functioning of the common market. Negotiations were hastily concluded while France was still favourably disposed. Few of the founders could have realized that they were creating a new liberal constitutional order with broad jurisdiction over nation states. In seeking parliamentary approval of the treaty Guy Mollet, the French *premier*, greatly exaggerated the social dimension.[11] Like most French leaders, Mollet never imagined the treaty would ever be implemented, certainly not in detail.[12]

Despite the obvious liberal bias of the treaty, social democrats like André Philip believed that the existence of common European institutions gave them the power to organize the market.[13] There was indeed an attempt in the 1960s to coordinate national planning, industrial and monetary policy under Robert Marjolin and his Medium-Term Economic Policy Committee, but the Germans were opposed to planning and the French to a common currency. French president François Mitterrand and president of the Commission, Jacques Delors, tried to introduce a social dimension in the 1980s but with little success. Socialists thought that in the EC they could obtain reforms they were unable to win at home.[14] Many condemned the monetarist bias of Maastricht but hoped that the dissatisfaction created by it would produce effective demands for a redistributive European government.

This hope is ill-founded. On the basis of a historical and legal analysis, this chapter argues that bias against social intervention in the market is systemic, inherent in the principles, institutions and practices of the EC constitutional order, especially since buttressed by the neoliberal revolution of the 1980s. The EC was not established by big business and multinationals; they had limited control over the political process and were doing quite well in the 1950s in penetrating national markets without it. But the EC has certainly served their interests – they have been the most enthusiastic supporters of the single market and currency – while subjecting wage earners to the organizationally dissolving and depressing wage effects of untrammelled competition.[15] The unstated aim of the single currency is to drive down wages and benefits.[16] The EC and the European Monetary System associated with it did constitute a constraint on Keynesian reflation and industrial policy under Mitterrand.[17] The failure of the EC to establish a coherent social policy is patent.[18] Yet, it has served as an alibi for national politicians to wash their hands of social policy and ignore growing division in their countries.

TREATY OF ROME (1957)

The best way to understand the Community is to begin with a legal analysis of its founding treaties. Article 2 of the Treaty of Rome lists its aims as harmonious and balanced growth, rising living standards and stability. The primary means for achieving these aims is the creation of a single competitive marketplace on the model of the domestic market.[19] The treaty incorporates the economic assumption that free trade leads to a reduction in costs and to increased productivity and wages. Rules are to be interpreted without prejudice to the system of property, but no policies except perhaps those of agriculture must be allowed to distort competition.

The other method stipulated in the treaty to achieve its aims is the progressive approximation of economic and monetary policy among the member states, but this does not authorize the creation of European institutions to regulate the market or promote a single policy. Under article 104 each member state was to pursue the economic policy needed to assure a balance of payments and maintain confidence in the currency while taking care to ensure a high level of employment and stable level of prices. Unlike the Spaak Report, which noted the twin dangers of deflation and inflation, the treaty seeks to hold down prices. The emphasis is on the harmonization of economic and monetary policy rather than counter-cyclical policies. The treaty contains provision for neutralizing the trade effects of competitive devaluations that by lowering interest rates may set up a growth cycle, as frequently occurred in France and Italy. The European Court (ECJ) held in 1977 that floating exchange rates were in breach of the obligation under article 105 to coordinate monetary policy.[20] Trade interdependence was expected to limit the effectiveness of national economic and monetary policy. Implicit in the logic of the treaty was the goal of fixed exchange rates leading to a single currency.

The liberalism of the Rome treaty was not applied with full force until the single market initiative was made possible by the neoliberal revolution of the 1980s. Until then the Commission, charged by treaty with the development of the common market, had to make accommodations with the neomercantilism of member states regarding capital mobility, nonquantitative restrictions on trade, state aids, public procurement and monopolies. Special arrangements were made to allow state aids with France and Italy, which flouted the obligation to notify. Public utilities, the major sector for public procurement, were exempted from new regulations. Article 67 had spoken of ending exchange controls only to the extent necessary for the functioning of the common market. Under the directives of 1960 and 1962 nations could still invoke safeguard measures to control short-term financial movements. Freedom of movement for capital was first declared as a principle in the 1987 Single European Act (SEA) and implemented by directive in 1990.[21]

SINGLE EUROPEAN ACT (1987)

The SEA aimed to facilitate the completion of the internal market which, with the exception of the freedom of movement of capital, was inscribed in the original treaty. Originating from the liberal turnabout of Mitterrand, the act reflected the collapse of interventionist policies in the major states. Liberalization has been a cumulative process in Europe with the common market forcing deregulation upon member states, which then pressed for more deregulation in the EC. In his shuttle diplomacy Mitterrand found a common denominator in the desire to complete the internal market. The idea was taken up in 1985 by the new president Delors, appointed by Mitterrand, and by Lord Cockfield, a Thatcher appointee to the Commission. Cockfield drafted a white paper with 300 specific proposals for eliminating barriers to competition – physical, technical and fiscal. To remove barriers the Commission relied on the principle of the mutual recognition of standards, first announced by the ECJ in *Cassis de Dijon* (1978), the setting of technical standards by non-governmental bodies and a minimalist approach – only the 'essential requirements' – to the harmonization of health and safety standards.[22]

The harmonization of national rules and standards was blocked by the requirement of unanimity. The SEA provided for the harmonization of regulations by qualified majority. In the absence of harmonization the principle of mutual recognition obtained. Under this principle no state could invoke its own standards to bar goods that were marketable in an exporting member state. This meant that the lowest level of regulation, usually that which imposed the least cost, would prevail. Regulations not notified by the Commission by 1992 were to be subject to mutual recognition; in 1992 the Commission failed to notify.

The Commission requested two reports from economists on the single market. Both reports predicted that the removal of barriers would reduce costs, which would increase demand, competition, productivity and growth. Both also acknowledged the need for macroeconomic stimulation and for special funds to reduce the regional inequalities caused by the increased competition.[23] The Cecchini Report attempted to quantify the benefits of market deregulation,[24] predicting five million more jobs, seven per cent supplementary growth and 'an upward trajectory of growth through the next century'.[25] Cecchini's figures, which represented the views of leading experts,[26] were wildly over-optimistic, ignoring the negative effects of competitive efficiency on protected jobs and wages.[27]

MAASTRICHT TREATY (1992)

The Maastricht treaty, by establishing a single currency with an independent bank committed to price stability, further restricted the economic functions of the EC to those of the liberal state. Article 3 defines its guiding principles as those of stable prices, sound public finances and monetary conditions and a sustainable balance of payments. Article 2 lists among its tasks the promotion of a high level of employment and of social protection, economic and social cohesion and solidarity among member states, which are also presented as aims of national economic policy in article 102a. However, the interventionism implicit in article 2 is severely constrained by the monetary convergence criteria on budget deficits, debt and inflation and by the requirements in article 3a that economic and monetary policy be conducted 'in accordance with the principle of an open market economy with free competition' and that price stability be the primary aim of monetary policy.

EUROPEAN LAW AS INSTRUMENT OF DEREGULATION

The new legal order incorporated free market ideology. The ECJ has found that the treaties confer fundamental rights to property and enterprise and to equal treatment before the law, rights which limit governmental intervention.[28] Law is much better at knocking down barriers to free trade than at erecting new protection. It was a main vector of capitalism in doing away with the remnants of the feudal and mercantilist state in early modern Europe.[29] Courts of general jurisdiction, as opposed to administrative courts, are better designed for establishing universal rules and are poorly qualified to evaluate individual or collective exceptions to the rules that are usually required by specific measures of social or industrial intervention.[30]

The emphasis of the treaties is on negative integration, the removal of discriminatory barriers in the marketplace, tariffs, monopolies, state aids, and safety and technical standards, rather than the creation of new institutions and the enactment of positive measures of social welfare.[31] The approximation of national regulatory laws is only authorized for the purpose of achieving a common market. Much of the negative integration written into the treaties was found to be either directly applicable in law, such as the bar against quantitative restrictions, or self-executory by the Commission in matters of competition, state aid, public procurement, and so forth.

Provisions for positive integration such as industrial or employment policy were either absent from the treaties or so vague and undefined as to require unanimous positive action from the Council of Ministers (council), which was the case for the common policies of agriculture, transport and commerce.[32] Actions under article 175 of the Rome treaty for the failure of the Community to act were far rarer than actions to overturn state regulation; even where the ECJ found failure it could not command the detail of action to be taken.[33] In any event, the ECJ held that Rome treaty provisions for industrial, transport or social policy – its upward harmonization by member states under article 117 – were too vague, undefined or unsubstantial to be justiciable.[34]

With its doctrines of direct effect, the supremacy of European law, preemption and absorption, the ECJ was a powerful instrument for trade integration and national deregulation.[35] Doubtless, if the Treaty of Rome were to be more than an intergovernmental agreement, the ECJ had to ensure uniform application of the law in the member states. Measures that were clear, precise and self-evident were held to have direct effect in national law. The instrument for achieving this uniformity was the preliminary ruling under article 177 of the Rome treaty. *Van Gend en Loos* (1963) found that individuals had the right to challenge national regulations in state court under European law. By enmeshing the state courts in the application of European law, the ECJ made the selective application of EC legislation impossible.

The ECJ held European law to be supreme even as against subsequent state legislation. Under the doctrine of preemption national law was precluded in areas of EC competence even in the absence of specific European law. The most extreme extension of jurisdiction was the doctrine of absorption that prevents national states from exercising their jurisdiction where it impinges upon an area of Community competence. The doctrine of implied powers embodied in article 235, by which the EC can assume powers not provided in the treaty if necessary to attain its objectives, is an open-sesame to the expansion of Community power.[36]

This exercise of EC judicial power is not checked by any countervailing doctrine of enumerated powers as in the US constitution.[37] The doctrine of subsidiarity written into Maastricht is not very restrictive of EC jurisdiction. The restriction that the EC shall take action only if the objectives of the action cannot be sufficiently achieved by member states and can, by reason of the scale or effects of the action, be better achieved by the Community only applied to areas not within its exclusive competence, which is very broad. In any event, the article on subsidiarity in the Maastricht treaty is probably too general and political to be justiciable. For this reason the Commissioner from Britain, Leon Brittan, proposed a body of national parliamentarians to act as guardians of states' rights.[38] There is an absence of an identifiable jurisprudence of states' rights. Judges appointed to the court, drawn from among experts on European law, are naturally inclined to expand its frontiers. They have a 'certain idea of Europe' which overrides other considerations.[39] The anonymity of decisions and absence of dissenting opinions makes it impossible to identify judicial parties as in the US. This may make the law more magisterial but also more removed and remote from the public.

Judicial activism in the EC may not pose as much danger as it might in the US to states' rights because member states enjoy the legislative power to limit law if not to reverse it.[40] The judicial activism of the 1960s and 1970s may have been balanced by the inactivity of council, but nothing was done to limit the scope of judicial power. In any event, there is a tradition of the *acquis communautaire* that makes it very difficult for council to reverse laws or ECJ decisions. Once the market is deregulated it becomes nearly impossible to reregulate it.

It is not only in the margins of legislation where courts ordinarily decide that the judicial bias against national regulation operates. The ECJ's judgment in *Cassis de Dijon* that Germany could not use its own compositional standard for alcoholic drinks to bar the sale of French cassis and that member states more broadly could not use their own standards to prohibit the sale of goods that were marketable elsewhere in the EC was a policy decision. The ECJ was careful, however, to qualify it with an even more peremptory ruling that states could prohibit goods that failed to meet 'mandatory requirements' of health, fair trade and consumer protection. The impact of *Cassis de Dijon,* endorsed by the Commission as the principle of mutual recognition, was however limited

by council, which incorporated in its policy the reservations of producer and consumer groups.[41]

AGRICULTURAL EXCEPTION

The only policy of positive integration that was successfully instituted was agriculture. Contrary to the principle of free competition, the EC subsidized farm prices and exports, protecting them
from outside competition. De Gaulle made the establishment of
the policy a condition of French membership. He had the help of
the vice-president of the Commission, Sicco Mansholt. Since all
members gave some form of assistance to farmers, a common policy
was indicated. But it was only achieved, with marathon bargaining
sessions – stopping the clock on New Years' Eve – and threats of
walk-out, after nearly twelve years. It raised agricultural productivity and incomes, but also created greater inequalities in the country-
side, benefiting the wealthy farmers and yielding huge surpluses.
Still, if agriculture and the food industry became the only major
sector that was self-sufficient it was because it benefited from the
only truly interventionist policy in the EC.[42]

SOCIAL POLICY

Other areas for positive integration were not so fortunate. The Rome
treaty did not contain explicit provision for social policy. Under
article 117 member states were to promote improved working conditions and standard of living for workers, but this was to follow
largely from the functioning of the common market. The protocol
for France, requiring upward harmonization of over-time pay, was
forgotten. The sole social prescription of the treaty concerned equal
wages for equal work between men and women. The social dimension of the law was largely restricted to cross-border mobility of
European citizens, who constitute a tiny minority of migrant workers
in the EC; the conferral of equal social rights to such workers did
not increase their numbers, which remained at about half of one
per cent of the population.[43] The first action program on social
policy by the Commission, issued in 1972, called for the upward
harmonization of labour standards and new European forms of
collective representation. The meagre results of this enthusiasm were

two minor directives on collective redundances in 1977 and transfers of undertakings in 1979.[44]

The social goals of the EC were confided in article 3 of the Rome
treaty to the European Investment Bank and European Social Fund.
The bank was to contribute to the balanced and steady development of the common market, which meant aiding less developed
regions and projects of common interest. It played a limited role
in the 1960s, making 1.8 billion dollars available for the modernization of transport, chemicals, coal and machine tools, mostly in
Italy. Thereafter the bank used its funds almost exclusively for
purposes of regional development – 7.8 billion ecu, which were
approximately equal to dollars, for that purpose in 1987. Aside from
references to regional disparities the treaty had not made provision
for regional policy. This changed with the creation of the European Regional Development Fund in 1975, a side payment for British
membership. Thereafter it became the token for social justice and
redistribution in the Community.[45]

The Social Fund was to contribute to improving employment
opportunities and raising the standard of living, specifically by increasing geographical and occupational mobility. Most of its funds
went to assist with the resettlement of Italian workers who were
already reemployed. During the years 1972–76 the fund was expanded by 500 per cent and used to assist the hard-core unemployed. The fund reached its peak relative to the EC budget in
1979. Its focus narrowed. In 1988, 75 per cent of its 2.8 billion ecu
went to young people under 25 and 45.5 per cent to backward regions. As the problem of unemployment deepened, member states
were increasingly reluctant to transfer resources to the EC.[46]

TRANSPORT POLICY

The Rome treaty provided for a common transport policy. Trans-
portation was treated as a business governed by commercial principles even though article 77 recognized the legitimacy of state aid
to fulfil the obligations of public service. The efforts of the Commission to promote competition ran up against the monopolistic
practices of member states, which subsidized transport as a public
service.[47] Transport policy was mostly concerned with assuring fair
terms of competition, removing barriers to carrying by private hauliers
and restricting rates within upper and lower limits, the 'two-pronged

fork', to avoid monopoly undercutting or overcharging.[48]

Public services do not operate under commercial principles. Under French law a public service has the obligation to provide continuous service to all users at equal and reasonable rates. It is also expected by tradition to provide secure and rewarding jobs for its personnel. Article 90 of the Rome treaty stipulated that public services would be subject to terms of fair competition to the extent that these did not interfere with the performance of their mission, which must not be contrary to Community interest. The Commission reversed the burden of proof, making public services the exception rather than the rule. Services must justify their mission and prove that restrictions on competition are necessary to fulfil it. France has had to abandon state monopolies in the import of tobacco, alcohol, gas, electricity and petroleum and France Télécom its monopoly of communication links. The substitution by the EC and ECJ of the duty of 'universal service' modelled on the divestiture of AT&T does not preserve the integrity of the public service.[49]

Directives on competition in the public services threaten the integrity of such motors of growth and innovation as the SNCF, the French railways, and EDF, electricity and gas. Only state investment could have produced the technological and commercial success of the TGV, the high speed railway, in France. French rail also fulfils an obligation to provide service to peripheral regions at the same rates as it charges on the better travelled lines. It has been forced to separate the management of infrastructure from rolling stock, making it more difficult to fulfil its mission. EDF, which has been perhaps the most socially efficient and innovative electrical and gas utility in Europe, must open up its service to the largest consumers – from 20 to 33 per cent of its market – to competition.[50]

STATE AID TO INDUSTRY

State aids were a major instrument of national social and industrial policy. Such aid, including tax relief and even equity investment under certain conditions, in so far as it affects inter-state trade is incompatible with the common market. Article 92 of the Rome treaty allows for limited exceptions and a wide degree of discretion for the Commission to help poorer and underdeveloped regions, to remedy a serious disturbance in the economy of a member state and to facilitate development of certain economic activities or economic areas. States are obligated to notify the Commission about their aid. In the early years there was little enforcement. Special agreements were negotiated for shipbuilding and the South of Italy, which gave up notifying the Commission.[51]

It is difficult to find coherence in Commission policy on state aids, but it is not sympathetic to long-term industrial projects. It has tended to be harsher on aid to a sector or industry than regional assistance. It has been more favourable to short-term relief that reduces capacity than restructuring programs that would expand it. It is been ruthless towards state aid for nationalized industries in which social and industrial criteria have been sacrificed for the need to reduce capacity and thus the size of the public sector.[52] On the other hand, since the SEA and Maastricht, it has been compelled to consider needs for research and development, for environmental protection and the promotion of small business.[53]

Enforcement was stepped up in the 1980s. Until then only twenty to thirty plans for state aid were notified annually and only one to three denied. The number rose to 200 notified and twenty rejected in the late 1980s.[54] The Commission encouraged other states to make complaints and required refunds from companies that were given aid contrary to law.[55] Many governments, arguing the sanctity of contracts, resisted. In return for the recapitalization of Renault the French government had to promise to impose the same requirements of profitability on the firms it aided as those used in the private sector.[56] Structural funds do not compare in importance to state aid; even after the 1988 Delors II Package they were only a fifth of the value of state aids.[57] Constricted in the 1980s, state aid has risen since 1992 to 43 billion ecu with the most coming from Germany and the highest per head from Italy.[58]

PUBLIC PROCUREMENT

Public procurement of goods and services was an even more important instrument of national economic policy, serving regional, technological, and employment objectives. It constituted 15 per cent of GDP of which only 0.14 per cent went to non-nationals. Directives providing for competitive bidding in public supply and public works in the 1970s did little to alter the situation. New directives passed under the SEA, which included the public utilities left out by the first ones, provided for monitored compliance, review procedures and open awards based on the criteria of the lowest price or most economically advantageous. The Commission negotiated with member states in 1989 to end the use of procurement for regional purposes.[59]

The new policy was reinforced by ECJ decisions such as *Ireland* (1989) that held that technical standards could not be set so narrowly as to restrict supply to nationals. In *Du Pont de Namours Italiana* (1990) the ECJ voided an Italian law requiring that public authorities purchase at least 30 per cent of their goods from the Italian South on grounds that it was a quantitative restriction to inter-state trade. This law provided 24 billion ecu in aid to the South compared to only one billion that comes from the European regional fund. Yet, the ECJ ruled that the need for unrestricted competition preempted regional considerations in the award of public contracts.[60]

Competitive tendering is not necessarily socially efficient; private contractors seek to maximize profits, even if at the expense of quality and service, or of wages and working conditions. Compulsory competitive tendering of public services in Britain has resulted in job losses and wage cuts.[61] It is unrealistic to expect that public authorities awarding contracts will not give consideration to proximity and effects on employment and economic development. Adopting a competitive approach that makes little allowance for social realities, the EC has made negligible impact on procurement practices.[62]

INDUSTRIAL AND TECHNOLOGY POLICY

The Rome treaty did not provide for industrial policy. The Committee on Medium-Term Economic Policy set up in 1964 to consider the coordination of national economies discussed the technological gap with the US, but the Commission under German influence ruled out positive intervention for sectors or nations. The French sought changes in commercial and tax law to facilitate transnational mergers. The Commission responded in 1966 by proposing a European Company Statute on the German model, a proposal that is still on the table after thirty years. In 1970 the Colonna Report urged support for an industrial policy to encourage industrial cooperations and mergers in order to narrow the productivity and technology gap with the US, but it was opposed by Germany.

Instead of considering a new French proposal for a voluntarist and protectionist policy in 1983, the Commission approved the privatization program begun in Britain that would eliminated the motors of industrial investment in Europe.[63]

One of the main purposes of the SEA was to overcome the technological deficit. A title was introduced to strengthen the scientific and technological base of European industry by encouraging research and development in firms, research centres and universities. This provision ran up against the reluctance of member states to transfer resources to the Community. Only 4 billion ecu were spent for the framework program and Eureka, an intergovernmental program to assist technological development, as against an estimated 67 billion spent for industry by the member states in 1990. Another estimate puts EC aid to R&D at 4.5 per cent of total R&D. Restricted to precompetitive projects, the policy was vitiated by the bias towards deregulation, a tough mergers policy, and public purchasing controls. The EU lacks the structural prerequisites for launching its own companies: research networks, public procurement, fiscal intervention, promotion, and public sector ideology and leadership. It was not accidental that more has been accomplished by intergovernmental arrangements like Eureka and Airbus in this domain than under the EC.[64]

The Treaty of Maastricht gave the council power under article 130 to take measures by unanimous vote to enhance the competitiveness of EC industry, to speed up structural adjustment, to assist small and medium-sized firms, and to foster cooperation and the better exploitation of innovation among firms. The EC is supposed to contribute to the achievement of these objectives through the policies it pursues under other provisions of the treaty. Since the EC was able to act in this area previously under implied powers, the new article may limit rather than extend its industrial competence. How the EC can assist individual firms without violating principles of fair competition remains to be seen.[65] Industrial policy is bound by the restrictions set in the Bangemann Memorandum, named after the German commissioner for the internal market, approved by council in 1990, which relied on the private sector to make necessary adjustments and limited EC intervention to the precompetitive environment – research, training and infrastructure. Industrial policy has been stymied by the unanimity principle and by the anti-interventionist attitude expressed by the Commission in its communication of 14 November 1994.

Delors' 1993 White Paper on *Growth, Competitiveness and Employment* tried to link it with regional policy with an ambitious 400 billion ecu scheme for trans-European networks in transport, energy and telecommunications. The aim was to create fifteen million new jobs by the year 2000 while improving infrastructure. The European Investment Fund – set up in 1994 – was to provide transnational finance, but it was never given more than nominal capitalization. The twenty-four projects planned by Delors were reduced to fourteen and left to wither. Led by the Germans, council has repeatedly refused to finance even minimalist versions of the trans-European networks.[66]

Under articles 3a and 102a of Maastricht the 'open market economy with free competition, favouring an efficient allocation of resources' (that is, the classical Smithian model), has become the guiding principle, not merely a privileged instrument, of the EU. When combined with the principle of proportionality in article 3b this means that nearly all regulatory policies except perhaps agriculture must give clear indications that exemptions from the principle of undistorted competition are justified.[67] Already under the old treaty the ECJ had subjected nearly all intervention to the competitive test. In *Continental Can* (1971) it held that a company cannot abuse its dominant position with commercial arrangements that substantially reduce competition. No attention need be paid to the usefulness of anti-competitive conduct. The Merger Regulation issued in 1989 allowed some consideration for technical and economic progress provided consumers benefit and there is no hindrance to competition. The Commission did not consider competitive efficiency when prohibiting the proposed take-over of a Canadian aircraft maker De Havilland by ATR, a French-Italian consortium.[68]

COMMERCIAL POLICY

Industrial development has not been assisted by European commercial policy, which is among the freest in the world. Under article 11 of the Rome treaty the EC must contribute to the abolition of restrictions on international trade and the lowering of customs barriers. Member states, under article 18, agreed to reduce duties below the level which they could expect from a customs union. The assumption was that the free internal market alone would prepare firms to face international competition. In the debates between the protectionist French and Italians and free-trade Germans and Benelux, the latter usually won, especially after the accession to membership of Britain. The US led the charge to open up the European market in the GATT rounds. The Kennedy Round concluded in 1967 achieved cuts of 32 per cent. By 1972 the average tariff on manufactured items was 8.2 per cent. Member states still retained export credits and there was greater protection for textiles. Today, after the liberalizing Uruguay Round, the average tariff is about 6 per cent, which is one half that of the US and a third that of Japan. The EC still disposes of anti-dumping duties, which are subject to the competitive test, and some voluntary export restraint agreements, but not the unilateral system of dealing with unfair trade practices that the US under section 301 of the Trade Act enjoys.[69]

LABOUR POLICY

Mitterrand had always wanted to correct the liberal bias of the EC by adding a 'social space' for the working class. His appointment of Delors in 1985 gave an impetus both to the completion of the internal market and to the construction of a social dimension. Delors was not a social democrat but a social Christian, who had come up through Catholic unionism. He valued the market as a guarantor of individual autonomy and responsibility and creator of wealth without which there could be no social improvement.[70] With his belief in the Catholic doctrine of subsidiarity, he preferred voluntary cooperation and social dialogue to state intervention; and qualitative issues such as working time and conditions to conflictual and materialistic wage issues. His vision of social policy contained an adequate level of social protection, rights of information and consultation, professional training and social dialogue, particularly on technology and work organization.[71] But he was more concerned with obtaining consensus than reform and his social policy was undercut by internal market reforms.

The SEA extended Community competence over health and safety, the first industrial sphere to be regulated by the nineteenth-century state and one in which employers had a concern for the standardization of products and machines. It also charged the Commission with fostering a dialogue between management and labour at European level which could lead to formal agreements. Discussions at the Val Duchesse created the illusion of bargaining. Neither employers nor unions were authorized to conclude agreements at a European level. UNICE, the employers' association, opposed in principle to EC labour regulation, interrupted the dialogue.

Seeking to rally British trade unions and Labour Party behind Europe, Delors talked of a social dimension and of the need for a basic set of social rights at the European trade union conference in 1988. Delors took up a draft for the Community Charter of Fundamental Social Rights proposed by the European Trade Union Conferation (ETUC), but it was watered down to accommodate the British, who then refused to sign.[72] Hedged with a subsidiarity clause that requires the conformity of all measures with national practice, the Charter of Fundamental Rights of Workers was careful not to expand EC competence. It was merely a statement of principles without the legal force promised by Delors and demanded by the European Parliament. Progress on implementation was impeded by the British veto, with only six of 24 legislative proposals, mostly on health and safety, being adopted by 1991.[73] At Maastricht ministers tried to extend majority voting to other social matters, but once again the British negotiators eviscerated the legislation and then rejected it.

The social protocol to the treaty of Maastricht extended qualified majority voting to laws on working conditions, information and consultation and equal opportunities, but excluded questions of pay and strikes and limited the new legislation with a subsidiarity clause and a stipulation that they were only to provide minimal protection. This latter limitation is a departure from article 117 of the Rome treaty, which calls for the improvement of conditions by member states, and could be used to undermine national social legislation.[74] The negotiators showed their dislike of state intervention by providing for negotiated law, laws resulting from negotiations between labour and management and directives implemented by such agreements. When faced with the Commission's proposal for European Works Councils, the last great campaign of the Delors' presidency, the ETUC and UNICE opted for direct legislation. After six years there is only one negotiated directive, that on parental leave. An accord has been reached on equal treatment of part-time employees, but it is questionable whether the encouragement of part-time employment is in labour's interest.[75]

Proposals for European works councils had been circulating since the 1970s. The draft Fifth Directive in 1972 and European Company Statute (ECS) of 1975 had provided for employee participation on the supervisory board and European works councils. The Vredeling proposal of 1980, limited to multinationals, offered existing local employee representatives rights of information and consultation on a range of issues. It was defeated in parliament and council by a barrage of employee lobbying.[76] The legislation finally approved in 1993 under the social protocol was a weakened version of Vredeling, more European but also less regulatory. Works councils were to be set up by negotiations between employees and employers and by default by national legislation, which had to respect minimal conditions of representation and consultation on management decisions likely to have serious consequences for employees.[77]

The legislation made no provision for enforcement, which depends on national law. There is a question whether workers have an effective remedy against a company that has a headquarters in another member state. That was the problem raised when Renault failed to notify and consult workers in Belgium about the closing of their plant in Vilvoorde. Workers in Brussels and Nanterre France were able to sue the company under national law, but they received only nominal satisfaction. The French appeals court held that Renault had to provide effective consultation to its works council before closing the plant.[78] The fracas caused by Vilvoorde did push the Commission into strengthening worker consultation provisions of proposals for the ECS and national works councils.[79]

Delors raised the profile of the ETUC and in return obtained its support for the single market and currency. Union leaders in the British TUC, German DGB and French CFDT were resigned to market regulation. Faced with declining membership, political support and bargaining power at home, they reached out to Delors as a kind of 'Jesus rail' – what you grope for when you are falling down the stairs.[80] Their faith – they are only now beginning to realize – was misplaced. They failed to obtain European collective bargaining and binding commitments from the social charter. [81] By strengthening unions at European and enterprise level the Commission may have diverted unions away from the sectoral level where their power to fix wages is greatest. EC labour policy may actually serve the employer strategy, which is to undermine sectoral solidarity and achieve enterprise and individualized wage setting.[82]

EC policy since Maastricht has become increasingly market-oriented. Delors' 1992 White Paper, proposing the trans-European networks, endorsed employer demands for labour flexibility, work-sharing, the diminution of social charges and wage reductions relative to productivity. Council, in December 1993, recommended to member states policies of pay moderation, beginning with the public sector, decentralized bargaining, controlling social expenditure and more flexible forms of work organization. The Commission under Santer has adopted the monetarist logic of Economic and Monetary Union (EMU), recommending budget cuts and deflation as the way to stimulate investment and create jobs.[83] The Commission has virtually abandoned the legislative approach to social policy, relying instead on non-binding recommendations.[84]

The employment chapter of the 1997 treaty of Amsterdam, revising Maastricht, provided for the coordination of national policy under pre-existing powers that subordinate it to general economic policy, which is deflationary. In response to French demands to put employment at the top of the agenda, the European Council adopted a resolution based on a British memo that would make job creation depend on market conditions and a reduction of taxes and social charges. The French failed to obtain any extension of EC competence or expenditure for employment.[85]

SOCIAL AND DEMOCRATIC DEFICIT

The social deficit of the EC is connected to the democratic deficit. Social policy requires democratic pressure and legitimation. But this process is thwarted by the institutional basis of the EC, the reliance on Commission initiative, inter-governmental assent, and a subaltern parliament. The complexity and elitist bias of decision-making makes it difficult to activate popular movements and opinion over European issues, Europe is regarded as a rich man's club for a self-appointed elite; it has always been regarded with suspicion by working people in most countries.[86] Decision-making tends to be technical, consensual and depoliticized. The public lacks the familiar signposts of Right and Left, government and opposition, that structures politics in their own country. Maastricht, in an attempt to reduce the democratic deficit, has aggravated it by making the legislative system even more complex and opaque, providing no less than six legislative procedures from consultation to assent, with council, whose decisions are largely unaccountable before public opinion, having the final say.[87]

The European Parliament is not about to replace national parliaments as a source of legitimacy and power. European elections have been called 'second-order' with a low turnout, an incentive to punish national incumbents and preoccupation with domestic issues. They are demotivating because they do not lead to a change of government or tangible legislation. The lack of transnational media and a common language renders the work of the parliament obscure. There is no party discipline in voting, with cross-cutting national, regional and sectoral interests deciding the result. Legislation controlled by rapporteurs is often passed without discussion.[88]

The complex procedure seems to demand a consensual mode. The working parliamentary majority is a centrist alliance between Socialists, who represent a broad spectrum of views from the neoliberalism of Tony Blair to the interventionism of the French, and Christian Democrats, who are open to employer influence. It resembles the cross-cutting class and regional consensual politics of post-war Belgium[89] rather than that of contemporary France and Germany, in which Socialists and Christian Democrats stand in opposition. No other majority could garner enough votes to pass the Community budget. The only strong interventionists are on the extreme Left, which is divided and little committed to Europe. The centrist consensus around federalism avoids political debates, gives resolutions an idealistic deracinated character, and fosters the illusion that integration is ideologically neutral.[90]

In this context well-resourced business lobbyists have a distinct advantage over labour or other popular organizations. They have the know-how and resources to master all the stops in the complex decision-making process through the Commission, council and Parliament. The Commission depends heavily on interest groups for the content of legislation. UNICE is the best financed lobby in Brussels. Associations of business vastly outnumber those of labour with 20 unions facing 332 associations of industry.[91] The consultative Economic and Social Committee on which labour is well represented has accomplished little. While labour is divided on national and political grounds employers are united in opposition to European industrial regulation. Their power was seen in the defeat of the 1980 Vredeling proposal on European works councils when they were able to coordinate pressure simultaneously on Christian Democrats in parliament and governments in council.[92]

Though its power is diminished, labour is still much better organized for political action on the national rather than on the European level. Unions depend on social norms, ideology and legislation that are not available on the European level, where they are divided by linguistic, cultural and political barriers.[93] Whatever unions may have gained from the EC – training schemes, works councils, health and safety legislation – they have lost through EC sponsored deflation and deregulation. Deregulation might have occurred to some degree without the EC – it was part of a profound sociopolitical transformation – but the EC provided an alibi and justification for governments, particularly social-democratic ones, disinclined to act alone. Rather than accept responsibility for economic and social policy, they chose to tie their hands with EMU.

Many social democrats hope that the discontent created by EMU will induce popular demands for European government such as the French have made, but the idea is anathema to the Germans and other members. There was only limited enthusiasm for extending co-decisional powers of Parliament at Amsterdam in June 1997. Further transfers of state sovereignty to the EU are highly unlikely for reasons discussed. First, as we have shown, the EC lacks the constitutional and institutional foundations for an interventionist government. Second, it lacks democratic legitimacy, the primary support and loyalty of a European people or demos. Third, policy divergences among the major partners, especially Germany and France, make agreement on macroeconomic policies problematic. Finally, states may have reached the limit of their transfer of sovereignty without losing their coherence as constituting bodies for society. They are especially unlikely to yield more control of social policy, which is a main source of their legitimacy.

Europeans still look to the nation state for their physical security and social welfare. Everywhere primary loyalty is to the member state and only secondarily to the EU. Europe is supported as an aid to, rather than a replacement for, the state. Globalization, which can ruin firms, industries and regions, makes the nation state even more important as the main focus of regulation and strongest bastion of solidarity. To say this is not to deny the pressure of international market forces, but to recognize the power of national governments based on popular coalitions to channel and tame them. The state remains the most powerful institution to regulate markets for the purpose of employment, education, research, health, financial integrity, job training, labour relations, infrastructure and justice. Even with globalization the state has the capacity to secure markets and industry and attract long-term investment. It has no peer as a source of public power for economic governance.

These basic facts about the EC and nation state have been obscured by a 'lib-lab' Europhilia that views the history, law and institutions of the Community through rose-coloured glasses. Nations have lost capacity to regulate markets on their own, but not as much as many believe. To the extent that more European and international cooperation is needed the EU, unless radically overhauled, may not always be the best framework in which to proceed. Much of the lost capacity of states has been self-inflicted, the result of partisan political choices. These choices have been sanctioned by certain illusions about the EC. To deflate these illusions is not to give up all attempts to reform it, but to put them into perspective so that they reinforce rather than undermine domestic policy and strategies.

Notes

1. Kapteyn *et al*, 1989, pp. 80–1.
2. Featherstone, 1988, p. 343.
3. Milward, 1992, ch. 2, and his 1995, p. 58.
4. Cited in Marjolin, 1986, p. 293.
5. Cf. Mazier *et al*, 1984.
6. Milward, 1992, pp. 36–7.
7. Moss, 1993.
8. Kindleberger, 1967.
9. Milward, 1992, pp. 189–98.
10. Marjolin, 1986, pp. 286–8.
11. Pineau and Rimbaud, 1991, p. 233.
12. Holland, 1980, p. 64, n. 23.
13. Philip, 1957, pp. 250–4.
14. See Dankert and Kooyman, eds, 1989.
15. Haack, 1983; Pinto Lyra, 1978, esp. pp. 193–6; Jaumont *et al,* 1973, pp. 10–12, 58.
16. Verdun, 1996, 65–75.
17. See Chapter 3 on France.
18. Streeck, 1995. Vogel-Polsky and Vogel, 1991. Cf. Ross, 1995.
19. Kapteyn *et al*, 1989, p. 76.
20. Snyder, ed., 1996, p. 96 (J. Usher).
21. Prate, 1995, p. 133. Oliver and Baché, 1989.
22. Moravcsik, 1991. Lord Cockfield, 1994.
23. Padoa-Schioppa, 1987, pp. 5, 18, 50, 109. Cecchini, 1988.
24. Cecchini, 1988, pp. 99, 105.
25. *Ibid.*, xviii.
26. 'It is highly unlikely that so many leading consultants, academics, officials, and experts would be all wrong,' *ibid.*, p. 116.
27. Martin, 1996, p. 42.
28. Mertens de Wilmars, 1993, II, 13–14.

29. Snyder, ed., 1996, pp. 157–8 (T. Heller).
30. Martin, 1996, p. 53. Mertens de Wilmars, 1993, II, 10.
31. Cf. Tinbergen, 1965, 77–9, with Pinder, 1969.
32. Pinder, 1969.
33. Hartley, 1994, pp. 340–1, 393–415.
34. Szyszczak, 1994, pp. 315, 325. Kapteyn *et al*, 1989, p. 82.
35. Weiler, 1993.
36. Weiler, 1991, 2413–17.
37. Cf. Krisler *et al*, 1986, pp. 11, 23.
38. Brittan, 1994, p. 94.
39. Judge Pascatore cited in Salesse, 1996, p. 58.
40. Weiler, 1993.
41. Alter and Meunier-Aitsahalia, 1994.
42. Prate, 1995, pp. 75–87. Dinan, 1994, ch. 11. Bourry, 1993.
43. *Le Monde*, 21 May 1997, IV.
44. Ross, 1993. Streeck, 1995, p. 400.
45. Hallstein, 1972, p. 79, Kapteyn *et al*, 1989, p. 214.
46. Kapteyn, 1989, pp. 637–41. Taylor, 1983, pp. 204–13.
47. Hallstein, 1972, pp. 277–8.
48. Holland, 1980, p. 11. Lindberg and Scheingold, 1970, pp. 163–81.
49. *Le Monde*, 24 June, 1997, II. Monnier, 1996. Cartelier, 1996, p. 89.
    Debène and Paymundie, 1996.
50. *Le Monde*, 12 June 1996.
51. Holland, 1980, p. 14.
52. Pernin, 1996.
53. Evans and Martin, 1991.
54. Padoa-Schioppa, 1987, p. 33.
55. Goyder, 1988, ch. 21.
56. Cohen, 1995, p. 42.
57. Martin, 1996, p. 77.
58. *Le Monde*, 18 April 1997.
59. Martin, 1996.
60. Martin and Stehmann, 1991.
61. Martin, 1996, p. 89.
62. *Ibid*., pp. 45–8.
63. Holland, 1980, pp. 23, 26, 75. Hayward, 1995, pp. 7–8. Monnier, 1996.
    Hallstein, 1972, pp. 194–6. Denton, 1969.
64. Sharp, 1993. Cohen, 1995, p. 34. Saint-Martin, 1996, p. 183.
65. Bourgeois and Demeret, 1995, pp. 72–3.
66. Coates and Santer, 1996. Holland, 1996. *Le Monde*, 16 Oct. 1996.
67. Snyder, ed., 1996, pp. 39–40 (P. Verloren van Thematt).
68. Bourgeois and Demeret, 1995, pp. 70–89.
69. Prate, 1995, pp. 92–103. Hine, 1985, pp. 75–9. Tyson, 1992, pp. 255–9.
70. Cf. Ross, 1993, p. 61.
71. *Ibid*., pp. 72–3.
72. Silvia, 1991, 634–9.
73. Ross, 1993, p. 52, Streeck, 1995, p. 403.
74. Shaw, 1994. Szyszczak, 1994.
75. *Le Monde*, 16 Apr., 16 May 1997.

76. Devos, 1989, pp. 178–9.
77. Hall and Gold, 1994. Hall, 1992. 'European Works Councils,' *European Industrial Relations Review*, no. 206 (March 1991), pp. 12–14, 29–32, no. 207 (Apr. 1991), pp. 23–7.
78. *Le Monde*, 9 May 1997.
79. Regan Scott, European Liaison of the TGWU.
80. Verdun, 1996, 72, 74.
81. Silvia, 1991, pp. 636–40.
82. Martin, 1995.
83. Coates and Santer, 1996.
84. Streeck, 1995, p. 426. P. Venturini, former advisor to Delors, UACES 27th Annual Conference, 6–8 Jan. 1997.
85. *Le Monde*, 18 June 1997.
86. Lindberg and Scheingold, 1970, pp. 264–75.
87. Neunreither, 1994, 304.
88. Jacobs *et al*, 1995, pp. 7, 90–3.
89. De Winter, 1993, p. 202.
90. Ladrech, 1996, pp. 292–6.
91. Streeck and Schmitter, 1991, 136–8.
92. Devos, 1989, pp. 175–9.
93. Lemke and Marks, 1992, p. 16.

References

Alter, K. and Meunier-Aitsahalia, S. (1994) 'Judicial Politics in the European Community: European Integration and the Pathbreaking *Cassis de Dijon* Decision', *Comparative Political Studies*, 26: 535–61
Bourgeois, J. and Demeret, P. (1995) 'The Working of EC Policies in Competition, Industry and Trade', in Buiges, P., Jacquemin, A. and Sapir, A. (eds), *European Policies on Competition, Trade and Industry*. Aldershot: Edward Elgar
Bourry, C. (1993) 'Existe-t-il une industrie européenne?', *Etudes et recherches, ISERES*, no. 131
Brittan, L. (1994) *The Europe We Need*. London: Hamish Hamilton
Cartelier, L. (1996) 'Services publics européens entre la théorie économique et droit communautaire' in Cartelier, L., Fournière, J. and Monnier, L., *Critique de la raison communautaire: utilité publique et concurrence dans l'Union Européenne*, Paris: Economica
Cecchini, P. (1988) *The European Challenge, 1992: The Benefits of a Single Market*. Aldershot: Gower
Coates, K. and Santer, J. (1996) *Dear Commissioner, Will Unemployment Break Europe?* Nottingham: Spokesman
Cohen, E. (1995) 'National Champions in Search of Mission', in Hayward, J. (ed.) *Industrial Enterprise and European Integration: From National to International Champions*. Oxford: Oxford University Press
Dankert, P. and Kooyman, A., (eds) (1989) *Europe sans frontières: les Socialistes et l'avenir de la CEE*. Anvers: EPO

Debène, M. and Raymundie, O. (1996) 'Sur le service universel: renouveau du service public ou nouvelle mystification?', in Cartelier, L. *et al* (eds) *Crtique de la raison communautaire*. Paris: Economica

Denton, G. (1969) 'Planning and Integration: Medium-Term Policy as an Instrument of Integration' in Denton, G. (ed.) *Economic Integration in Europe*. London: Weidenfeld and Nicolson

Devos, T. (1989) *Multinational Corporations in Democratic Host Countries: US Multinationals and the Vredeling Proposal*. Aldershot: Dartmouth

De Winter, L. (1993) 'Socialistes belges entre région et Europe' in Telo, M. (ed.) *De la nation à l'Europe: paradoxes et dilemmes de la social-démocratie*. Brussels: Bruyand

Dinan, D. (1994) *Ever Closer Union? An Introduction to the European Community*. London: Macmillan

Evans, A. and Martin, S. (1991) 'Socially Acceptable Distortion of Competition: Community Policy on State Aid', *European Law Review*, 16: 79–111

Featherstone, K. (1988) *Socialist Parties and European Integration: A Comparative History*. Manchester: Manchester U.P.

Goyder, D. (1988) *EEC Competition Law*. Oxford: Clarendon Press

Haack, W. (1983) 'The Selectivity of Economic Integration Theories: A Comparison of Some Traditional and Marxist Approaches', *J. of Common Market Studies*, 21: 365–87

Hall, M. and Gold, M. (1994) 'Statutory European Works Councils: The Final Countdown?', *Industrial Relations Journal*, 25: 177–86

Hall, M. (1992) 'Behind the European Work Council Directive: The European Commission's Legislative Strategy', *British J. of Industrial Relations*, 30: 547–66.

Hallstein, W. (1972), *Europe in the Making*. London: George Allen & Unwin

Hartley, T. (1994) *The Foundations of European Law*. Oxford: Clarendon Press

Hayward, J. (1995) 'Europe's Industrial Champion', in Hayward, J. (ed.) *Industrial Enterprise and European Integration: From National to International Champions*. Oxford: Oxford University Press

Hine, C. (1985) *The Political Economy of European Trade: An Introduction to the Trade Policies of the EEC*. London: Harvester

Holland, S. (1996) *The European Imperative: Social and Economic Cohesion in the 1990s*. Nottingham: Spokesman

Holland, S. (1980) *Uncommon Market*. London: Macmillan

Jacobs, F., Corbett, R. and Shackleton, M. (1995) *The European Parliament*, 3rd ed. London: Catermill

Jaumont, B., Lenègre, D., and Rocard, M. (1973) *Le Marché commun contre l'Europe*. Paris: Seuil

Kapteyn, P., Gormley, L. and Verloren van Thematt, P. (1989) *Introduction to the Law of the European Communities after the Coming into Force of the Single European Act*. Boston: Kluwer

Kindleberger, C. (1967) *Europe's Post-War Growth: The Role of Labor Supply*. Cambridge, Mass.: Harvard U.P.

Krisler, S., Ehlermann, C-D. and Weiler, J. (1986) 'The Political Organs and Decision-Making Process in the US and European Community' in

Cappelletti, M., Seccombe, M. and Weiler, J. (eds) *Integration through Law*. Berlin: Walter de Gryter

Ladrech, R. (1996) 'Political Parties in the European Parliament', in Gaffney, J. (ed.) *Political Parties and the European Union*. London: Routledge

Lemke, C. and Marks, G. (1992) 'From Decline to Demise? The Future of Socialism in Europe', in Lemke, C. and Marks, G. (eds) *The Crisis of Socialism in Europe*. London: Duke U.P.

Lindberg, L. and Scheingold, S. (1970) *Europe's Would-Be Polity*. Englewood Cliffs, N.J.: Prentice Hall.

Lord Cockfield (1994) *The European Union: Creating the Single Market*. London: Wiley Chancery

Marjolin, R. (1986) *Architect of European Unity*. London: Weidenfeld and Nicolson

Martin, A. (1995) 'European Institutions and the Europeanization of Trade Unions: Support or Seduction?' European Trade Union Institute

Martin, J. (1996) *EC Public Procurement Rules: A Critical Analysis*. Oxford: Clarendon Press

Martin, J. and Stehmann, O. (1991) 'Product Market Integration versus Regional Cohesion', *European Law Review*, 16: 216–43.

Mazier, J., Basle, M. and Vidal, J.-F. (1984) *Quand les crises durent*. Paris: Economica

Mertens de Wilmar, J. (1993) 'The Case Law of the Court of Justice in Relation to the Review of the Legality of Economic Policy in Mixed Economy Systems,' in Snyder, F. (ed.) *European Community Law*. 2 vols. Aldershot: Dartmouth

Milward, A. (1995) 'Approaching Reality: Euro-Money and the Left', *New Left Review*, no. 216, pp. 55–66

Milward, A. (1992) *European Rescue of the Nation-State*. London: Routledge

Monnier, L. (1996) 'Politique économique et raison communautaire', in Cartelier, L. *et al* (eds) *Critique de la raison communautaire*. Paris: Economica.

Moravcsik, A. (1991) 'Negotiating the Single European Act', *International Organization*, 45: 19–56

Moss, B. (1993) *Labour and Economic Growth under the Fourth French Republic*. Birmingham: Aston University Papers

Neunreither, K. (1994) 'The Democratic Deficit of the European Union: Toward Closer Cooperation Between the European Parliament and National Parliaments', *Government and Opposition*, 29: 299–311

Oliver, P. and Baché, J.-P. (1989) 'Free Movement of Capital Between the Member States: Recent Developments', *Common Market Law Review*, 26: 68–81

Padoa-Schioppa, T. (1987) *Efficiency, Stability and Equity: A Strategy for the Evolution of the Economic System of the European Community*. Oxford: Oxford U.P.

Pernin, A. (1996) 'Des dysfonctionnements de la raison communautaire: une analyse à partir du contrôle des transfers Etats-enterprises', in Cartelier, L. *et al*. (eds) *Critique de la raison communautaire*. Paris: Economica

Philip, A. (1957) 'Social Aspects of European Economic Cooperation', *International Labour Review*, no. 76, pp. 244–56

Pinder, J. (1969) 'Problems of European Integration', in Denton, G. (ed.) *Economic Integration in Europe*. London: Weidenfeld and Nicolson

Pineau, C. and Rimbaud, C. (1991) *Le Grand Pari: l'aventure du traité de Rome*. Paris: Fayard

Pinto Lyra, R. (1978) *La Gauche en France et la construction européenne*. Paris: Librairie générale de droit et de jurisprudence

Prate, A. (1995) *France en Europe*. Paris: Economica

Ross, G. (1995) *Delors and European Integration*. Oxford: Polity Press

Ross, G. (1993) 'Social Policy in the New Europe', *Studies in Political Economy*, 40: 41–72

Saint-Martin, O. (1996) 'L'Anti-Politique industrielle de l'U.E.' in Cartelier, L. *et al* (eds) *Critique de la raison communautaire*. Paris: Economica

Salesse, Y. (1996) 'Institutions européennes, déficit démocratique et intérêt général.' in Cartelier, L. *et al* (eds) *Critique de la raison communautaire*. Paris: Economica

Sharp, M. (1993) 'The Community and New Technologies', in Lodge, J. (ed.) *European Community and Challenge of the Future*. London: Pinter

Shaw, J. (1994) 'Twin-Track Social Europe – The Inside Track?' in O'Keefe, D. and Twomey, P. (eds) *Legal Issues of Maastricht*. London: Wiley

Silvia, S. (1991) 'The Social Charter of the European Community: Defeat for European Labour', *Industrial and Labour Relations Review*, 44: 634–9

Snyder, F. (ed.) (1996) *Constitutional Dimensions of European Economic Integration*. The Hague: Kluwer

Streeck, W. and Schmitter, P. (1991) 'From National Corporatism to Transnational Pluralism: Organized Interests in the Single European Market', *Politics and Society*, 19: 133–64

Streeck, W. (1995) 'From Market Making to State Building? Reflections on the Political Economy of European Social Policy', Liebfried, S. and Pierson, P. (eds) *European Social Policy: Between Fragmentation and Integration*. Washington, D.C.: The Brookings Institution

Szyszczak, E. (1994) 'Happy Tale or Remaking the Fairy Tale?' O'Keefe, D. and Twomey, P. (eds) *Legal Issues of Maastricht*. London: Wiley

Taylor, P. (1983) *The Limits of Integration*. London: Croom Helm

Tinbergen, J. (1965) *International Economic Integration*. Amsterdam: Elsevier

Tyson, L. (1992) *Who's Bashing Whom? Trade Conflict in High Tech Industries*. Washington, D.C.: Institute for International Economics

Verdun, A. (1996) '"Asymmetrical" Union', *Revue d'intégration européenne*, 20: 59–81

Verloren van Themat, P. (1996) 'Propositions on the Legal Analysis of Economic and Monetary Union', in Snyder, F. (ed.) *Constitutional Dimensions of European Economic Integration*. The Hague: Kluwer

Vogel-Polsky, E. and Vogel, J. (1991) *L'Europe sociale 1993: illusion, alibi ou réalité*. Geneva: Institut d'études européennes

Weiler, J. (1993) 'The Community System: The Dual Character of Supranationalism', in Snyder, F. (ed.) *European Community Law*, 2 vols. Aldershot: Dartmouth

Weiler, J. (1991) 'The Transformation of Europe', *Yale Law Journal*, 100: 2403–83

8 The Economic Limits of European Integration

John Corcoran

The abolition of internal tariffs in the early years of the European Economic Community failed to remove all the non-tariff barriers (NTBs) to trade, and consequently a single integrated market failed to emerge. After many years of making no further progress with the single market as an issue, it was revived as part of the EU's policy agenda in 1985. The Milan European Council resulted in the drawing up of the White Paper *Completing the Internal Market*, setting the target date of 31 December 1992. The single market campaign saw the EU return ostensibly to its essentially economic foundations as set out in the Treaty of Rome. This was strengthened by the Single European Act, and most recently by the Treaty on European Union in which a clause calls for:

> the elimination ... of customs duties and quantitative restrictions on the import and export of goods and all other measures having equivalent effect ... [and] an internal market characterised by the abolition of obstacles to the free movement of goods, persons, services and capital. (*Treaty on European Union*, article 3)

Yet it is clear that the 1992 project for the removal of NTBs and the creation of a single market also served the clear political purpose of advancing the aim of European unification.

The main impetus behind the initiative came from the European Commission, one of whose key roles is to advance and defend the process of deeper European integration. The path towards deeper integration had advanced rapidly in the 1950s and the 1960s. By the 1970s this process had slowed considerably, as the Community entered a period characterized by the term 'euroscllerosis', an era of slow decision, hindered by the consequences of the Luxembourg compromise, and overshadowed by the economic uncertainties of oil price hikes, a downturn in world trade, and growing unemployment across Europe. The 1985 White Paper on the completion of the internal market envisaged a reinvigorated European Community returning to its original ideals of liberalized trade between the member states. But this aim cannot be separated from the political changes essential within the decision-making process in order to allow the removal of the NTBs; thus the achievement of an economic advance necessitated a significant political adjustment.

In the Single European Act, approved in July 1987, two major adjustments were achieved. Firstly, the removal of the requirement for unanimity on the Council of Ministers removed the log-jam that had previously bedogged the decision making of the Council. Secondly, after the famous *Cassis de Dijon* case (1978), the principle was established that any goods 'lawfully produced and commercialised' in any member state could be transported and retailed in any other member state without the necessity of being modified, tested, certified or renamed. In the 1985 White Paper this principle was further elaborated into the principle of 'mutual recognition' of technical standards for manufactured goods. In achieving this the way was made clear for the removal of national technical standards as a barrier to the importation of goods from other member states. The establishment of the principle of mutual recognition is represented by the Commission as the 'the first tool the Commission has . . . to ensure the free flow of goods' (EC 1985, p. 135).

The creation of the Single European Market, with the formal abolition of physical and technical barriers to trade, did not however address the continued existence of fiscal barriers; the EU consists of a number of distinct tax territories, each with its own system of taxation. The physical barriers that existed between the member states of the EU before 1993 played an important role in the collection of taxes. However, the wide disparity in standard VAT rates was thought to threaten tax competition between states, with business and private transactions influenced by the differential in tax rates. The logical solution to this problem would be to move towards the harmonization of tax rates; this however represents a sensitive issue since the setting of tax levels is an issue that underpins each member state's national sovereignty. From 1993 there was an agreed minimum standard rate of VAT of 15 per cent throughout the EU, but otherwise progress towards any significant degree of tax harmonization within the EU has been slow.

In 1997 a finalized EU-wide VAT regime is due to come into being, based on the principle of collecting VAT in the country of origin. The advantage of this system is that a British company sending goods to any EU member stage would charge the UK level of VAT. The recipient of the goods will then reclaim the VAT (if there is a differential) from its national VAT return system. The problem with this method is that with the VAT being collected where the goods are produced, this automatically favours those countries with balance of payments surpluses within the EU. Countries with a trading deficit will lose out unless an adequate system of compensation is established.

The continued existence of duty free sales is an anomaly, and the practice is due to end in 1999; the agreement to retain duty-free sales was designed to assist the producers of luxury items such as perfumes and spirits; its continued existence and its unsurprising popularity cannot hide the fact that it represents a tax break to the travelling public who generally consist of the more affluent members of society.

There has been no effective harmonization of excise duties on alcohol and tobacco products, and this has led to significant problems, notably the difficulties faced in the case of cross-border trade between the UK and other EU member states.

From 1993 a very high limit was placed on the quantity of duty-paid items that individuals could import from other member states. The basic rule was that whatever was imported had to be for the individual's personal consumption. This had made it worthwhile for individuals to take shopping trips from the UK to France; more significantly, due to the fact that in 1994 the duty on beer in the UK was 30 pence per pint compared with only 4 pence in France, the transfer of beers, wines, and spirits from France to the UK has become a multi-million pound business involving well organized groups, with very few parts of the UK not now supplied with illicit beers, wines, and spirits. The UK Brewers Society claims that 1.9 million hectolitres of beer was imported into the UK in 1994, amounting to 15 per cent of the UK take-home market. Although this figure is almost certainly an over-estimate, this trade is estimated to represent a loss of £250 million per year to the UK exchequer (*Financial Times*, 9 June 1994).

There has also been little real progress in the process of harmonizing company taxation. An independent committee named the Ruding Committee reported to the Commission in 1992 on three areas of concern arising from differentials in corporate tax levels. Firstly, did the corporate tax differentials distort the single market?

Secondly, will market forces, in the form of competition between nations to lower their corporate tax burden, eventually lead to natural harmonization caused by the member states competing to create the most favourable fiscal climate for their business sectors? Thirdly, what measures should the EU take concerning this issue? The findings of the Committee were predictable, but nevertheless confirmed that the continued differentials in corporate tax levels did indeed represent a barriers to the greater economic integration envisaged by the Single European Act. Firstly, significant differentials in the level of corporate taxation did exist both in the tax rates and tax base. Secondly the lack of harmony could, it was said, become a significant distorting factor in determining where companies situated themselves. Thirdly, it seemed unlikely that 'tax competition' would iron out the anomalies since governments needed to maintain income; instead it would be likely that governments would compete for foreign direct investment by offering lucrative tax concession packages to prospective investors.

The Single European Market investigation into the relative prices of virtually homogenous goods and services found many sectors still affected by barriers. These barriers may well reflect genuine differences in the nature of these national markets, which no amount of legislation will eradicate entirely. An example of this problem can be seen in the case of the general insurance industry. From July 1994 insurance companies were permitted to compete across national borders. The insurance industry was now deregulated and comparisons between different national markets could be realistically made, yet a significant degree of price divergence remains between the various national markets, indicating that the deregulation of EU member states' markets alone may not remove the barriers preventing market convergence, since unique commercial and cultural features of national markets continue to exist.

Car prices for identical models also vary widely within the EU. While individuals can visit another EU state to purchase a car to import into their own country, they will often find the price advantage taxed away by their home state in the form of import duty. The automobile manufacturers successfully lobbied the European Commission to accept that in order to maintain a high quality service network, the mass import of cars by unauthorized dealers would be 'unacceptable'. The result of this corporate lobbying is illustrated by the variation in the price of cars at the time of the launch of the Ford Mondeo in the spring of 1993, with price differentials

Table 8.1   Differential pricing in the EU: Ford Mondeo 1.6 CLX, tax excluded prices, adjusted for differing specifications

Country	Price cheapest = 100 in May 1994
Germany	118.7
UK	110.5
France	109.2
Netherlands	106.2
Portugal	100.4
Spain	100.0

Source: European Commission quoted in *The Economist*, 27 August 1994, p. 31.

within member states of 22 per cent. By the following year the retail price of the Mondeo 1.6 CLX was still 19 per cent higher in Germany than in Spain. Table 8.1 illustrates the differential between various members states after taking into account tax differences and specifications. Generally the more affluent the national market the higher the price charged; differential pricing is a multinational pricing strategy which should have become an anachronism after the creation of the single market, but clearly has plenty of life in it yet.

It is however in the Common Agricultural Policy (CAP) that the EU demonstrates most dramatically the selectivity of its commitment to the creation of a free trading single market. From the signing of the Treaty of Rome the central aim of the CAP has been to 'ensure a fair standard of living for the farming community' (article 39). To achieve this the CAP consists of a price support policy for agriculture throughout the EU. All EU producers are protected from competition from beyond the EU by the setting of 'threshold prices' for agricultural imports so as to ensure that any more cheaply-priced agricultural products are automatically forced up in price and to ensure that the EU-generated product is not disadvantaged in the European marketplace. This ensures a guaranteed income and future for farmers throughout Europe. The result of the CAP is import substitution, paid for by the consumers of the EU being forced to buy more expensive food products, due to the market support which is in turn transferred to the producers of the EU. This amounts to a tax on the EU's consumers.

CAP has a regressive income effect, as lower income households throughout the EU spend a higher percentage of their income on food, and thus the impact of the higher food prices caused by CAP falls disproportionately on those poorer sections of society (Table 8.2).

Table 8.2   How Europe's poor pay more for the CAP

Country	Average Household (% of income spent on food)	Low Income Household (% of income spent on food)
France	19	32
Germany	20	46
Italy	19	43
Spain	28	52
Ireland	23	45
United Kingdom	32	38
Average	23.5	42.6

Source: *Are You Paying Too Much?* (1991), Publication of the Government of Australia (Australia House, London).

No attempt was made in the 1992 programme to fundamentally reform CAP and as Cutler *et al* (1989) point out, 'it would be difficult to imagine a set of arrangements which could be more diametrically opposed to the avowed objectives of 1992 than are those for the CAP.'

THE SINGLE MARKET PROGRAMME

The 1985 White Paper contained a large number of assertions about the likely economic benefits of the 1992 Programme. In 1986 the Commission sought to add weight to these general assertions through the commissioning of a massive research project, published in the Spring of 1988, entitled *The European Challenge*, 1992 subsequently known as the Cecchini Report. The terms of reference for this massive research undertaking were to investigate 'the costs of non-Europe'; thus from its very inception it was likely that the findings of the report would heavily favour the removal of NTBs. The introductory material and the summary of the results of the investigation were firm in the belief that the 1992 programme would bring large benefits. According to Lord Cockfield in his foreword, the removal of NTBs offers:

'a prospect of significant inflation-free growth and millions of new jobs . . . . . There would be a medium term increase in GDP of seven percent, unaccompanied by inflation, and the creation of 5 million new jobs'.

(Cecchini, 1988, p. 102)

The Cecchini Report was in fact a political document designed to encourage progress towards the creation of the single market. The researchers employed by the Commission produced the most favourable estimates that were likely to materialize if all barriers were removed. The European Commission reassessed its view of the Cecchini Report in 1994 when it published *The Community Internal Market – 1993 Report*, making it clear that the macroeconomic benefits of the programme to complete the single market would in fact take far longer to emerge than at first had been hoped. A number of factors were identified as having been responsible for the relatively low rate of return on the 1992 initiative.

Firstly, in many member states the legislation concerning the single market was still being brought into effect, and although by February 1995 the EU average for the implementation of single market measures reached over 90 per cent of the 282 measures which made up the 1985 White Paper, there was evidence of very different rates of progress and implementation in different member states. For example, Denmark had passed legislation on 209 of the 282 measures, whereas Germany had by the same date enacted only 184.

Secondly the macroeconomic environment had altered considerably since the launch of the 1992 programme. A number of macroeconomic shocks had reduced the benefits of the single market – events such as the unification of Germany and the subsequent strain placed upon the German economy, the liberalization of trade with Central and Eastern Europe, and the move into recession throughout Western Europe, all contributing to confounding the optimism which had once surrounded the single market programme.

The single market has largely disappointed those who anticipated that it would bring enormous benefits. Far from being the catalyst for a strengthening of the EU's economy, with more employment and greater prosperity for all, the SEM appears to have merely increased the rapidity and gusto with which corporate Europe has set about driving down costs through the paring back of their workforces. This is reflected in the persistence of the problem of mass unemployment in the EU. Obviously the scale of the unemployment problem varies from region to region in the EU, and this gulf between the affluent regions of Europe and those most severely affected by unemployment and structural decline is a major challenge facing the EU as it continues to progress down the road to economic and monetary union. In recognition of the severity of this problem a commitment was made in the Treaty on European

Table 8.3 Unemployed as a percentage of the civilian labour force (July 1994)

	1983–91	1992	1993	1994	1995
Denmark	9.2	11.2	12.2	11.0	10.5
Germany	7.3	7.7	8.9	10.0	10.0
Belgium	11.0	10.3	11.9	12.8	12.7
Greece	7.6	8.7	9.8	10.7	11.0
Spain	19.0	18.4	22.7	24.5	24.4
France	9.7	10.4	11.7	12.3	12.2
Italy	11.2	11.6	10.4	11.7	11.9
Luxembourg	1.5	1.6	2.1	2.7	2.5
Netherlands	9.5	6.7	8.1	9.8	9.5
Portugal	6.7	4.2	5.5	6.4	6.9
UK	9.4	10.0	10.3	9.6	8.9
Ireland	16.0	16.3	16.6	15.7	15.4
EU	10.2	10.3	11.3	12.0	11.9
USA	6.7	7.4	6.8	6.3	5.8
Japan	2.5	2.2	2.5	2.9	2.8

Source: European Economy

Union to introduce measures that would ensure a return to a high level of employment within the EU. The commitment was however remarkably vague; there was no attempt to quantify the level of unemployment that was to be the target, nor any commitment to take action, or any serious intention of removing responsibility for the maintenance of employment from the responsibilities of the member states, despite general assertions that economic and monetary union would be 'a good thing':

'The Community shall have as its task, by establishing a common market and an economic and monetary union and by implementing common policies or activities ... to promote throughout the Community ... a high level of employment.'

(Article 2)

As Table 8.3 shows, levels of unemployment vary considerably across the EU; nevertheless the trend since the early 1980s has been that, far from diminishing as a problem, unemployment has in fact tended to worsen. The European Commission Report on the *Employment Situation in the EU in 1993* showed that unemployment rates in the objective 1 regions (regions lagging in economic development) rose more quickly than in the other regions in the early 1990s. Partially in response to this fact the EU established the cohesion fund to direct EU assistance at the four poorest member states in order to bring their per capita GDP to within 75 per cent of the EU average. However, the European Commission has itself estimated that, in order to achieve this, it would require an increase in its budget of more than 100 billion ecus per annum, equivalent to a figure in excess of 1 per cent of total EU GDP. It is estimated that even by 1999 the cohesion fund will still only account for an annual expenditure of 2.6 bn ecu or only 3.1 per cent of the total EU budget. Even the increases in the structural and cohesion funds agreed at the Edinburgh summit in 1992 are retrospectively being resisted by the German and UK governments. By the end of 1993 the German current account deficit had reached DM 39.5 billion, more than half this deficit being directly accountable to its financial contribution to the EU. Clearly if the national interest of the wealthier member states prevail, then the EU will not have sufficient financial resources to the able to reduce the socioeconomic disparities which exist between the regions. Furthermore, as the single market becomes established it seems likely that the process of economic divergence will intensify, permitting the wealthier and more affluent regions of the EU to progressively become more advantaged in terms of attracting high technology investment and high 'value added' employment, whilst other regions become progressively more disadvantaged. The EU itself summarizes its failure to seriously confront this issue in its report *Community Structural Policies*:

> 'In summary statistical data indicate that overall progress over time has been far from satisfactory.... Regional disparities in the Community remain wider than those within most unitary states or federal systems. Differences ... are greater ... given the lack of specific distributive mechanisms'.
>
> COM(92)84, p. 6

IDEOLOGICAL ROUTES

The EU is committed to a liberal market ideology, as exemplified by the enormous political and economic momentum which resulted in the single European market programme. On the other hand, the EU trusts in the benefits of market intervention, a belief which highlights its simultaneously held credo of liberal collectivism. The original signatories of the Treaty of Rome wished to create a liberal market organization because their avowed determination to remove tariffs and quotas was to a considerable extent the Community's *raison d'être*. Yet from its very inception the principle of 'free trade' was far from sacrosanct. Article 109 of the Treaty of Rome anticipated the possibility of protectionist policies being permitted to assist member states with severe balance of payment difficulties. The treaty also identified a positive role for macroeconomic policy, article 104 making the well-intentioned wish that 'economic policy should ensure full employment'. These iterations of the 'liberal collectivist' aspect of the Community have never, though, been applied in such a way as to challenge the more muscular 'liberal market' instincts of the institution.

When aid has had to be provided to a member state with balance of payments difficulties, as occurred with Greece in 1985, the Community has linked the aid to the implementation of orthodox deflationary policies, and in other cases has strenuously resisted any tendency to resort to protectionism.

In 1988, partially as a response to the success of the European Monetary System (EMS) in the 1980s, the European Council established a working party under the chairmanship of the President of the European Commission, Jacques Delors to investigate the means by which the EU could advance towards the realization of Economic and Monetary Union (EMU). The Delors Report laid down a number of proposals for moving towards EMU, involving a three-stage progression towards monetary union. At the Maastricht summit the EU agreed to the text of the Treaty on European Union. The implications of the agreement to proceed to EMU were significant since it marked the start of the involvement of the EU in directly influencing the national economic policies of its member states. This came about through the fact that the three-stage process leading up to EMU involved a period of 'convergence', where the member states would seek to achieve specific targets for key economic indicators such as fiscal deficits, inflation rates, interest rates, and stable exchange rates. To fulfil the convergence criteria, many states would be forced to embrace economic policies befitting the orthodox economics behind the treaty itself. Strict control of public expenditure, control of inflation as the overriding priority of government, and so on, set an agenda not only for monetary union but also for an economic environment in which the interests of corporate Europe would be paramount.

It has long been the case that corporate interests have been profoundly influential upon the policy direction of the EU. This is demonstrable in the drive towards the creation of the single market, and is further demonstrated in the period of internal European Commission discussion which preceded the finalization of the EU's decision to proceed towards the establishment of European Monetary Union (EMU). EMU can be seen as an inexorable continuation along the road travelled since the creation of a Common Market and the European Community; the desire to create a single currency for a single market was an inevitable spillover from the anticipated establishment of the SEM on 1 January 1993.

The European Commission's study *One Market One Money* was enormously influential and effectively set the keynotes for the movement towards EMU in the years ahead. *One Market One Money* represented a substantial shift since the first EMU launch in 1970, containing specific policy advice in two key areas: firstly the priority it attached to the maintenance of price stability above all other economic targets, and secondly the emphasis it placed upon the need to enhance the credibility of key monetary institutions, this to be achieved primarily through central bank independence.

There was a strong connection between the contributors to the study and the European corporate lobby. Commission officials developed close links with UNICE, the organization that brings together national employers' associations such as the Bundersverband der Deutschen Industrie (BDI) and the Confederation of British Industry (CBI). Through UNICE's EMS/EMU group the corporate voice was an influential one from the earliest stages of the research associated with *One Market One Money*. The corporate contributors emphasized the microeconomic benefits to be derived from a single currency, the most important being the fact the EMU would remove the costs of hedging against exchange-rate uncertainty, of commission fees, and of the company costs of retaining the services of foreign exchange departments. The EC Commission estimated that the total direct transaction cost savings (corporate and non-corporate) of the transition to EMU would amount to between a quarter and a half of one per cent of the EU's GDP; a figure roughly the same as their previous estimate of the savings from the abolition of frontier controls as part of the creation of the single market. As a result of this influence, national employers' confederations throughout the EU gave great weight to the transaction cost argument in their lobbying in favour of EMU with their own governments.

However, the criteria for admission to the monetary union will be difficult to achieve for the bulk of the EU's current membership. The first condition is having a rate of inflation less than one and a half percentage points higher than the mean of the three lowest. After Finland and Austria joined the EU, their low inflation rates reduced the mean, making the test more difficult. The second condition is somewhat more automatic, in the sense that markets will bring down the 10 year Treasury bond rate of such countries as look likely to fulfil the other conditions and be accepted into EMU.

The third condition, concerning public expenditure, is a matter of judgement for the ECOFIN examiners; attention will be paid as to whether a candidate nation's budget deficit is no greater than 3 per cent of GDP, and how near public debt is to 60 per cent of GDP, but it is becoming clear that the examiners may not adhere absolutely rigidly to these criteria. Instead, consideration will be taken as to the 'sustainability' of the public finances of each candidate nation. This particular criterion has created the most difficulties, since in countries such as France and Spain there has been a widespread popular backlash against the Maastricht-imposed attacks on the welfare state and public enterprise. In France in particular, the popular resistance to the strictures imposed by attempting to meet the Maastricht criterion has spread far beyond the organized working class to incorporate significant sections of middle class opinion also. The last condition, concerning exchange rate stability, makes it impossible to enter the 'irrevocably fixed exchange rate period' with a final devaluation. The candidate currencies must have stayed within the limits of the EMS exchange rates for a minimum of two years.

It will be difficult for all but a hard core of member states to achieve these criteria by the target date, and it seems inevitable that European Monetary Union will be something of a piecemeal process creating an inner core and outer core of EU membership.

As the single market programme progresses, and as the EU moves towards monetary union, it seems entirely likely that the future for the weaker and less competitive EU member states will be one of greater unemployment. The EU does not possess the fiscal muscle to offset the regional economic divergence which the single market process will encourage. The priority for the EU should, though, be to increase and redistribute employment so that the low income and high unemployment areas of the EU benefit. If monetary union goes ahead in the manner proposed it will reinforce the centripetal tendencies already triggered by the SEM. What is required is an EU whose policy priority favours secure employment. For this to be achieved, the EU as an institution will have to assert its democratic nature by actively defending the interests of ordinary Europeans. Such a defence can only be mounted if the grip that the corporate lobby has hitherto had upon the policy-making process of the EU is greatly reduced.

References

Cecchini, P. (1988) *The European Challenge, 1992: The Benefits of a Single Market*. Aldershot: Wildwood House

Cutler, T., Haslam, C., Williams, K. and Williams, J. (1989) *1992 – The Struggle for Europe*. Oxford: Berg

Delors, J. (1987) 'Introduction of the Commission Programme for 1987', *Bulletin of the EC*, Supplement 1/87, Luxembourg, EC

European Commission (1985) *Completing the Internal Market*, COM (85) 310 final

European Commission (1990), 'One Market One Money', *European Economy*, 40, May. Brussels: Commission of the European Communities

European Commission (1991) *The Regions in the 1990s. Fourth Periodic Report on Economic and Social Progress in the Regions*, COM (90) 609 final

European Commission (1991b) *Treaty on European Union*, Luxembourg

European Commission (1992) *Community Structural Policies*, Luxembourg

European Commission (1993) *Reinforcing the Effectiveness of the Internal Market*, COM (93) 256 final

European Commission (1993) *Making the Most of the Internal Market*, COM (93) 632 final

European Commission (1993) *Employment Situation in the EU in 1993*, Luxembourg

European Commission (1994) *Do You Believe All You Read in the Newspapers?*, London Office

European Commission (1994) *The Community Internal Market – 1993 Report* COM (94) 55 final

European Commission (1995) *One Currency for Europe*, COM (95) 333 final

9 EMU and the Democratic Deficit

Bill Morris

Ron Todd, my predecessor as general secretary of the Transport and General Workers' Union, once told the British TUC conference that Europe is the only card game in town. I shared that view then and I share it now. However, only a radically recharged vision can secure the backing of the people and give 'Europe' the momentum to fulfil its mission.

At the heart of the debate about Europe today, there is one problem which overshadows all others. It relates to the introduction of a common currency for the continent. This is a shifting debate. As late as 1996, it appeared to many of us that Europe was on course for the introduction of a single currency, proceeding on schedule and on a sound basis. Events since then have, however, forced a modifications of this view. In particular, two of the pillars on which a single currency would have to rest have shifted.

The first was the understanding that Germany would not countenance the introduction of the single currency on anything other than a rock solid, D-Mark-writ-large basis. The totally unexpected decision to seek the revaluation of the country's gold reserves in order to meet the deficit reduction criteria have now called this into question. Secondly, the election of the Socialist government in France led by Jospin has given rise to adjustment, to say the least, in the established Franco-German axis at the heart of the whole single currency project.

So those of us who are concerned, above all, with employment prospects have been forced to take account of the changing terms of the debate. As that debate unfolds, it is an opportunity to reinstate the jobs issue at its heart. For far too long, the whole question of a single currency for Europe has been discussed without any reference to its possible impact on employment – both the preservation of existing jobs and the prospects for new job creation. The absence of this element from the debate is surely one of the reasons for the decline in popular support for the European

181

Union and the rise of Euroscepticism, in one form or another, across so much of the continent.

For the ordinary man and woman in the streets, the people the trade union movement represents, the debate about Europe is not, primarily, a debate about sovereignty or federalism. It is about jobs above all else. This is the issue which must now be given the most serious consideration. No one can pretend that all the weight of evidence is on one side alone. There have been a number of alarmist predictions of job losses as a result of participation in European Monetary Union (EMU), yet there is also good reason to fear redundancies if the project goes ahead without Britain as a part of it. The cost of going in must be balanced against the cost of staying out. And for me the real criteria against which all claims need to be tested is jobs. So the EMU debate needs to be sober and balanced.

The terms for this debate were, alas, set at Maastricht in 1991. The treaty signed there focused on the twin issues of budget deficits and national debt, with ancillary targets for inflation and interest rates. Thus defined, it was inevitable that progress towards a single currency should be seen as an exercise in austerity, with cutbacks in social spending centre-stage. Yet then, as now, the principal economic problem confronting the member states of the European Union was jobs. Throughout the decade unemployment has remained at or near post-war highs across the continent – even in Britain, where the last government repeatedly manipulated the figures to make the dole queues seem shorter than they in fact were, joblessness is higher than it was in 1979, when the Tories came to office. The waste, economic chaos and injustice of mass unemployment, the myriad social ills which come from long-term joblessness, is the most important issue not just for trade unionists, but for the governments of all the EU member states.

There are twenty million without work in the EU today, even on government statistics which, in some cases, are more than a little economical with the counting. Between 1991 and 1994, six million jobs were lost in the EU – 4 per cent of the workforce and twice the size of any contraction in employment since the last war. Over 11 per cent of the European workforce is unemployed, compared to 6.5 per cent in the USA and less than 3 per cent in Japan. Amongst women workers, unemployment is running even higher, at 12.5 per cent. And, in what is perhaps the most worrying aspect of all, as many as 48 per cent of Europe's unemployed have been out of work for over a year. Parallel to all of this has gone an increase in part-time work, ranging from 8 per cent of those employed in Portugal to nearly one job in four in Britain.

The impact of this situation is immense. It is a drain on the resources of welfare budgets, a major brake on the development of the productive economy and inextricably bound up with a host of problems from crime to drug abuse to racism. It is at the heart of the problem of 'social exclusion', now exercising politicians across Europe. The trade union movement has always said – and needs to keep on repeating – that there can be no viable programme of 'social inclusion' which does not have a return to full employment as its centre-piece.

Now is the time for a serious evaluation of the impact that EMU will have on this situation. Will the introduction of a single currency help or hinder efforts to solve the jobs crisis? I do not deny the resonance of issues of national sovereignty and democracy which are also raised by the move towards a common currency, but I believe that for the trade union movement, they are largely considered in terms of their impact on the prospects for the economy and employment.

The election of a Labour government in Britain and a Socialist-Communist-Green government in France, alongside the previously-elected Centre-Left coalition in Italy, creates the possibility of the traditional concerns of the labour movement, including unemployment, securing a far greater hearing in the debate about EMU. While conservatives held undivided sway over most of Europe's governments, it was likely that any views other than those of bankers and businessmen would be marginalized.

It is also the case that in Britain there is far from being a political consensus around the benefits of the putative 'euro'. Even if the British economy meets the debt-and-deficit criteria laid down at Maastricht, there will still be a great deal of political work to be done if the British people are to be convinced to vote to ditch the pound in the referendum which my union was the first to propose on the issue. Looking at the consequences for employment of EMU will be central to this whole debate – particularly, I believe, in Britain, where memories of the enormous job losses which accompanied sterling's membership of the Exchange Rate Mechanism (ERM) at an over-valued rate remain fresh and painful.

The employment issue arises out of EMU in two distinct ways. The first is job losses which result directly from austerity measures and budget spending cuts imposed in order to ensure compliance with the Maastricht criteria. The second is the consequences of the introduction of the single currency itself. The principal concerns of the trade union movement should be around this second aspect. It can be argued that Britain (and, by this stage, most other European countries) have already endured most of the pain associated with meeting the requirements of the convergence criteria. The cuts made in government spending flow, in any case, from the sort of policies that right-wing governments would have pursued even were there no single currency project. Who can forget the savage squeeze imposed on public spending in Britain by Margaret Thatcher and Geoffrey Howe in 1980–82, when there was little or no talk of a single currency? What is, of course, true, is that the requirement to hold fast to the convergence criteria, if it is allowed to become a dogma of national economic policy, can prevent left-led governments from taking action to cut unemployment which they might otherwise have done. This is obviously a matter of particular controversy in France at present.

This argument leads into the fundamental concerns regarding the impact of a single currency on jobs. My most immediate anxiety is that the German government, in particular, will try to forge ahead towards a single currency in order to meet an entirely arbitrary launch date, when the necessary economic preconditions are not in place. A single currency without real convergence would be the worst scenario of all, yet that spectre was clearly raised by Chancellor Kohl's botched attempt to bludgeon the Bundesbank into massaging its gold reserve accounts in order to create the appearance that Germany is in conformity with the Maastricht criteria.

Such behaviour would give the green light to all sorts of accounting tricks in countries with deficits still further off course than Germany's. That would leave a single currency born as an act of political will, without a sound basis in economic reality. It would be a weak currency, which the new central bank could only prop up through fierce deflationary measures. To go down that road would risk a re-run of the ERM nightmare of 1991–93, with all the attendant bankruptcies and redundancies. I do not believe that the European Union could easily withstand a repeat of that experience. Far better for the protagonists of the euro to acknowledge that the main European economies are not ready for such a fundamental step.

I believe that it would be wrong for Britain to sign up to the single currency at the present time and without the present criteria being firmly underpinned by a Treaty on Jobs. We cannot afford to see Russian roulette played with the jobs and futures of tens of thousands of our members.

However, that should be a starting point for debate, rather than a conclusion, because the single currency issue is going to remain with us. If, as I believe, the British government does not dissolve the pound into the euro at the outset, the question of joining at a later date will inevitably remain on the table. If and when a stable euro is up and running, British trade unions will have to soberly weight up the advantages of going in against the advantages of staying out. This would mean a long-term examination of the impact on employment and on the prospects for a return to full employment – something we have not seen in Britain for around thirty years.

Historical experience indicates that there have been relatively few periods when anything like full employment has been actually achieved under a capitalist system. When it has been, one of the most important factors leading to that achievement has been the willingness and ability of a national government to intervene in the management of the economy.

This can take a variety of forms, from exchange rate control to public spending increases aimed at stimulating economic activity. Once national governments lose effective control of these levers of economic policy, a programme to restore full employment starts to look less and less plausible. Whilst the European Union could itself, through the commission, lead an attack on unemployment, there are nevertheless two fundamental problems with seeing the EU as the new agency of a full employment economy. Firstly, the resources concentrated in Brussels are very small indeed compared to those held by national governments and, secondly, the proposals for a single currency and the establishment of an effectively unaccountable European central bank to manage the euro would mean that the currency would be outside democratic control.

So the European Union will lack both the resources and the power to conduct an interventionist economic policy, despite all the right-wing rhetoric about 'interference' from Brussels bureaucrats. The Maastricht treaty was tailor-made for bankers by politicians who have, to far too great an extent, accepted the prevailing wisdom that nothing much can be done about economic policy in the new globalized economy.

Under the conditions, the creation of the euro would not mean transferring the power to intervene to ameliorate the employment position from one set of democratic institutions to another. It would mean removing that power from those who could – if they wished – use it, to . . . nowhere. Paradoxical as it may seem, the process of constructing what is called a European 'super-state' actually goes hand-in-hand with a major reduction in the power of the state to manage the economy in the interests of the people.

At present, trade unions can lobby national governments to take measures to cut unemployment or reduce inequality, and we can seek to elect sympathetic members of parliament and governments. EMU would effectively take away much of that right. National governments would declare themselves powerless to do anything, while decisions would be taken by a bankers' committee insulated from any form of accountability or popular pressure.

So the single currency will actually enthrone the dogma of *laissez-faire* economics ever more securely in Europe. If the experience of the last 15–20 years worldwide proves anything, it is that the free market is not the road to full employment. Rather, it has lead to a combination of higher unemployment and a larger section of those actually in work being stuck in low-paid jobs with minimal security and social protection.

We have argued that by introducing greater democracy into the working of the EU, and establishing political supervision of a European Central Bank, these issues could be addressed. These ideas may have some merits. However, I feel that such a dilution of the bank's independence will prove unacceptable to German public opinion. Furthermore, democratizing the EU would still not make it an effective lever for job creation, since it would still lack any real resources to give effect to any good intention it may have. The European Union budget amounts to just 1.27 per cent of gross domestic product, scarcely enough to make any serious dent in the mass of continent-wide inequality and unemployment I have referred to. The budget is only 2.4 per cent that of the total budget of the member states. The great majority of even this limited amount is already ear-marked, primarily to farm-price support through the Common Agricultural Policy, and there is little or no public support for an increase in the funds the member states remit to Brussels. Thus, while the European Commission does play a role through regional aid and funding for research and development, it does not have the resources for a serious extension of this role.

The single currency would also mean economies in widely diverging real states of health being forced into a common strait-jacket. That is the problem of the narrow definition of convergence prescribed at Maastricht. It takes no account of a range of vital factors, like productivity, investment, labour costs and so on. As the *Financial Times* recently noted, 'the Maastricht tests concentrate on financial criteria with little attention paid to real convergence in growth rates, productivity growth and unemployment levels'. (*Financial Times*, 19 September 1997)

The management of the currency by a Bundesbank writ large, with an unaccountable committee looking solely at the inflation rate, could prove far too constrictive to allow the healthy growth of some economies, thereby contributing to a rise in unemployment. Comparisons with the situation in the USA are ill-founded, since labour is naturally far more mobile on that side of the Atlantic. For a host of cultural, linguistic and historical reasons, we are generations away from a situation where a family can move from Birmingham, England to Bremen as readily as from Birmingham, Alabama to Boston. A one-size-fits-all interest rates policy could artificially inhibit growth in some countries, with employment suffering as a result, as even the governor of the Bank of England, Eddie George, has acknowledged. (*T&G Record*, May 1997).

Whilst the employment case against EMU is formidable, particularly in the light of the developments indicated at the start of this chapter, it is also important to consider the other side of the argument. It could be argued that the risks to jobs would be greater if the UK stays out. Outside the euro, sterling would be vulnerable and unstable. Inside, we would be part of the largest currency union in the world. Outside EMU, sterling would only be stabilized if we practiced a sterner monetary policy than in the euro area, and thus maintained our parity. Any flicker of a rumour about devaluation might well cause a surcharge equal to the devaluation to be placed on British exports to the single market. A more positive position on the concept of the euro would at least increase our ability to influence events. Total rejection of the single currency would be one more example of the 'too little, too late' approach which has governed Britain's approach to the most important European decisions. Britain did not join the Coal and Steel Community at the outset. We delayed entry to the Common Market and were, as a result, lumbered with the Common Agricultural Policy. We rejected the ERM and then went in too late and at too high a rate. It is a sorry record.

The British TUC has also argued that British involvement in EMU would help boost American and Japanese inward investment in Britain and secure our position in the relentless moves towards industrial and commercial integration and the globalization of the world economy. Lower risk premia on cross-border investment, comparability of prices in the euro area, ending destabilizing exchange rate speculation, influencing European and global monetary policy and lower transaction costs on trade and travel must also count as factors in favour of EMU. So the calculation of the balance of advantage is a complicated one, and it is not enough for the trade union movement to simply criticize the present EMU proposals and walk away. That is not a credible option for the British trade union movement, however seductive it may sound. We must recognize the over-arching realities of today's global economy and devise policies which address them.

I believe that we have to recognize that Europe remains central to our future well-being. It is our major market and trading partner – our travel-to-work area and our investment zone. Increasingly, for trade unionists it is also going to become our negotiating area, as cross-border bargaining through European Works Councils and other means becomes more widespread. Sixty per cent of our visible exports go to the EU, compared to 36 per cent in 1973. France and Belgium alone buy as many British goods as the whole of Asia. Germany buys £2 billion more British goods than the USA does each year. If you are concerned with the real economy, then it is clear that our economic destiny lies in Europe. It is true that British capitalism remains more international in scope than that of other EU states. This reflects the particular role of the City of London in the world economy.

However, this globalism is not necessarily a great source of strength to the British economy. The export of capital from Britain has been a feature of the last twenty years, and it has gone hand-in-hand with a neglect of investment in manufacturing industry, in particular. As a consequence, the whole shape of the British economy has become distorted and unbalanced – something which also has an obvious impact on employment prospects and possibilities. Rebuilding our industrial, as opposed to our rentier, economy cannot be achieved by turning our back on Europe. The development of economic and trading blocs is a trend of growing importance in the world. The North American Free Trade Area may expand to include the whole of the western hemisphere, and a Japan-dominated yen bloc in the far east looks a possibility. These developments have not been favourable to the labour movements in the countries affected. Nevertheless, they are entrenched.

Could Britain prosper while standing outside the European Union? I do not believe so. There are millions of jobs in Britain dependent on the European market – not the single currency, but the free trade zone already in place. To lose that access, or to be competing on disadvantaged terms, would be suicidal, and there are now few voices in the labour movement seriously advocating withdrawal from the EU. Export-oriented jobs would be lost and inward investment would surely be affected. So what is needed is an approach towards the single currency which makes a priority of rebuilding the productive economies of Europe. I believe that, while some trade unionists will oppose a single currency out of principle and under all circumstances, for me and many others, the critical issue is one of timing and the conditions underpinning it. Get these right, and much opposition will fade. After all, it has never been part of the tradition of the trade union movement to celebrate competition between nation states. 'Workers of the world, hang on to your separate currencies' does not have much of a ring to it.

Creating better conditions for a genuine social programme of economic integration would have several elements. We need to see progress towards an Employment Chapter in the Maastricht Treaty which aims to prevent long-term unemployment and social exclusion, ensures that demand across Europe grows at an adequate rate to ensure sustainable growth, and promotes flexibility by providing workers and job-seekers with the skills needed to adapt to a constantly changing economy and labour market. Such a fresh approach would have to be mainly the work of national governments, which is why the political shift away from free-market ideologues and conservatism in much of Europe is so important. However, the EU could also have a positive role to play, if it acted on the call by Commission President Jacques Santer for a confidence pact for employment.

The commission could help stimulate private and public sector investment. For example, it could prioritize the development of trans-European networks in transport, information technology and the energy sector. The Delors jobs package, to be funded by eurobonds, could be revived and extended. Of course, these measures will not on their own eradicate unemployment. But they would begin the creation of a different dynamic within the EU – one which puts the satisfaction of people's needs first, and which recognizes that a positive European 'project' can only rest on prosperous national societies at peace with themselves.

Over-ambitious constitution-mongering and a Europe built by and for financial interests alone have lost the support of the people. The EU and its member states must have the thriving economies, cohesive societies and security for all which alone can give people the confidence to tackle the new issues raised by globalization.

10 Why 'Employability' Won't Make EMU Work

Andy Robinson

'You could say we have rescued EMU although I would be grateful if you didn't say it too loudly'. The remark – off the record, of course – was made to the *Financial Times* by one of Tony Blair's Ministers at the European Union's Amsterdam summit in June 1997.[1] However smug, the statement is quite accurate. The language of Blairism provided a makeshift bridge between Bonn and Paris in what at one stage appeared to be a clash over European unemployment that might have scuppered the whole EMU project. French Socialist prime minister Lionel Jospin had won the May 1997 election with promises to change the thrust of European integration and put jobs back on the agenda. If that meant renegotiating the fiscally restrictive stability pact – 'an absurd concession to the Germans', in the words of Jospin – so be it. The French unemployment rate had risen from 9.5 per cent to 12.8 per cent between 1991 and 1997, and the victory of a Left coalition that embraced the Eurosceptic Communist Party showed just how many French citizens put the malaise down to preparations for monetary union. Jean-Marie Le Pen's europhobic and racist National Front's 15 per cent share of the vote rammed the point home.

Jospin offered the electorate an expansive monetary union founded on a flexible interpretation of the Maastricht convergence criteria, the inclusion of Spain and Italy from January 1999, and the abandonment of the Stability Pact which proposed to fine those members of the union whose budget deficits exceeded strict limits, even in recession, evoking the disastrous 'economics of retribution' of post first world war reparations. On the domestic front, Jospin pledged he would create over 700 000 jobs for young people by the year 2002, half of them in the public sector. The Socialist manifesto also set out plans to cut working hours with no reduction in pay. This was light years away from the consensus that had prevailed in the EU for so long, that unemployment was a structural phenomenon which could only be remedied by labour market deregulation and lower wages for less skilled workers. Jospin, following Keynesian economists such as Jean-Paul Fitoussi at the Observatoire Français des Conjontures Economiques, actually proposed wage increases, to boost consumption. The implication in Jospin's manifesto was that the problem was less the supply side than weak demand for labour, stemming from a chronic shortage of aggregate demand in a French economy that had only managed a 1.3 per cent average annual growth rate since 1990. Employers federations (CNPF) and Jean-Claude Trichet at the Bank of France screamed that the problem was not consumption but investment, which had fallen by 5 per cent since 1990.[2] Trichet dismissed the very idea that French business's reluctance to invest might have had something to do with the central bank's *franc fort* policy which had pushed real interest rates up to 5 per cent between 1993 and 1994 in a stagnant economy – all in the name of mercantilist 'competitive disinflation' and a 'hard' single currency.

Cynics muttered that Jospin's Keynesianism was the reflex action of a party still reeling from the electoral debacle of 1993, surprised by President Chirac's decision to call elections and quite sure that it would not win them. But there it was, almost embarrassingly, on paper after the Left's convincing victory in June 1997. A week before the Amsterdam summit, Dominique Strauss-Kahn, Jospin's finance minister, announced that he would not sign the Stability Pact until a chapter on employment was written into it. German chancellor Helmut Kohl, under intense pressure back home to stop the slide towards a 'weak' euro, said the pact was not negotiable. Rumbling discontent from the Bundesbank stressed the old adages: unemployment could not be countered by a looser fiscal or monetary regime but only by structural reform. Amsterdam looked more and more like a battleground where the German–French axis would be blown apart and with it any chance that EMU would start in January 1999, or maybe ever. That was when Britain's New Labour took the stage, fresh from its May 1997 election victory.

Gordon Brown, the New Labour chancellor, had already spelt out his policy on employment the week before Amsterdam. Macroeconomic stability and coordination were essential conditions for employment growth but so were flexible labour markets. Anglo-American experience proved that only a careful combination of generous monetary policy and deregulation could deliver the goods. The key concept for Blair and Brown, as it had been for Bill Clinton, was an exotic term plucked straight from the business bestsellers that filled the shelves of airport bookstores: employability.[3] In the new global labour market, governments could not guarantee employment growth, never mind full employment, but instead could only create the conditions in which labour would adapt continuously to the changing needs of business. It was all about managing change, any corporate CEO could tell you. That meant no rigidities that might stop shifts in nominal wages or non-wage labour costs clearing the labour market, especially at the lower-skilled end of the earnings table. It also meant abundant investment in education and training ('lifetime learning' was one of the sexiest phrases of the employability thesis). European labour legislation was anathema to all this. High hiring and firing costs in Europe hindered employment creation. Employability could compensate European labour for losing mandatory dismissal compensation and other statutory means of job protection. Privileged insiders in European labour markets – that is, those in stable employment – should be equipped to sell their wares at regular intervals rather than given job security at the expense of outsiders, the precariously employed or longterm unemployed. Flexibility and mobility would become all the more important once monetary union was established.

Even *Le Monde* admitted that Gordon Brown had inspired the final text of the Resolution on employment that emerged from the discord of the Amsterdam summit.[4] New Labour's touch even survived translation from management guru English to diplomatic French: 'It's necessary to give priority to the creation of a competitive, well trained and mobile workforce and allow the labour market to adapt to change. . . . Welfare systems and tax structures should be adapted to improve the functioning of the labour market', ran the unofficial French translation. True, there was not much for the French Keynesians in the policy recommendations. But at least the resolution recognized the 'need to improve the efficiency and broaden the scope of intergovernment cooperation by placing a greater emphasis on employment'. There was also a vague reference to the development of an economic pole to square up to the European Central Bank. Anyway, in its most ambitious versions, the flexibility–employability thesis promised to smooth out skill shortages and other capacity constraints, and enable more expansionary fiscal and monetary policies. Clinton's former Labour secretary Robert Reich claimed that 'maximum flexibility' for employers and 'workforce adaptability' could eliminate bottlenecks in labour markets and allow governments to run the economy 'at full tilt'.[5]

More important than anything for Jospin and Strauss-Kahn, facing the music back home, was that the resolution sounded radical.

Strauss-Kahn signed the Stability Pact and hoped Germany would at least yield on the 3 per cent deficit criteria. But by July 1997 it was clear that Kohl needed a French deficit very close to 3 per cent of GDP if he was to fend off the ever wider alliance of forces – the Bundesbank and sections of his own government coalition – clamouring for postponement of EMU. EMU 1999 was the imperative. Strauss-Kahn, proving that Tony Blair's obituary to 'tax and spend socialism' was premature, at least in France, announced a 15 per cent increase in corporate tax and cuts in defence spending to bring the deficit down.

The problem, of course, was that meeting the convergence criteria, even with progressive fiscal measures, meant ceding acres of ground to the orthodoxy that, for all its new age neologisms, lay at the heart of the employability thesis, just as it had dominated most of Brussels thinking on labour markets since the late 1980s. EMU plus the Stability Pact effectively meant the disappearance of macroeconomic levers which had consistently compensated the real structural differences between European economies. Nothing was better guaranteed to give even greater credence to the most drastic supply-side solutions than the maintenance of deflationary fiscal (and possibly monetary) conditions in a monetary union with inadequate demand for productive labour. Economists across the political spectrum agreed that nominal convergence based on the Maastricht criteria – inflation, and debt levels – had not actually led to real economic convergence of productivity rates or social institutions, such as wage bargaining structures. Relative productivity levels between different regions were still widely discrepant. Wasn't this, after all, the main reason for the 30-year long depreciation of Europe's peripheral currencies (the lira, peseta and pound) and even the franc against the D-Mark?[6]

Until EMU, unit labour costs, in different EU states – a measure of competitiveness – had traditionally been brought into line by exchange rate fluctuation and higher wages in the high productivity core. Nominal exchange rate depreciation had helped less competitive economies avoid balance of payments crises. Losing the right to devalue – and the corresponding margin for independent monetary policy – would mean that only real wages could shift to correct imbalance and offset the effects of what economists called asymmetric shocks.[7] Either wages or people – via mass emigration

– would have to shift. There would be nothing else left to give. The alternative to greater downward flexibility for real wages (or fluid labour mobility) was more unemployment in less competitive regions. Placed in the context of the massive demand-related Keynesian unemployment that Jospin had hinted at in his electoral programme, the adjustments would inevitably be traumatic. The historical precedent was there in gold standard Europe in 1920–30. Spanish chief economist of the European Monetary Institute, Jose Viñals, a fervent supporter of EMU, candidly stated:

> Among the adjustment mechanisms available to cope with real asymmetric shocks in the future EMU – labour mobility, fiscal policy and relative wage flexibility – it is unlikely that labour mobility will play an important role since the numerous historical, cultural and linguistic differences across European countries constitute a formidable barrier to international migration. The Maastricht treaty grants only a limited role to national fiscal policies to cushion the impact of asymmetric shocks. What about real wages?[8]

For many EU countries real wage flexibility in EMU inevitably meant deregulation, the withdrawal of employment protection legislation, and cuts in unemployment benefit and non-wage labour costs (most likely through the contraction of welfare). Some had been there before: this was the British road to low productivity employment.

Indeed, British Eurosceptic supply-siders such as Patrick Minford and Alan Walters made the same point as the Europhiles. But, ironically, Minford and Walters, Margaret Thatcher's most class conscious advisors, were far softer on the workers than pro-EMU economists, many of them Social Democrats, however fervently these professed to believe in a 'progressive' monetary union. Minford[9] stressed that exchange rate flexibility should be used as a cushion while labour market deregulation was in progress. Devaluation would at least create room for demand and GDP growth while the unions were emasculated and labour legislation dismantled. Economic advisors to centre-left governments in Gonzalez's Spain, Mitterrand's France and Olive alliance Italy made the Iron Lady's advisors seem like namby pambies. 'We have been trying to deregulate the Spanish labour market for the past 20 years without much success, monetary union will make it a necessity', said Viñals in an interview with the Spanish daily *Cinco Días*. The single currency as 'discipline',[10] and unemployment as *force majeure* would be all the more decisive in a monetary union with a clear deflationary bias and without a central budget or any centralized macroeconomic instruments outside the independent central bank.

Fiscal transfers in the truly federal monetary union of the USA compensate up to 30 cents of every $1 fall in GDP in a state affected asymmetrically by economic slowdown.[11] In the EU, with a centralized budget of only 1.27 per cent of EU GNP, fiscal transfers are negligible. No cushions there either. As for cohesion funds, designed to improve infrastructure – and so help increase productivity rates – in the poorer regions they were still set at a measly 0.46 per cent of EU GNP.

What both the Eurosceptic and Europhile supply-siders agreed on was the need for deregulation of European labour markets if unemployment was to be brought down, from 11 per cent (1996) of the EU work force and from far more in Spain and southern Italy. Whether to do this with the aid of the exchange rate as an anaesthetic (Thatcherite softies) or by using EMU as electro-shock therapy (Social Democratic hawks), was all that was under discussion. Critics from the Left were also divided over the long term desirability of EMU but at least agreed that giving up the exchange rate cushion without establishing a substantial EU budget and probably a federal structure to compensate regional imbalances (both structural and cyclical) could be disastrous, particularly for the peripheral economies. Nor would deregulation be the solution. Both pro-and anti-EMU Keynesians pointed out that the Anglo-American model of labour flexibility – even in its new labour employability garb – might just mask the problem by creating low wage, low productivity service sector employment that, according to Joan Robinson's term, would fall into a category of 'disguised unemployment'.

DEREGULATION IS WASTE

In France and Germany where minimum wages, high firing costs, and relatively high employer social security contributions prevent the creation of extremely low wage jobs, productivity levels in services have been held stable or increased. Deregulation in Europe, argues John Eatwell,[12] would just shift the openly unemployed into disguised unemployment, 'clearly a waste of human resources since labour is working at a level of productivity below its true potential'. The problem throughout the G7, Eatwell stresses, is that 'the rate of growth of effective demand is everywhere too low'. European Monetary Union could, in theory, create more favourable conditions for sustained expansion of effective demand in a European economy freed of some of the constraints imposed by global financial markets and currency speculators. Internal EU trade after all is equivalent to over 60 per cent of GDP so fluctuations in euro rates versus the dollar or yen would not be so harmful to macroeconomic policy as internal exchange rate volatility has been. But labour market deregulation in the context of an EMU, hemmed in by deflationary targets for monetary policy and by the stability pact, would just compound the problem.

Deregulation may also be incompatible with the high tech, knowledge-based economy that employability proponents claim to value so highly. First because, as Eatwell mentions, 'very low wages may discourage productivity-boosting innovation'. The UK does seem to provide evidence that when choosing between a cheap labour force or long term investments in labour-saving technology, giving employers freedom to do as they please may not be the most advisable course.[13] Second, because the kind of external flexibility associated with the US and UK labour markets may actually be damaging to the education and training programmes that defenders of employability propound. The effect on investment in training caused by worries about free riders is well documented. 'Fear of losing trained workers can lead to lower investment in skills (which) in turn may lead to higher turnover, further discouraging training', writes the Danish economist Keld Holm in a recent study for Lehman Brothers.[14]

But this is just one of the glaring weaknesses of a conception of labour market flexibility based upon the ease with which an employer can hire and fire. Holm notes that stringent job security regulations in European economies are typically accompanied by alternative flexibility in the form of variable working hours and 'higher internal job rotation and job progression'. Anglo-Saxon firms tend to adjust to changes in output by altering the size of their workforce while German and other European companies adjust the number of hours worked:

These differences in adjustment patterns are probably the most important reason for questioning the conventional wisdom of the

1980s. Traditional measures of labour market flexibility focus more or less exclusively on external flexibility, instead of looking at the complete picture of labour market flexibility including changes in working hours and internal mobility. . . . Internal flexibility has been almost completely ignored by economists, partly because of a lack of reliable statistics, information and economic theory. This is underlined by the fact that macro economists have a tendency to treat the firm as a black box.[15]

Immersed in the 'conventional wisdom of the 1980s', policy recommendations for European labour markets from the European Commission and the OECD embraced the most ideological proselytizing versions of Anglo-American deregulation and waxed lyrical about the British labour market 'miracle'. As unemployment climbed in Europe's hard core, all eyes turned to the UK where the jobless rate had fallen from 10.4 per cent to 5.7 per cent (between 1993 and June 1997) with no discernible effect on wage levels. Economists the world over detected a 'structural break' – a new relationship between wages and unemployment – apparently brought about by the Conservative's supply-side reforms.[16] The OECD's 1994 *Jobs Report* paid barely nuanced homage to UK external flexibility as the way out of an 'explosive' situation in Europe. The vast majority of economists agreed. MIT economist Paul Krugman, a leading critic of Reagan's supply-side revolution, held Thatcher's UK up as the only way forward for Europe – 'Anything else would be an act of faith', he said.[17]

Support for deregulation in European Commission employment reports became less and less conditional. But closer analysis showed the UK labour market miracle in less favourable light even when compared with France, the sickest man of Europe. Income inequality had soared in Britain. In the mid 1990s the richest 10 per cent of British society received a quarter of total income while the poorest received just 3 per cent, a level of inequality far higher than other European countries and well above the UK itself of just 10 years earlier.[18] Worse still, the UK's jobs miracle appeared in part to be a statistical *trompe-l'œil*. Empirical research by economist at the British National Institute of Economic and Social Research (NIESR) showed remarkably that France had created more employment in the first two years of its miserably weak, *franc fort*-constrained 1990s recovery than Britain in the same period of its own expansion that had benefited from a competitive pound and far lower interest rates.[19]

The precipitous decline in the British unemployment rate, said the NIESR, was entirely attributable to a declining work force (all those working or actively seeking work), caused by a stricter welfare regime that appeared to have encouraged the long-term sick to leave the dole (and the work force) and sign on for sickness benefit. In France the workforce had grown by 1.7 per cent in the same period. Economists in Brussels, Paris and Bonn began to wonder what the UK employment figures would look like without the comparatively healthy growth of GDP (at least, in relation to the European hard core) between 1993 and 1996 driven by a monetary policy free of the ERM and EMU. In October 1996 a pro deregulation Commission report mechanically relating high unemployment levels with greater statutory employment protection was withdrawn at the last minute and branded facile. The OECD *Employment Outlook* reports also began to challenge some of the linchpins of the Anglo-American model of external flexibility.[20]

The 1996 report noted widening income differentials in the US and the US and the UK (the difference between bottom and top decile income has risen by 15.7 per cent and 14.8 per cent respectively between 1979 and 1994) as against stable and low wage inequality in continental Europe. Low wage junk jobs (Eatwell and Robinson's disguised unemployment), at least for older workers, were not a gateway to higher productivity employment (a euphemism adopted later in New Labour's welfare-to-work programme) but could be a 'trap from which they would never manage to escape'. Nor were temporary jobs, so widespread in Spain since partial deregulation in the early 1980s, necessarily a bridge to permanent employment. The report also almost inadvertently questioned yet another key feature of the employability, external flexibility thesis: that the concentration of unemployment amongst the less skilled was a result of technological advances that had increased demand for skilled, qualified labour and spurned the less qualified.

In the US 32 per cent of workers with upper secondary education had low paid jobs, noted the 1996 OECD report, against 10 per cent in France. Maybe the explanation for junk jobs and junk wages was more down to earth: where there is a general lack of demand for all sorts of labour, low wage jobs are taken by the better qualified of the unemployed who displace the unskilled.[21] The 1997 OECD *Employment Outlook* – noting that low paid workers in the US and the UK showed less upward mobility than in continental Europe – even went so far as to question the same organization's 1997 *Jobs Strategy* that had emerged from the deregulatory *Jobs Study* of 1994:

> Equity concerns about earnings inequality which several European governments have identified as an important barrier to implementing some of the policy recommendations of the OECD *Jobs Strategy* cannot be dismissed simply with an appeal to increased labour mobility. (p. 50)

In plain English (clarity of expression is risky when you're challenging the policy recommendations of the organization that pays your wages): 'There is nothing in the Anglo American deregulation model that makes up for its ugly propensity to make the poor poorer and the rich richer'.

Confusion spread amongst European policy makers still transfixed by the US employment performance – American unemployment had fallen below 5 per cent by the mid-1990s with negligible wage inflation and an economy that posted a 5.8 per cent growth rate in the first quarter of 1997 – but nevertheless relieved at the OECD's nuances. In June 1996 Padraig Flynn's Employment Commission produced a robust defence of the German model which flew in the face of that conventional wisdom shared by German business leaders and Anglo-American financial analysts and journalists: 'The German economy does not have a fundamental competitiveness problem. It has a balance of trade surplus and stable unit labour costs . . .'.[22] Germany, the report noted, had invested 21 per cent of GDP in 1990 compared with 15 per cent in the UK:

> The German system contrasts with the UK model – based on flexible labour markets, relatively low levels of social protection and flexible exchange rates – which is often offered as the alternative. However, the UK model can be seen as a response to competitive weakness given its low levels of capital and human resource investment – as much as a political choice.

It was a confidential document and Flynn's spokespeople back-pedalled furiously when it was leaked to the press, denying any attack on the UK deregulatory model. The withered reference to the UK's dependence on flexible exchange rates also sounded like sour grapes now that almost everyone agreed that ERM and the desire to create a 'hard' euro had held German and French interest rates far too high for far too long. But the really remarkable thing about Flynn's report was that, despite being published in the same month, it appeared to contradict quite bluntly the employability resolution of the Amsterdam summit, by proclaiming the virtues of German internal flexibility.

HAPPINESS AMONGST THE TULIPS

As the UK lost its shine, Holland became the beacon for European and OECD labour market supply-siders. The Dutch unemployment rate had fallen from 12 per cent in the mid-1980s to 6 per cent in 1997, a performance on a par with the UK. Employment had grown by around 2 per cent in the 1990s, no great shakes compared with the US but at least it had not fallen as in the EU as a whole. Nor had Holland attacked its welfare state with the same venom as the UK nor had income inequality soared as it had in the Anglo-American model. Europe's centre left media saw the light at the end of the tunnel. 'Hope rediscovered in Holland', ran one headline, 'Happiness is amongst the tulips'.[23] But the Dutch miracle was actually a way of sidestepping the real problem – weak demand for labour – by taking older and less physically able workers out of the labour force (the participation rate of 60–64 year olds is just 20 per cent) and by encouraging part time work which accounted for 35 per cent of total employment in 1994, the highest in the OECD. The employment rate in Holland was just 50.7 per cent in 1994 against 59.4 per cent in 1970. Broad unemployment (defined by the OECD as all those unemployed and inactive of working age receiving social security benefits plus those in subsidised employment) had risen from 7.1 per cent of the work force in 1970 to 26.6 per cent in 1985 and then to 27.1 per cent in 1994. All of which has placed some strain on the Dutch welfare state, aggravated by the policy of reducing employment taxes and employer insurance contributions.[24]

Holland did prove that collective wage agreements at sectoral level could hold down wages in a way that would not discriminate as cruelly against the low waged as Anglo-Saxon deregulation.[25] It also proved that falling unemployment was compatible with a fair minimum wage, relatively generous dole payments and the internal flexibility model (greater employment protection) of adaptation to economic change. But it was more a rearguard action than a miracle and, despite the headlines, the light in the tunnel was dim.

Few denied, either, that the European internal flexibility model got stuck where entry into employment was concerned. Once you had a job, the system helped you to keep it. But just as Anglo-American external flexibility made it easier for employers to fire, it gave greater incentives to hire too. The German model, by contrast, gave few incentives to take on new workers, except those entering through apprenticeship. This tended to reinforce the insider–outsider dichotomy which so appalled the employability school, and made long term unemployment a serious problem in Europe compared with the US. The outsiders in Germany (and Holland, with the exception of those in part time employment) were generally women whose access to the labour market was limited. In France, where the unemployment rate for 15 to 24 year olds had reached 28 per cent by 1997, they were more particularly the young. In Spain, where partial deregulation had created the most ruthlessly segmented labour market on the continent, they were both.

Indeed, Spain was a source of fascination and outrage for labour market students. How could a society survive with over 20 per cent of its labour force on the dole, with youth unemployment rates of around 40 per cent, and employment population ratios of just 46 per cent? Since partial deregulation under the first Socialist Governments in the early 1980s, Spain appeared to have developed a grotesque hybrid labour market with almost limitless external flexibility for the employers of that third of the employed with fixed term labour contracts and vast job security for the other two thirds. A constant reserve of unemployed enhanced the flexibility – or heightened the insecurity, depending on your point of view – of the temporary segment. What was a mystery to analysts was how Spain had avoided either a social explosion or, alternatively, an explosion of welfare costs. The answer, strangely, highlights further weaknesses in the Anglo-American deregulated market: these have been extensively researched by Paul Gregg at the LSE.

Spain's privileged insider labour force – protected by far-reaching labour laws – is made up fundamentally of family breadwinners. The outsiders are more often than not married women or youths who share the family home with the breadwinner. Unemployment amongst breadwinners is around half the general rate (11 per cent compared with 22 per cent in 1997). Generous dismissal compensation and dole payments for insiders meant that those breadwinners who did lose their jobs could still maintain their families, at least in the short term. The result was actually a relatively equitable distribution of Spain's very scarce employment amongst households, comparatively high social cohesion given the circumstances, and a quite inexpensive welfare system built around the family. Compare that with the UK where deregulation had caused wages to fall dramatically for unskilled workers, concentrating unemployment in impoverished, welfare-dependent households.[26] Twenty-two per cent of British households with children lacked any wage earner compared with just 12 per cent in Spain. Job-seekers in these welfare-dependent workless households faced marginal tax rates of up to 100 per cent on entry wages, huge disincentives to taking up low paid work. All of which pushed up social security expenditure despite the constant attempts by Thatcher and Major's governments to rein back welfare spending. Spending on social security rose from 9 per cent of GDP in 1979 to 13 per cent in 1996.

The lesson from Gregg's work was another body blow to the deregulators. Deregulation and external flexibility appeared to atomize society, destroy non-market institutions such as trade unions, break up families[27] and concentrate poverty amongst welfare-dependent households, and employment amongst multi-earner families. Granted, in the process, it created more service sector jobs as child care and domestic work was farmed out to the market: 'There is a burgeoning demand for services in the US – from takeaway food to personal fitness trainers – that has its roots in the growth of individualism and the breakdown of the family'.[28] But the result was, paradoxically, a more expensive welfare state. The internal flexibility model, on the other hand, placed greater emphasis on the social fabric both by fostering consensus between different social agents (unions, employers and government), maintaining income equality, and, in some countries by protecting more traditional family structures which enabled a more equitable distribution of employment amongst households.

Despite all this, both unashamedly orthodox economists and the new employability school urge full-blooded labour market deregulation in countries or regions like Spain if their economies are to survive in EMU without even higher unemployment. Spain will have to 'cross the river' and make insiders' wages responsive to changes in unemployment and the economic cycle. The implications for anyone acquainted with how Spanish society hangs together are hair raising. Removing protection for labour market insiders seems likely to undermine Spain's family-based employment distribution system with disturbing consequences for social cohesion. But the family – just as Keld Holm noted with respect to the firm – is a black box for most labour market economists. Nor, if the truth be told, is maintaining the insider–outsider system a viable option within EMU. Spanish insiders' wages are barely responsive to unemployment levels or the economic cycle. Nor were they able to compensate the effect on Spanish firms' competitive position during the overvaluation of the peseta before the devaluations of 1992–95 during the ERM crises.

In fact, exchange rate depreciation has been a lifeline to Spain throughout the 1980s and 1990s given its relatively low productivity levels *vis-à-vis* the European core, quite low skill levels and meagre investment in innovation and R&D. The immediate agenda should be to improve these aspects. That is, to promote real convergence with the more quality-competitive (as opposed to cost-competitive) centre, before joining monetary union, at least in its present monetarist mould. The same might well be said for Southern Italy and other less competitive areas.

These critiques of the implications for training, investment and innovation, on the one hand, or employment distribution and welfare viability, on the other, have taken some of the shine from the Anglo-American model in the eyes of European Social (and Christian) Democratic governments. Thinly disguised as 'employability' in Amsterdam's makeshift Employment Resolution it is unlikely to regain adherents. But rather than look to the more expansive macroeconomic policies in the US, for some explanation of its superior employment performance in the 1990s, policy makers on the centre left – at least before Jospin's victory in the 1997 elections – appear to have drawn the most pessimistic conclusions from recent theories of globalization and technological advance. Prophets of techno apocalypse such as Jeremy Rifkin and Stanley Aronowitz have won influential followers in the European Social Democratic parties, most notably Michel Rocard and Felipe Gonzalez. Work sharing figures in most centre left manifestos in the mid-1990s. But, rather than propose shorter working hours as a means to improve the quality of life – or, more mundanely, safety levels in the work place – for potentially overworked labour, European social democrats see it defensively as the only alternative to mass unemployment given the impossibility of creating jobs in high wage economies in the context of globalized labour markets and the new technological revolution.

Both of these apparently irresistible forces of destruction of European labour have actually been questioned by recent studies which place globalization and technological change in a less alarming perspective.[29] Rifkin's terrifying visions, of techno-apocalypse and the disappearance of human labour in the age of the smart machine, appear exaggerated given the comparatively slow rise in productivity in the OECD over the last two decades. Wood's thesis[30] that competition from developing countries has created unemployment in OECD manufacturing is far more convincing but hardly grounds for renouncing full employment policies. What appears to have sown the seeds of such pessimism on the European centre left is monetary union itself. Fatalism has inevitably prospered where the mere suggestion of independent expansionary macroeconomic policy has been denounced as useless or selfish. French Socialists accused Italy, Spain and the UK of competitive devaluation as their economies emerged from recession after the devaluations of 1992–95. Unemployment, rather than being the key criterion for eligibility for monetary union, has become the price Europe has had to pay for a 'hard' euro. Jospin's 1997 victory was a crucial break with such a view but, as we have seen, his employment programme is bound to clash with the deflationary underpinnings of EMU in its present guise.

Two alternative agendas to this orthodox, fatalistic EMU have emerged. The first, hinted at in Jacques Delors' *White Paper* of 1992[31] is a kind of Eurokeynesianism, based on a fast track federalization and an EU-wide reflationary programme financed by euro bonds designed to compensate the deflationary effects of convergence and monetary union. Stuart Holland and Ken Coates have tirelessly pursued this New Deal for Europe[32] hinted at in the White Paper's pledge to create 15 million jobs before the year 2000 through debt financed infrastructure work, urban regeneration, venture capital for small and medium sized enterprises and work sharing. The idea has foundered time after time on the jagged reefs of Commission orthodoxy but for a European Left generally supportive of the EMU project and suspicious of opponents of the single currency, it is a possible way forward. Less ambitious Eurokeynesians count on an inertial expansion of the EU budget and the abandonment of the Stability Pact, as the real implications of monetarist EMU become clearer. As Charles Wyplosz put it, 'The stability pact does not make sense and things that do not make sense do not survive'.[33]

The most powerful argument of these pro-EMU Keynesians is

that any national attempt to pursue full employment macroeconomic strategies are destined to fail in the context of near omnipotent global financial markets whose penchant for deflationary macro policies is well documented.[34] A single currency would provide some protection from financial speculators, and a greater margin for expansionary macro polices, especially given the high level of internal trade in the EU. But the problem of internal imbalance would remain, creating a pressing need for compensatory policies in less competitive regions as an alternative to sweeping deregulation and real wage cuts. Cohesion polices would have to be far more ambitious. Active labour market policies with regional bias – labour subsidies for weaker regions – have also been put forward. Some[35] have even gone so far as to propose selective import controls for uncompetitive regions within the single market, a suggestion that would provoke outrage amongst most of the EMU strategists.

The second agenda with far more support in the British Left is the wholesale rejection of EMU and a return to the national stage in the struggle against unemployment. The death of national macroeconomic sovereignty was prematurely announced, say these economists. In any case, an autopsy would show it was suicide. European governments gave up exchange controls in the 1970s and 1980s and liberalized financial sectors, even before trade restrictions were lifted and the single market created. Complaints about financial speculation undermining national policy, and making EMU an absolute necessity, ring rather hollow in these circumstances. Exchange rate flexibility should be used to enable expansionary macroeconomic policies and ease the transition for deficit countries (those with structural deficits on their balance of payments) towards higher productivity and greater quality (as opposed to cost) competitiveness, the result of effective industrial policy, widespread use of state enterprise and massive investment in education and training.

This would create the conditions for real convergence between poorer and richer economies which might ultimately, but not necessarily, be accompanied by the creation of democratic federal structures in Europe, and EU-wide fiscal and monetary policy, under democratically accountable bodies. Only then could EMU be placed on the agenda for a Europe committed to full, high productivity employment.

Notes

1. 'Britain helps keep EMU on track', *Financial Times*, 17 June 1997.
2. *Le Monde*, 10 July 1997.
3. To name but two: Moss Kanter 1989, and Handy, 1995. Handy has participated in brainstorming sessions with Tony Blair.
4. 'Le compromis d'Amsterdam met fin à la crise qui menaçait l'euro', *Le Monde*, 18 June 1997.
5. Reich, R., *The Guardian*, 14 July 1997.
6. Italy's effective exchange rate fell by over 60 per cent between 1970 and 1996, the UK's and Spain's by 50 per cent, France's rate fell by about 10 per cent, Germany's rose by 150 per cent, and the Netherlands and Austria's rose by around 50 per cent.
7. Asymmetric shock: a term used to refer to any disturbance that might unevenly affect an economy, creating a need for a varying monetary and fiscal policy in different areas.
8. Viñals and Jimeno, 1996.
9. Patrick Minford. See his contribution to the *Report on EMU* by the panel of independent forecasters (UK Treasury, 1995).
10. Viñals and Jimenez, 1996.
11. Kenen, 1995.
12. Eatwell, 1997.
13. See Michie and Grieve Smith, 1996.
14. Holm Keld, 1997.
15. Holm Keld, 1997.
16. The 'structural break' presumably predated the Lawson boom-slump of 1989–92. UK inflation of nearly 10 per cent in 1990 had silenced defenders of Thatcher's supply-side reforms. Supporters of the 'structural break' thesis in the mid-1990s argued that labour market conditions had enabled a non-inflationary reduction in the unemployment rate in the 1980s but that British chancellor Nigel Lawson had allowed demand to grow too fast. With speed limits the Lawson boom would not have occurred, they claimed, and there was no reason for it to be repeated in the 1990s.
17. Quoted in 'Crear empleo o repartilo? Esa es la cuestión *Cinco Dias*, 1 July 1996.
18. Goodman, 1997.
19. 'International comparisons of labour market response to economic recoveries' NIESR 1996.
20. OECD, *Employment Outlook* July 1996 and July 1997.
21. See Grieve Smith, 1997. To support Grieve Smith's point, the meteoric rise in average unemployment rates in Spain from 2.9 to 22 per cent between the periods 1950–73 and 1984–96 coincided with an increase in the number of workers with secondary education from 1.9 million (1979) to 4.6 million (1991) and of university educated workers from 0.4 million to 1.2 million. Youth unemployment in 1991 was around 40 per cent.
22. German unemployment and the European Social Model (Internal Working Document, 11 June 1997).

23. *Le Monde*, 3 December 1996.
24. 'Miracle ou mirage en les Pays Bas', *Le Monde Diplomatique*, July/August 1997.
25. While praising Holland for cutting payroll taxes, the OECD's Job Strategy team could not bring itself to acknowledge the success of the Dutch incomes policy. 'Wage moderation (through collective agreements) cannot be a substitute for more fundamental measures to correct structural rigidities'. 'The problem of high wages has largely faded at the macroeconomic level albeit not in microeconomic terms', the OECD continues in confusing fashion before recommending euphemistically that the minimum wage be 'relaxed', wage negotiation decentralized and the labour market further deregulated. Not surprisingly, the other economic 'miracle' of 1990s Europe, Ireland, was generally praised for its supply-side reforms rather than its incomes policy.
26. Gregg and Wadsworth, 1996.
27. See Rowthorn, B. and Ormerod, P. *The Guardian* and Rowthorn interview in *Cinco Días*, 22 January 1997.
28. Hutton, W., 'Let's not get too rigid about flexibility', *The Observer*, 13 July 1997.
29. On the myth of globalization see Thomson and Hirst. For critiques of techno and globalization apocalyptics see Krugman, 1996 and Henwood, 1997 and 1997a.
30. Wood, 1994.
31. European Commission, 1993.
32. Holland, 1997.
33. Quoted in *Cinco Días*, 21st March 1997.
34. On the global financial markets' penchant for deflationary macro policies, see Singh, 1997.
35. Eatwell, 1994. Eatwell has since rejected this solution.

References

Eatwell, J. (1997) 'Effective Demand and Disguised Unemployment', in Michie, J. and Grieve Smith, J. (eds) *Employment and Economic Performance*. Oxford: Oxford U.P.

Eatwell, J. (1994) 'The Coordination of Macroeconomic Policy in the European Community' in Michie, J. and Grieve Smith, J. (eds) *Unemployment in Europe*. London: Academic Press

European Commission (1993) *Growth, Competitiveness, Employment*. Luxembourg: European Commission

Goodman, A. *et al.* (1997) *Inequality in the UK*. Oxford: Institute of Fiscal Studies and Oxford U.P.

Gregg, P. and Wadsworth, J. (1996) *It Takes Two: Employment Polarization in the OECD*, LSE Centre for Economic Performance Discussion Paper, September

Grieve Smith, J. (1997) *Full Employment: A Pledge Betrayed*. London: Macmillan

Handy, C. (1995) *Beyond Certainty*. London: Hutchinson

Henwood, D. (1997) *Wall Street*. London: Verso

Henwood, D. (1998) 'How Jobless the Future', *Left Business Observer*, no. 75

Holland, S. (1997) *A New Deal for Europe*. Brussels: European Labour Forum

Holm, K. (1997) *Labour Flexibility: Solution or Misperception?* Lehman Brothers Global Economic Structural Series. London: Lehman Brothers

Kenen, P. (1995) *Economic and Monetary Union in Europe*. Cambridge: Cambridge U.P.

Krugman, P. (1996) *Pop Internationlism*. Cambridge, Mass.: MIT Press

Michie, J. and Grieve Smith, J. (eds) (1996) *Creating Industrial Capacity: Towards Full Employment*. Oxford: Oxford U.P.

Moss Kanter, R. (1989) *When Giants Learn to Dance*. London: Simon & Schuster

Singh, A. (1997) 'Liberalization and Globalization: An Unhealthy Euphoria', in Michie, J. and Grieve Smith, J. (eds) *Employment and Economic Performance*. Oxford: Oxford U.P.

Thompson, G. and Hirst, P. (1996) *Globalization in Question*. Cambridge: Polity Press

Viñals, J. and Jimenez, J. (1996) *Monetary Union and European Employment*. Madrid: Federación de Estudios de Economía Aplicada

Wood, A. (1994) *North-South Trade, Employment, and Inequality: Changing Fortunes in a Skill-Driven World*. Oxford: Clarendon Press

Index